With a Good Heart

A Walk From LA to Brooklyn

To Karen and Pat!
Thanks for your
hospitality!

[signature]

Tom Griffen

for katie—

you are (i hold you) in my heart

1

I have always known
That at last I would
Take this road, but yesterday
I did not know that it would be today.

- Ariwara No Narihira
9th century poet

Day 1

LATELY I'VE BEEN FEELING CLINGY and sentimental. One thought away from inexplicably bursting into tears. But this morning—the day I'll finally begin my walk across America—I feel nothing. I just want to get it underway.

*

At sunup, my brother Joel and his wife Brittany drive Katie and I from their place in Glendale to the Santa Monica pier. We park on Ocean Avenue, south of the boardwalk, then walk to Cafe Demitasse where we kill time before my scheduled start. Joel discusses upcoming work projects as my mind wanders. I imagine my blue Osprey backpack crushed in the trunk of his Prius. I visualize what's in each specific compartment: some snacks in the outside pouches, my raincoat in the main hold, a brand new Buck knife in the waist belt. This silent inventory removes me from the table conversation, yet briefly distracts me from the nervous energy constricting my chest. "Hey," Katie says. "You alright?" Her words startle me and I nod without looking at her. I reach for my americano, then raise it to my lips with trembling hands.

*

Carrying a pack is definitely unnecessary today. The route will be loaded with restaurants and I'll be at Joel and Brittany's place again tonight. But starting this journey lugging no gear feels like cheating. So I'll be heaving a fully-loaded backpack as I take my first steps away from the Pacific. Katie's agreed to join me for day one and will carry nothing.

*

I slouch in the rigid chair at the cafe four-top. Bursts of fever, then chills, then fever again roll over me like waves. I am overcome with doubt, and struck by thoughts I have not had before. *Why am I doing this? Wouldn't I rather be home, relaxing? Who do I think I am? What the hell am I trying to prove?* I sense that something bad is going to happen. And I sort of wish it would. Something dire and chaotic that will force me to change plans. Like maybe today the big one will finally knock California into the ocean. That would definitely be a good enough reason to quit before I start. Nobody would ever question my decision to throw in the towel under those circumstances.

*

Amidst the whiz of the steaming espresso machine, and the circular chatter at my table, I fully disassociate and imagine a grim future. What if I get mowed over by a car going 80 mph? Or mugged at gunpoint? What if I am mauled by a hungry mountain lion or bit by a diamondback? Shit, I don't even have a snakebite kit—how can I possibly be ready for this adventure without something as simple as that? I visualize these fatal scenarios in an effort to jinx them from happening.

The prospect of my demise on the roadside isn't far-fetched. Nearly 6,000 pedestrians were killed in the United States in 2016, a 10% increase over the previous year. This year, assuming the math remains constant, there will be more than 7,000 pedestrians killed. Maybe I will be one of them? Vehicles fly by at ridiculous speeds, drivers eat or text or sleep or try to grab something from the back seat, lose their trajectory, and take out whatever's on the shoulder. In January 2017, Mark Baumer, a young man walking across the country to raise awareness for climate change, was struck and killed by a vehicle as he walked across Florida's panhandle. It's very possible that my overall preparedness won't matter one bit.

*

Gripping surges of panic pulse through me and draw me deeper inward. My vision tunnels as the rush pins me down. I sit motionless and hope nobody notices. I try to lift a finger, but I can't. Try to move my toes. Impossible. As the clamp tightens, I have one coherent thought. *My efforts will very likely kill me.*

But rather than stew on this gruesome thought, I use it as a foothold. In a moment of clarity, I straighten up, look down at my watch, and stammer, "Um...we'd better get going." Everyone jumps up as if they've been waiting for my cue. Katie looks at me and raises her brows. "I'm fine," I snap as we file out the door.

A block from the pier, the solar-powered Pacific Wheel comes into view alongside the steel West Coaster. I hold up my hand to block the low sun as my pace quickens into the boardwalk's tractor beam. "Hell yeah!" I shout as my body rejoins itself. Then I clap my hands and holler, "Come on now! Let's get this fucking party started!"

*

I had previously posted on social media that I'd begin my walk across America with a fingertip dip in the Pacific at 8:00 a.m. on the north side of the pier. I don't know many people in this area, and certainly none of my Orange County connections will want to brave early morning traffic into Los Angeles on the first workday of the new year. Nobody'll show, I'm sure of it.

But as we near the pier I see familiar human shapes. People from my past and present who have come to see me off. My throat flutters and Katie puts her hand on the small of my back and tells me I shouldn't be so surprised. I tug at the straps of my backpack and am suddenly self-conscious of the Walking Across America sign around my neck. I wish I could duck into an alley and start without fanfare. Why did all these people come, anyhow? Don't they realize how uneventful this will be? I feel bad that they've interrupted their day to watch me hoof it from the Pacific waterline to the sidewalk. Walking really isn't much of a spectator sport—not anymore, anyhow.

*

Back in the 1800s, pedestrianism, also known as foot racing, drew giant crowds. Competitive walkers trod endless circles on indoor tracks while onlookers waged bets on their cumulative distances covered. In 1809, Captain Robert Barclay Allardice walked one mile every hour for 1,000 hours. His feat drew more than 10,000 curious people to witness the endeavor. Another walker, Ada Anderson, earned the nickname "Champion Lady Walker of the World" after completing 1,500 miles in 1,000 hours. An accomplishment that, up until that point, had only been matched by her trainer, William Gale. Centurions walked 100 miles in less than 24 hours and earned celebrity status. In the modern era, runners compete in ultramarathons where covering 100 miles within a 24-hour span is a coveted triumph. I've attempted—and finished—a couple of these races in less than a day. But I damn sure can't imagine walking the distance in a similar span of time.

I'm no Captain Allardice or Ada Anderson. I'm not trying to squash any speed records or break new ground. I'm just a guy with a heavy pack and a wobbly plan. And even though I'm embarrassed by the arrival of friends who've come to watch my first steps, their presence humbles me. Among the group are Frank and Mary, an older couple I refer to as my adopted parents. They arrived via limousine, an hour's ride from their home in Newport Beach. My best friend Kent and his partner Alicia make a surprise appearance, too. So does Chandra, an old work friend. She brought along her boyfriend, Kevin. None of these people know each other, so they stand around awkwardly, laugh graciously at my anxious jokes, then snap photos as I dip my hands in the surf, turn around, and backtrack the wintry beach, trying not to fill my meshy shoes with cool sand. I love them all for being here, but what I really want to do is to put them in my rearview.

*

My supporters peel off until it's just the original four of us standing where the pier meets the hardtop. I suggest we go back to Cafe Demitasse—I'd definitely enjoy my drink this time around. But that's not happening. Katie and I give Joel and Brittany giant hugs. I press the crosswalk button and choke back tears even though we'll all be reunited for dinner this evening. "Let it out," Katie says. But I don't let it out. I hold it in like I always do.

*

We're barely across the street when a man reads my sign and asks if I'm starting here because Forrest Gump did. It's never crossed my mind that this was where his fictional cross-country running journey began. I chose this spot because it seemed like the perfect walking distance from my brother's place. Exactly 20 miles. Which, in actuality, is probably too far for day one.

Moments later on Colorado Avenue, another man squints to read the sign dangling from my neck. "Oh, I see," he says. "You're one of those walk across America guys." In his tone I hear, *another one of those dime-a-dozen fools.* I say nothing in return because it feels ridiculous to proclaim my intention to walk to the Atlantic when I'm literally minutes into the journey. So I just smile and nod like some kind of moron. He shakes his head.

More people break their necks to watch us pass and I bashfully wave like a C-list celebrity. I am a spectacle. Completely out of place with my clean clothes and pristine gear. To make things worse, my pack is already starting to hurt my back. And my new Dodgers hat, a gift from my brother, is so tight it's giving me a headache. I am conflicted. I badly want to share what I'm doing, but I also want to hide from the attention its earning me. I know I need to get used to being vulnerable, but right now I'd give about anything to be invisible.

With the ocean out of sight, we break at a covered bus stop where I remove my sign and am immediately overcome with relief. For the rest of the day I'll be just another guy wandering through LA with my life on my back. But unlike vacationers, the homeless, and pretty much everyone else, I still stand out. My goddamned trekking poles are to blame.

Trekking poles speed me up, make my walking form more efficient, and allow me to absorb miles with ease. But they also serve a diplomatic role. In my various test walks back home, passersby would notice them and replace iffy looks with cheerful greetings. Icebreakers like "Hey! Ya going skiing?" or "Where's the snow, buddy?" often led to folks sharing items on their own bucket lists. Had I been a guy on the roadside wearing just a backpack, I doubt I'd have received such upbeat receptions.

The poles, it seems, give me purpose. They keep me from being perceived as a drifter. Though I generally feed off being in the limelight, today it's annoying. Each comment about my poles needles me until I'm tempted to pack them away, too.

*

My phone's GPS guides us through Santa Monica, Westwood, and Century City. Soon we're in Beverly Hills walking past skyward mansions. Lawns are pristinely groomed, bushes and trees shaped just so. An excess of double-parked work vehicles makes it tricky for drivers to navigate the narrow streets lined with freshly waxed Ferraris and Maseratis. There's suddenly no evidence of people living on the street. No cardboard bed mats or discarded shopping carts. The surreal opulence resembles a movie set more than a neighborhood where real people live. In fact, we see very few people at all besides laborers. I interrupt their stares with a toothy "Buenos dias!" and get nonplussed responses.

On Hollywood Boulevard, a car passes us honking then flips a U to park. My friend Derek jumps out of the driver's seat and runs over to join us. He's been zipping around for more than an hour, tracing the route he figured we'd take from the pier. The blaring sun beats down on our grinning faces as Derek points to a sagging adjacent building. "Man, I used to go dancing there! Who'd have thought I'd be back here now cheering you on? Life's so weird, isn't it?" He gets back in his car and drives off, beeping more until he's out of sight.

In the wake of Derek's uplifting energy, I nearly start to cry again. But, like before, I don't. For a while Katie and I walk silently. My throat hurts and I don't say a word. I keep having to slow down because my pace is too fast. Even when I try to stay mindful and keep a similar stride, the gap between us widens. And though I tell myself it's fine, that it's no big deal, it still bothers me.

*

Katie and I are eight years into a relationship that has been themed by stagnation. We've spent the majority of our time together giving lip service to a partnership we've never truly worked on. Our platonic compatibility is obvious, but trouble arises whenever we consider a future together. There's simply too much self-serving space dividing what she wants from what I want.

Katie seeks a quiet and predictable routine with a limited footprint, while I tend toward a frenetic and unpredictable life on the move. Katie doesn't believe in marriage and doesn't want kids, and I find myself considering both possibilities with increased yearning. Any of our myriad compromises have fallen flat and increased the psychic distance between us. Now this rift has become a main character in our story. And though we are both aware of the negative effects it has on our tranquility, we allow it to persist, year after year.

But we've reached a breaking point. We've grown more independent than ever and can't come up with any particulars to make staying together make sense. So we've decided to officially end things. And even though leaving on this long walk would be a perfect time for us to finally cut the cord, neither of us want this day to mark the end of our togetherness. So we've agreed to hold off on things until I return home.

For the next six months or so, both of us will exist on pause—in a liminal space. I trust the empty time on the roadside will help me figure some things out. But I also know that expecting a revelatory moment to appear is the plan of a fool. Though I worry our waffling is all going to come crumbling down at some point, I'm still fine to push it all to the side. I'll deal with the hard stuff later.

*

We make it to Glendale as the sun sets. The 20 miles took longer than expected and my body is thrashed. My legs burn and my shoulders are chafed and raw. I take a moment to savor the pain because it's physical proof the walk finally exists. Katie's flying home tomorrow morning and, barring any sort of hitch in the plan, the next time we connect will be on the coastline of another ocean. This thought steals my breath.

We set up our bed again on the hardwood floor and Katie conks out in a blink. I'm committed to documenting this trip with a daily Instagram post, so I knock out a quick recap. "Today I began my walk across America. Twenty miles are officially in the books. Can't lie, my body is a bit wrecked." I share a group photo from the pier and another of a gas station sign on Los Feliz Road that says, "Because your best miles are still ahead of you." Comments start ringing in. I read a few supportive hurrahs before tucking away my phone. Lay down feeling proud.

*

I spoon up against Katie one last time. Maybe ever. Her breath deepens as my mind races. I've finally started the thing I've been talking about for 25 years. I mouth words I hope to scream in six months or less. *I did it. I did it.* But there's so much between now and then. So much walking. So many unknowns. And even though I know better than to celebrate at the starting line, I can't help but do it anyway. I move my mouth like a puppet. *I did it. I did it.*

Brittany left a window cracked to allow in some fresh air. From the dark outside and beyond all that can be seen, I hear occasional remnants of people laughing. Quiet bursts of joy like shooting stars whisper into my fading ears.

Day 2

It's like I'm hungover. Everything is swollen. My legs feel bruised, my joints ache, the soles of my feet have a twinge of plantar fasciitis. Maybe I should be using shoe insoles. Because I always use insoles. But I don't have any with me so I'll have to make do.

Overnight I woke up coughing and this morning I'm hacking up gritty gobs of LA smog that stick like glue to the sink basin. I nudge them down the drain with a finger and splashes of warm water. If my immune system could talk, I know exactly what it would say: *You pushed too far. Twenty miles was a bit ambitious for the first day, don't you think?* Still, I plan to cover similar mileage today. I want to get as far from the ocean as possible.

*

Everyone is up before the sun, and we all pinball though the narrow hallway, taking turns in the bathroom and filling each others' coffee cups. Joel insists he and Katie leave for the airport extra early to beat rush hour. I'll start my day when they hit the road. Silence blows in with cool air through an open window. I sit on the couch with my mug of French roast and watch as steam rises. My knee bounces. I wonder where I'll end up stopping today.

Brittany goes back to bed while Joel, Katie, and I walk outside together. We exchange goodbyes and Katie takes me into her arms. Her embrace tells me everything's going to be OK. As she lets go, she says she left me an audio message on my phone's recorder. "Something to listen to later when you forget the things you shouldn't forget." They drive away and I'm alone.

I consult my phone maps to get my bearings, then follow East Broadway out of Glendale. In Pasadena, temporary bleachers line streets littered with wilting red carnations. Leftovers from the Rose Bowl parade two days ago. I walk toward the sound of workers banging solitary hammers, then leave the racket behind as I cross Colorado Street Bridge, also known as the suicide bridge. I stop multiple times to look over the rail. I'm overcome by vertigo as I imagine plummeting 150 feet into the Arroyo Seco. I wonder how long it would be before someone found my body. Not a single car passes as I walk the quarter mile.

*

The dark length of the San Gabriel Mountains to my north keeps me oriented. I've spent a lot of time in Los Angeles over the years and this landmark is extra familiar. A few years back I attempted the Angeles Crest 100-mile footrace. Of all the events I ever ran, the AC100 remains the most problematic and yet the most memorable. Mistakes are easy to name after the fact, and these were mine: I didn't eat enough, didn't drink enough, didn't pay attention to trail markings, and ran way too fast. I suffered from extreme dehydration, which led to hallucinations that included apparitions of Mexican cowboys on horseback who offered me endless words of encouragement. "Buenos suerte, amigo! Corre, corre corre!" I recall their garb: glimmering coin-studded chaps, colorful vests and crisp ruffled shirts, the intricate embroidery of their hatbands. And though these spectral memories now make for a good laugh, they represent me spinning out of control. My desperate mind making it easier to accept the failure of my physical faculties. I eventually collapsed when I reached the aid station at mile marker 89. EMTs promptly took my blood pressure and cut off my wristband, disqualifying me. When Dusty, my pacer, said we were being evacuated off the mountain, I wept. But my tears were joyful. "So this is what the edge looks like," I said. How often do we get to witness the boundary of our human potential?

*

In Monrovia I stop at a Mexican restaurant. And even though it's brisk and breezy, I sit outside. The server is curious about my backpack and asks what I am doing. It doesn't feel right to tell her I'm walking to the east coast, but I do anyhow. She stops chewing her gum and stares at me, incredulous. Then she asks *why*. I stammer over words as I try to offer a coherent answer. "Because I can. Because I want to. Because life is too short not to do the things that make me happy." As the statements blurt from my mouth, I realize they are meaningless. She tells me I'm "straight-up crazy" as she sets down a heavy plate of cheese enchiladas.

I take a big scoop of salted rice, lean back, and bask in my reality. I can eat when I want, where I want, and what I want. I can walk if I want to, or sit on my ass if I want to. *This is freedom*, I think as I savor the server's words. I finish my plate, mindlessly scroll through social media feeds, and enjoy another few minutes of doing absolutely nothing before formulating an afternoon plan. I leave my business card with a cash tip for the server and hit the road again.

Back on the sidewalk, a truck driving past slows for a red light. A man wearing a cowboy hat hollers at me from his passenger window. "Hey! What are you doing?" I tell him I'm walking to the Atlantic Ocean. His face squinches. "No really, where are you going?" I rephrase my answer and say I'm walking across California, then eventually all the way across the United States. He pauses. Looks away then back at me with giant eyes. His voice bites in disbelief. "Across the US? No fucking way!" He waves his hand dismissively. "You're fucking nuts, man!" The light turns green and he peels off. A bellow of black smoke fills his truck's wake.

My pace quickens when I see the Asuza Starbucks sign ahead. Today's stopping point. When I arrive, I send Joel and Brittany a pin. It'll take them at least a half hour to drive the 20 miles I walked, so I go inside to order a drink. I fidget with backpack straps as I nervously tell the barista what I'm doing. "No kidding? Why?" My answer is about as jumbled and unintelligible as the one from lunch. She brushes me off. "That's cool," she says, obviously unimpressed. "How about a name for that drink?"

Outside I sit in the shade of a green umbrella, watch the lowering sun spark the mountains aflame. My calf muscles twitch, and for the first time all day I'm aware of pain. I pull back the neck of my T-shirt and find a length of raw flesh from shoulder to chest. The thought of tonight's shower makes me cringe. I pick a crumb of salt from my hairline. Touch it to my tongue. Then, out of habit, I pull out my phone and mindlessly check Instagram, Facebook, email, texts. I even click on an app that lists the earthquakes that happened today around the world. There was a cluster of little ones near Mount St. Helens this morning, which reminds me of the little bag of ash my grandparents sent me after the 1980 eruption. I remember being in awe of the minuscule pouch of gray dust. My imagination piqued by the thought of its provenance and how it ended up here in my hands.

When I run out of new things to click on, I remember Katie's audio message. Nobody's around, so I play it at full volume through my phone's speaker. Her voice is clear but a little shaky. "Hey, I'm just going to give you a few brief reminders. First, I love you. For a long time. And second, I am not the only person who loves you. Don't be afraid to ask for help—and not just from strangers, but also from your people. Remember that you are physically and mentally strong and you've done a lot to prepare yourself for this trip. But that doesn't mean everything's always going to go smoothly. It just means you are ready to deal with things as they pop up along the way. You'll make good decisions, I know that you will. I know you want to be safe. And don't forget to drink water! I hope you really enjoy this experience and feel alive and connected and engaged and I look forward to hearing about it as you go. It's just walking! Everything's going to be alright. OK, bye now!"

I can't hold back any longer. My belly and back shake uncontrollably as water spouts from my eyes. My high-pitched bellyache sounds like laughter and I look around to make sure nobody sees me. When it passes I feel lighter. "I should do that more often," I say out loud. Then I sip my iced americano and pass the remaining time considering the difference between happiness and sadness. I wonder if they can be mistaken for each other?

When Brittany pulls into the parking lot, I raise my drink to her. She parks and pops the trunk for my pack. I apologize in advance for stinking up the car. "Dude! I can't believe you walked this far," she says. Which is funny, because I can't believe it either.

Day 3

Today I'm on my own. For the first time I'll walk with my pack fully loaded with the extra 10 pounds of gear I've been leaving behind at Joel and Brittany's. I have no idea where I'll sleep tonight. Maybe I'll stealth-camp like I did while hiking the Oregon Coast Trail? I'll wait for the sun to go down, secretly set up my tent somewhere, sleep with one eye open, then split before sunrise. I imagine stealth camping in Los Angeles is a bit different than the barren coast of Oregon. Here I'm more likely to have to compete with the local homeless population. And since I don't know the protocol for such things, I'm bound to break their rules and draw attention to myself. Thinking about these unknowns makes the morning ride with Joel to yesterday's stopping point a quiet one. I'm afraid of what the day will bring. Of the unknowns. But I play it off because I don't want my little brother to know I am scared.

When we arrive at the Starbucks parking lot, I stall. Ask Joel about his workday until there's nothing left to say. "Well, I guess I hope I don't see you for a while." I wrangle my pack onto my sore back and we both make dumb jokes to ward off an emotional farewell. Then I march away. I look back as Joel joins the flurry of commuters. "Well. Here goes," I say.

*

Around late morning, a friend who's local to the area sends me a Facebook message recommending I hit up the Donut Man in Glendora—an area staple for more than 45 years and, according to their website, "One of the most iconic culinary experiences in all of Southern California." I'm a sucker for donuts. When my brother Mike and I worked together in the late '90s, we'd take turns bringing donuts for the sales and finance teams. I'd usually show up with two dozen. Twelve for the teams, and 12 for Mike and I to split. Growing up, on any given Sunday my family would share a platter stacked high with Boston cremes, glazed old fashioneds, powdered jellies, and tiger tails. Our donut game was strong. Thank God for my equally strong metabolism.

I reluctantly stop at the iconic shop. Reluctantly because it's inconveniently located on the opposite side of the street, which means I have to break stride, wait for a crosswalk, and backtrack to it. All for a dang donut. Frankly, all I want to do is keep charging ahead. And now I'm interrupting my flow to make a friend happy. I want to be able to tell her I hit up her spot, but the minor detour feels like a major inconvenience.

*

I duck into in a shady bus stop and open Apple Maps on my iPhone. Swipe east from my location along old Route 66 into the thickening suburban sprawl. There's not much green space or anything else that may offer enough cover for a stealth camping spot tonight. The stretch looks even less accommodating when I shift the settings to satellite. I'm sure this journey will afford plenty of random places I'll call home for a night, but I'm not quite ready for this much adventure. At some point I may lay my head down behind a dumpster, or tuck into a baseball dugout, or alleyway between abandoned buildings. But not yet.

I lob my need for a place to stay into the social media ether. "Anyone know anyone in the Ontario area who might be willing to put me up?" I hear back from a handful of people including Michelle, a long-ago coworker whose parents live nearby. Also get a message from my second cousin, Gary, who I haven't seen since I was a teenager. Gary offers to use his reward points to book me an upscale hotel room. It's off my route but not by much. I take him up on it. When I hit 20 miles on the day, I note the cross streets and order a Lyft to the hotel property. A large pizza and salad go perfectly with a marathon of *American Pickers* on the History Channel. When I'm freshly showered and wrapped in the hotel robe, sipping a Sierra Nevada from the reception fridge, I promise myself I'll start camping tomorrow.

Day 4

I Lyft back to yesterday's stopping point and walk through the Asuza Pacific campus—a rare oasis from the white noise of passing cars. I absorb the silence from a park bench and wave to campus security cart as they drive by multiple times. Eventually the driver stops to ask if I need anything. "Thanks, but I'm all set." Then I preemptively answer his question. "I'm just taking a quick break. I'm walking across America." He asks why. I answer with another tangled variation of my string of recent self-serving responses to the same question. He tells me to be careful and drives away.

*

The tepid morning turns into a baking afternoon. It's probably only in the mid-80s, but a pack adds an extra 10-15 degrees. January suddenly feels like July. As distances increase between towns, manicured yards are replaced by dry, brown earth. Palatial dwellings turn modest. There's a shift in industry. Run-down shops linger along dusty streets. Fruit stands on every corner. Lots of places to fix a flat. Instead of saying *Hello*, I say *Buenos días*. I whisper rehearse a few lines of my limited Spanish in case I need anything. "Por favor, necesito ayuda. ¿Dónde está la tienda mas cercana? ¿Tienes agua? ¿Dónde hay un lugar seguro para dormir?" I worry someone might ask what the heck I am doing. Or worse, why. A hard enough question to answer in English, let alone in a language I only sort of know. During a break I Google translate the word *across*. *Atravesar* pops up. A verb meaning *to cross*. I could say, *Estoy atravesando*, which means, *I am crossing*. But something about it sounds wrong. Plus, it doesn't quite roll off my gringo tongue. I decide to go with, *Estoy caminando al océano Atlántico*. Which translates to, *I am walking to the Atlantic Ocean*. Not perfect and pretty grandiose, but enough to get my point across.

*

This stretch resembles Baja California, one of my favorite places on the planet. A whiff of burning trash transports me to one of my many adventures there with my best friend, Kent. The time we went to the Pool of the Virgin in the north near Mexicali. We parked his truck and gazed in the direction of Cañon Guadalupe where we planned to hike. Then we turned around to take in the expanse behind us. A horizon to horizon rippling sweep of bitter flats. Nothing but emptiness. My eyes were tricked by the impossibility of distance. Far away landmarks only registered when viewed indirectly, like stars. I squinted as waypoints melted away. As mirages danced and fed into the optical illusion. All in view was uncertain. The lack of trustworthy details reminded us to be wary. But it also asked us to have faith. I stared across and through the rippling breadth, blinking my eyes repeatedly trying to focus on something. Told Kent that I wanted to walk into it. Across it. Kent didn't question my comment. Didn't ask, "Across what?" or question why. He simply nodded and stared at nothing, too. Because he was thinking the same thing.

In 2012, Kent set out to walk across the United States. He towed a cart attached to his body while managing a leashed dog. The cart became tangled with the dog's lead, so he wheeled everything into the deep shoulder, disconnected his gear, and began unraveling things. At the same time, a lone car crossed over the solid white line and made full-speed contact with his cart. Everything exploded into a thousand pieces. The driver never stopped. Had it happened a few seconds earlier, Kent and his dog would have been connected to the mayhem. The difference between life and death is slight. In Kent's case it was decided by something as simple and inconvenient as a tangle.

After it happened, Kent called me from a pay phone and for the first time I heard him cry. I contacted a nearby hotel and booked a room for him and his dog and he returned home the next day. It was another two years before he tried again. But this time alone. Just him and a different cart setup. Took him 175 days to go from ocean to ocean. Maine to California. When he finished, I told everyone who'd listen that my best friend had just walked across the United States. Folks were amazed he'd walked so far, but also impressed I knew someone who'd accomplished such a feat. Telling his story warmed my face. I relished this secondary attention, using his story to make me sound more interesting. I wondered what it would be like to be him. To be able to prop myself up having accomplished such a magnificent feat. To be the one who could rightfully say, "Yes, I walked all the way across America." When he did it, I knew I could, too. And now, here I am.

Day 5

The satellite view of the 18-mile length of San Timoteo Canyon Road makes my heart race. I swipe a dozen times following the lengthy, desolate road and have a minor anxiety attack. My hands tremble as I load my pack with more food and water than will likely be necessary. I know my apprehension is nothing compared to the coming barren stretches in the desert where I'll have triple-digit miles between services. Still, the number scares me. Eighteen miles of nothing. But saying yes to risk is the first step in moving beyond fear. So I tighten down my shoulder straps, cinch up my waist belt, and find a steady pace as the cool morning air turns into a heater vent.

*

San Timoteo parallels a railroad track and trains rumble by all day. Conductors blow their thunderous horns and, at times, lean out the engine's side window to give me a raised arm wave. They are an antidote for the loneliness that's taking hold. After a few hours of walking, it often feels like the rest of the world has been sucked away. Like I'm the last one. Such thoughts are compounded by a fenced-in herd of zebra on the road's south side. A surreal moment to make me further question reality. I take a token photo to prove they are not figments of my imagination. Even still, I don't quite trust what I see.

*

I've been knocking out more than four miles per hour when I encounter Sergio, a roadside fruit vendor. Every weekend for 15 years, he and his wife, Griselda, pack up fresh fruit and a sun umbrella and drive 65 miles from their home in LA to this corner of the canyon road. I tell him about the zebras. He shakes his head. "Never seen zebras out here before." He looks deep into my eyes like he can see into my empty tank, then insists I join them in the canopy shade. He gently grabs my arm and leads me to a large cooler, tells me to take a seat. "You need to rest, amigo."

I do as I'm told, and immediately worry that I'm wasting time. This isn't a planned break and I need to get off this stretch of road before I run out of sunlight. Griselda runs back and forth from the stand to the never-ending line of drive-thru customers. Sergio works at the cutting board, fills plastic bags with watermelon, jicama, papaya, kiwi, and other cooling fruits. His movements are meditative. He hands me a plate and a fork. "Here. Eat up. You need it." He flexes his arm like a body builder.

Griselda chats with a driver who cranes his neck for a better look at me. I imagine she's telling him about the crazy, heat-stricken guero droning on about zebras while trying to walk the length of the canyon. I give him a half wave and he returns it. Suddenly I feel ill-prepared. I can only imagine how people must be perceiving me. Like I'm some kind of moron.

Sergio deftly slices more fruit and asks what I'm doing out here. I grunt and point to my full mouth. Griselda plops down next to me and our bare legs touch. She points at the bag of fruit in my lap. "This is just what I needed," I say. "Thank you." Another car pulls up and she hops up again. I tell Sergio I'm walking across the US. "What's in your pack? It looks heavy," he says. I explain it's mostly water, then rattle off my list of gear. Griselda returns and I scoot over to give her extra room. She taps her hand on my knee then starts messing with her phone. "I want to show you photos. My grandchildren." She looks way too young for grandkids and I tell her so. She smiles as she taps the screen. She turns the phone in my direction and her face beams. Most of the images are poorly-composed and out of focus, but she doesn't care. I look at them with her and it feels nice to sit so close to another person. My salty face dries as a breeze snakes through the canyon, kicking up little devils in the dirt lot.

Sergio interrupts. "Tom, I think what you are doing is a hard thing," he says. "But that's what makes it important." His words throw me off. Because shouldn't I be the one thanking him?

I stay for an hour and eat as much as my body can take. Cars come and go as Griselda runs out to deliver bags of fruit. A few customers turn off their engines and join us beneath the tent to ask about my journey. Like all the other people I've spoken to so far, everyone wants to know what inspired me to do this crazy thing. But as usual, my response is obscure and they drive away looking confused.

When I tell Sergio I need to leave, he frowns, but nods, too. "Make sure you eat good food every chance you get," He says. "And shoes—good shoes are *huge* if you are on your feet all day." They give me goodbye hugs and Griselda tells me they'll pray for me. Sergio bends down and grabs two oranges from a tall mesh bag, hands them to me, and sends me on my way.

2

Is it right to go? Is it right to stay?
Just have strong faith. Have lofty ideals.
In addition, have a sound body.
Think about the universe and life.
Think about how really, really short a person's life is.

- Takamure Itsue
The 1918 Shikoku Pilgrimage of Takamure Itsue

Day 6

NEAR THE WHITEWATER SECTION of the

Pacific Coast Trail, but still within earshot of Interstate 10, I finally bust out my brand new tent. Until tonight, it's been overpriced hotels. As I lay in each cushy bed, I kick myself for not diving headlong into the stealth camping scenario. In theory it's not difficult. But when I seriously consider secretly plopping down in some unexpected place for the night, I'm flushed with a fear that causes me to promptly inquire about nearby hotels. Once, years ago, I screamed at what I thought was someone lurking around my illegal campsite tucked in the corner of a private back yard. "Hey! Who's there!" I screamed. No response. When I finally got up the courage to peek my head out the zipper door, the intruder turned out to be a grocery bag snagged on a bush catching a hint of midnight wind. Fear invents ghosts.

As I lay in my sleeping bag, I text Kent and confess my regret for staying in so many hotels right out the gate. I call myself out for taking a full week to finally get my tent dirty. For not being brave enough to give in to my new reality. He texts back. "If I had extra money during my walk, I'd have paid for more rooms, too. You're being too hard on yourself. You're still walking across America."

*

It starts to rain. A soft drizzle. This worries me since I pitched my tent in a sandy wash, the perfect place to get swept away in a flash flood.

I settle into the hard ground—not particularly flat or smooth—adjust my position to accommodate the dents and divots of earth beneath my weight. I nestle my head atop my dirty clothes bag, a makeshift pillow. My heartbeat slows. I promise hereafter I'll do this as much as possible.

I listen to distant coyotes, yipping and howling. Their calls inspire other song dogs to join in from all directions. Some respond with shrieks, some dismal whimpers. The ending yowl finishes on an up note, which makes it sound like a question.

Finally, and for the first time on this trip, I feel like I'm really doing something. The day's effort combined with my body's ripening aroma proves an adventure is at hand. Things will be even better in the morning. I'll wake up early, my skin greasy and grimy. My body will feel extra sore and derelict. I'll break into my unopened stash of instant oatmeal I've been lugging for six days, make a cup of Nescafé instant coffee, and down it all cold. Afterwards, I'll dig a hole for my morning dump, breathe in the entrancing creosote and sage, still fragrant from the night rain. My gear will start to have purpose. This first night outside will make the next ones easier. Make me forget about my desire for luxury.

The coyotes go silent and I stop worrying about the possibility of being swept away by a rainy deluge. I focus on the soft tapping on the tent's rainfly. The sort of noise that never exists indoors where beds are warm and bellies are full. The sort of noise I could listen to forever.

Day 7

Back when I was in my 20s, I took a summer trip to Ireland. While staying at a hostel in Drogheda, I met Catherine, a solo traveler from the Netherlands. We made dinners together in the shared kitchen, sampled local beers, and became quick friends. Years later, she was one of my first Facebook connections. We've remained in loose touch ever since.

As I near Palm Springs, I get a message from her. She connects me with Joanna, her long-time family friend who resides in the desert oasis. Joanna wants to put me up for the night. She's reluctant to have a stranger in her house, so she offers to cover my stay at the Caliente Tropics Resort Hotel on the south end of town. She also insists on buying me lunch. "Meet me at the Sunny Bono statue on Palm Canyon," she writes. "There's a great Mexican place nearby." I inhale a plate of carne asada tacos while we get acquainted, then she drives me to the hotel and covers not one, but two nights. After seven days of walking, I desperately need an off day.

Day 8

I spend my first official down day looking for a route through the Mojave. It's illegal to walk on Interstate 10, so that's out. And I'd prefer to not follow the dirt path below electrical lines that parallel the freeway. I also don't want to backtrack to Morongo Valley even though that's where most transcon crossers enter the desert. I reach out to a few veteran cross-country walkers for their two cents. They all advise me to do a 180 and go through Joshua Tree. They assure me it's the only option given its regular services. But I don't buy it. I ignore their collective recommendations because I don't want to retrace my steps. I've come too far to make a damn U-turn.

After hours of consulting maps and satellite images, I settle on a plan. One I've never heard of other crossers attempting. I'll continue through Palm Springs to the Salton Sea, then follow the Bradshaw Trail, an old stagecoach road. It's 70ish miles long and has no options for refueling. I'll have to carry approximately four days' worth of provisions. The plan is frightening, but also thrilling. And mostly because it's atypical. Making my mark on the remote and desolate Bradshaw Trail will certainly underscore my tenacity. I take pleasure in the imagined chatter that's sure to ensue on the USA Crossers Facebook page.

After locking in my decision, I make a note in my journal. "Apparently I always have to be different and go against the grain (and ignore good advice). Is this Bradshaw Trail a bad decision? There's probably a reason people don't go that way. Hopefully this isn't where life comes calling."

Day 9

I leave Palm Springs before sunup and arrive in Coachella hell-bent on finding a place to camp. It's a big mileage day—28—my biggest so far. I've covered nearly 200 miles in just over a week. Not sure I ever ran this much in as many days. Makes me wonder if I'm overdoing it.

I lean against the side wall of a gas station and close my eyes. The sun is setting, and through my eyelids I see the sky burning orange. I'm lost in the roar of the 10 freeway and the clicking of gas caps. I'm nearly asleep when a truck's pitchy horn draws me back. It's too dark to press on. And even though a mile east would put me into desert scrub, I'm too spent to bring myself to do it. I reluctantly book a hotel two miles up the road, then order a Lyft to retrieve me. The driver says I did the right thing. "Coachella is crawling with desperate desert rats," he says. "They'll stab you for a liter of water. No telling what they'd do for a nice pack like you got there. Here, let me show you." He turns off the navigation app and detours to a squat camp where makeshift structures are built tall with scrap wood and pallets, blue tarps, and rusty sheet metal roofs. It's the magic hour, and dusk gives the camp a cinematic glow. Coachella's tent city looks dystopian. Romantic from the back seat of the Honda Accord. My driver sees the look in my eye and interrupts. "Make no mistake, friend, this place is bad news. If you'd have walked a half mile out of town they'd have seen you and well…I'd probably be reading about you in the paper in a few days."

We set a 6:30 a.m. pick-up for tomorrow. I crash hard on my giant bed, sleep dreamless. The next morning, I find the driver parked under the awning as if he never left. In a blink we're back at the gas station. He shakes my hand and wishes me good luck. "Tell me again why you are doing this?" I admit that I'm not quite sure. Say something about making unlikely connections with strangers. He adjusts the ball cap on his head. "Well, OK brother, good luck with that." He stops me as I'm about to close the door. "Hey—remember what I said about the desert rats. They ain't no joke."

Day 10

After a cup of weak coffee and a bear claw from the gas station, I walk under the interstate overpass, then approach the encampment from last night. Skinny plumes of smoke stream upward from a few broken structures. A man, shirtless in shorts, stands outside and looks in my direction as he scrubs a pot. He gives me a head wave. I raise a trekking pole. Minutes later, as the road starts to widen, I turn back to see if he's still there. He is, and he throws another wave. But this time by lifting the pot in the air and moving both arms like slow jumping jacks. Like some sort of SOS. I mirror his moves, then turn back to face the wide shoulder. I pick up my pace and march deeper into the desert.

*

By midday I'm parched. I stand in the shade of a liquor store in the townlet of North Shore. I hold off on going in because I hear a woman angrily hollering inside, presumably at another person. I'm not looking to interrupt someone else's beef.

All day I haven't said a word, and my ability to strike up or maintain a conversation with anyone has lately been scrabbled. Folks want to know where I'm going or where I'm coming from, and I often can't recall this most basic information. All the random towns blend into the next. My answer to the most common question, *Why are you walking across America,* fluctuates from day to day, never getting any clearer. Twice in the past few days the question has triggered a snarky response. I've flat out told folks "I'm just walking because I want to." Both times afterwards I've felt like a jerk. Not only was my response crass and dismissive, but it was infused with a real assholish vibe. I wish I'd just kept my big mouth closed. But more than that, I wish I had a solid answer to what everyone wants to know.

*

I wait patiently for the voices to mellow. I just want to go in and grab a few things then be on my way. I'm not looking for conversation. But unless I leave my pack outside, which I won't, one of the people inside will undoubtedly inquire about what I'm up to. Right now I don't want to be seen, but I'm short on water and, according to my phone, still a solid 10 miles and two scorching hours from the services in Mecca. Online, this liquor store doesn't even exist. It's the sort of place that only materializes when you're standing right in front of it. Maybe it's a mirage. Shoot, maybe all of this is. Including the International Banana Museum next door.

I make a mental list of what I need and push the door open. A string of holiday bells jingle from the doorknob. Cool air fills my nose. The loud woman stops her tirade midsentence. I look around to gauge where the others are, but I only see the one woman. She's skeletal, tan-skinned, has longish hair, she's maybe young, maybe old, and she's standing behind the counter with hands on her hips. Below her a sign says "Ice Bait Beer." A thick black holster on her skinny hip is weighted down by a black handgun. I say hello and she returns the greeting, I think. Then she responds with something incomprehensible.

I make my way down a narrow aisle, trying not to swing my pack into merchandise. I find a few bottles of water, some cans of Chef Boyardee, a couple Snickers bars, and a big bag of salt and vinegar chips. Set it all on the scratched glass cash wrap. I say something about the heat and tell her I'm happy her shop is open. No response. Then I tell her I've walked here from LA. Still nothing. I ask how far I am from the campground even though I know the answer. She stops ringing up my things and fiddles with the lottery ticket dispenser. "It's just up a'ways. You can't miss it," she says. Her monotone voice not much louder than a whisper. Then she looks up and locks her eyes onto mine. I want to look away, but I can't. "You run off any tweakers yet?" she says. I shake my head. "Cuz just an hour ago I saw a couple of 'em dip into the desert. Surprised they haven't found you. They will." She starts to bag my goods and I tell her not to bother. She looks over my shoulder. "Hear that?" she says with a twinge of sarcasm. "Says he doesn't need a bag." I turn to see who she's talking to and there's nobody there. Her lips move as she taps her long fingernails on the touchscreen. I pay with cash because it seems like the right thing to do. She drops my change on the countertop like dice. Offers me a stick of cinnamon gum. Unwraps one for herself. Doesn't break eye contact. "You see this gun?" Her voice turns loud again. "I'm illegally packing, goddammit. And I don't even give a fuck." She says she opens and closes the shop every day and regularly has to deal with people high on methamphetamines. "I'm sixty-five years old. They all look eighty. And I've known most of them since they were kids." She's drawn her weapon on them plenty of times. "I tell them if they keep actin' up, I'll kill 'em. And you know what, I fuckin' would." She says in this part of the world there's nothing for folks to do. That good people get caught up doing the wrong things. "And if you think I'm gonna dick around with getting a license to protect myself from these desperate bastards, think again!" I ask if it's really that bad out here. She snorts. Looks past me again and shakes her head. "Yeah, mister. It's bad. And when you see 'em coming you gotta fight 'em." She asks if I have any weapons. I tell her I don't want to carry anything I'm not prepared to use. "All I have is a length of PVC to scare off dogs," I say. Her eyebrows raise. She leans toward me. "Mister, look here. They come after you, you're going to have to beat 'em down with that pipe, you hear me? Just like one of them fuckin'

31

dogs." I head toward the exit with my items. And before I'm out the door, she's back to yelling at people again.

*

The entire shoreline of the Salton Sea is covered with sand-sized broken fishbones. Dried up and rotting fish carcasses lay everywhere. The receding water is brackish. Oily and dark. The internet says the water is slowly disappearing. That it kills wildlife. The air is rich with a putrid stench. Earthy sewage. I find it soothing. It's far less wretched than me and I breathe it in deeply, filling my lungs.

For 20 bucks, I camp in the recreation area. Ranger says I've got the place to myself. No surprise. Set up my tent in a dirt patch near the water then sprawl out on my tarp draped atop crunchy bones. I watch the sun dip into a waxy, brown murk lurking like a grudge on the horizon. I can make out the sun's full orb as it fights the dense atmosphere. I stare directly at it. And once I lock on, I can't look away. When the sky turns to pitch, everything I see is marked with a blinding white mirage. A visual memory like a scar blotting out a blanket of stars.

I send a text to Katie with a photo of a rotting tilapia glowing in the orange sunset. "Something poetic in all of this," I write. Minutes later my phone vibrates with Katie's response. "There's beauty in change if you are open to it," she writes.

Day 11

At the fence line of the Coachella Canal, I ignore the No Trespassing signs and cross the barricade onto a footpath. My steps are heavy and crunch like I'm walking on dry cereal. After a couple hours I start to feel light-headed and woozy. Momentum pulls me forward like I'm drunk. I take a break in a patch of shade made by another warning sign. No Loitering. I fall into a deep sleep, then wake up startled and confused to the sound of squeaking brakes. An electrical line service truck idles next to me. The driver leans out. "You OK?" I perk up. "I know I'm not supposed to be out here," I say. "Just making my way to the Bradshaw Trail." He asks if I need anything. I tell him I'll happily take some water if he has any. "All's I got's this open Pepsi," he says. He hands it to me and I take a sip. Wipe my mouth with my sleeve. "Man, this is delicious," I say. He laughs. Tells me I've been out here too long. I ask if he knows the Bradshaw Trail. "Yeah, it's just ahead," he says. "But I've never really been on it. Can't miss it though. You'll see the signs."

*

It's deathly quiet out here. Not even any birdsong. The wind is hot, but even when it blows nothing moves except the dust kicking up in the distance. The interstate is only a few miles north, and yet I hear nothing. Even the occasional airplane overhead is too high to make any sound. Too high to see me, too. "Maybe I'll die watching planes go by," I say aloud and crack myself up. I can't shake a slight sense of dread.

I follow unused paths, snap photos of random waypoints, and text them to Katie. "Just reached this trail intersection...now at this fence...now this fork near a pile of rocks." If something goes awry, at least she'll have some visual evidence of where I had been. Maybe help the authorities find me quicker.

The sandy footing on the Bradshaw Trail slows me down. I have to work harder to walk. It's got to be more than 90°. I drape a handkerchief under my hat to keep the sun off my neck. Calculate my water rations and realize I need to go easy on my stash. It's not even midday and I'm already halfway through today's allotment. Four days is a long time to be without replenishment, but if I push the pace and average 20 miles per day, I'll make it to Blythe in three. I keep my head down and charge forward, increasing the clip. I think about Helga Estby who walked across the United States in 1896 with her daughter, Clara. No backpack, no cans of refried beans, no CamelBak water bladders. Not even comfortable shoes. If she can walk for seven months in those conditions, I can do four days on this damn trail. I make up a song and sing it until my throat hurts. "I don't need to drink lots of water. I don't need to eat lots of food. I just need to keep moving forward. Just like Helga would do. Just like Helga would do."

Hours later I cross paths with another work truck. I tell him about his coworker on the canal. I secretly hope he might hand over his soda, too. Instead, he opens up a mini cooler and offers me two ice-cold waters. I celebrate the score like a lottery win. Don't even mind the brain freeze. I ignore my lurking worries about my inadequate water stash as the blazing miles melt behind me in slow motion.

*

The Bradshaw Trail parallels the Chocolate Mountain Aerial Gunnery Range. Black and red danger signs every 100 meters warn to stay north of the fence and be aware of any unexploded ordnance. "Violators Will Be Subject To Prosecution." I veer off the safe side of the trail hoping to find shade beneath an abandoned train trestle.

As I near the old tracks, I hear voices. It's a group of helmeted men sitting on quads, engines off. When these me, they flip up their visors to give me a closer look and ask me what the heck I'm doing out here. "Taking a shortcut to Blythe," I say. "But ultimately walking across America." They think I'm kidding. "You crazy or something?" one asks. I assure them I've been asked that before. An older man offers me a bottle of water, and the rest follow suit, mumbling to each other as they dig into their pockets for spares. I walk from one man to the next and cradle the bottles in my arm until there are too many to carry. I lick my parched lips as I accept their gifts.

*

All this liquid generosity makes me feel like I'm beating the system. I also feel like I deserve the good tidings. My ego has increased with my swelling thirst, and rather than hike harmoniously, I mock the trail with every step. "Bring it, fuckin' Bradshaw Trail! This all you got?" I curse the single track. Shake my first and point my poles at the surrounding mountains. I taunt the landscape as it tightens its grip. "See! I can take it! I've managed worse!" I descend into some kind of self-righteous, self-preservation mode. Hyper-focused on making it to the end of this trail which, after one tough day, is making me question my worthiness of its challenges.

Between fits I'm aware that I'm slipping. I'm losing my edge. I've stopped caring how I navigate the Bradshaw and am only concerned with my commitment to get it done at all costs. My stubbornness pushes me forward. I once had a coach tell me I am more mentally strong than physically able. I think he was probably right. Which isn't necessarily a good thing. Especially not right now, anyhow. I take more photos and sent them off to Katie. "Just in case," I write.

*

I think I've got a few more miles left in me, so I make my way from the trestles back to the main trail. I find a pace again. The stabbing of my poles into the loose sand, the dull crush under my shoes, my raspy and labored breathing. "Fuck yeah," I say. "Here I go." I hum the tune to my Helga song before belting it again. "Just like Helga would do!" Then, zapped, most likely, by my extra energetic output, I start to doze off while walking. Like I've been driving too long and can't stay awake. I punch myself in the legs and shake my head. "Come on, Griffen, get it together." But still, every few steps my eyes go dark, my knees buckle, and I catch myself mid-collapse. Once, I drop a trekking pole and have a split second dream that I've lost an oar in the rapids. I pick it up and am not sure which end is the handle.

The sun is low behind me, and now is as good a time as any to stop. I find a place to camp off the trail. Soon as I take off my pack, the corded muscles of my calves and hamstrings lock up. I stretch my foot on a rock to keep the cramps at bay, but they keep coming. Squatting is impossible, so I have to lay down to hammer in tent stakes. I drain the day's water ration and crave more. Pine for a sip. I down a quick dinner and go directly to bed. Because if I'm sleeping I won't think about drinking.

Day 12

I'm barely five miles in when I start seeing water bottles everywhere along the trail. Repeatedly, I rush to pick one up— only to realize it's actually a rock. One time it's a weathered Dasani bottle with a few ounces of gray backwash sloshing at the bottom. I drink it, then shake my fist at the desert, laughing like a maniac. "Haha! Is that all you got, motherfucker?"

Before lunch the heat reaches the mid-90s. My vision tunnels and I stumble along the trail. My heart pounds, racing erratically. The mountains in front and behind look the same and I wonder if I'm going the right direction. "Shake it off, man!" I shout. I rattle off my food inventory to the blue sky. "Beans! Tortillas! Cholula! Apples! Fruit cocktail! Oats! Instant coffee!" I struggle doing simple math as I confirm my water ration. "Seven bottles at one and a half liters equals how many days' worth of water?" I thought I brought enough to complete the Bradshaw. But now I'm unsure. A reflection in the far eastern distance catches my attention. "See, Griffen. That's Blythe. You can make it that far." But it's not Blythe. Not even close. Just some house or shack a couple miles ahead. And though I know this, I don't want to admit it.

*

I sit in a swatch of tumbleweed shade. All I can think about is water. Sweet and wet and gloriously delicious cold water. I'm so thirsty I'm livid. I lay down in the dirt and feel the cool dust on the side of my face. My breathing stirs it up. I watch a large ant race away. "I need a break. Just a few minutes. Just a few fucking minutes." I take off my pack and use it as a pillow. Close my eyes.

*

I jump awake. The shade is gone. A thin layer of desert talc covers my face. I try to spit but I can't. My tongue is dry. I rub dirt from my eyes. "Fuckin' dehydration," I whisper. I know this feeling. I scoot my body back into the shade of the weeds. I try to rationalize my situation, but I can barely hold onto a thought besides my craving for water. I want water. I need water. And all I need is in my backpack. But if I drink it, I can't keep going. I'll have to turn around. I lay down and fall asleep again. Wake up gasping. Choking. The walls of my throat pinched together. The colorless landscape. It's all too bright. My lips are rope. I just want a sip. One sip. I want water. I think of Katie. Her words. "Make good decisions. I know you will." I sit up. Rub my numb cheeks. Reach one shaky arm toward my pack. Unzip the top. Pull out a tall bottle, stare at the sloshing liquid within, and salivate. "Fuck it," I say. I break the seal. I raise the spout to my mouth, and whimper as I fill my belly with warm water. It leaks down my chin like I've forgotten how to drink. Rivers through my beard, into the neck of my salty shirt, onto my chest. I swallow mouthful after mouthful until my stomach is full. Until my vision clears and I come back to life.

I remember a northbound turnoff from this morning. Maybe two or three miles back. I'll follow it out to the freeway. Probably make it there by tomorrow afternoon. Drink as much water as I want between now and then. I failed this trail. But at least I'll live through it.

*

I load up and turn around. After an hour I start to doubt my memory because I should have made it to the intersection by now. When another group of off-road vehicles stops, I ask about the road to the interstate. "Oh yeah. Gasline Road. It's still maybe seven more miles ahead." They ask if I'm OK. I say I'm not. A couple in a two-seater says they live out here and have never seen anyone trying to walk the trail before. "Hop in," they demand. "We'll ride you there." They say I'm a rockstar for giving it a go. "More like an idiot, maybe," I say. I pile into the back with my pack still strapped on. They give me a couple cold waters and tell me to hold on tight. The driver hits the gas and suddenly there's a breeze. I press the waters against my cheeks and go limp.

At the crossroads they cut the engine and dismount. We exchange handshakes and hugs. More cold waters. "Be careful, bro. This place ain't no joke!" When the dust clears I start walking north. I want to cry but it's like I've run out of tears. So I just make the noises of crying. I drink three liters of water before I finally have to pee.

*

It's a miracle my phone has service out here. It's been spotty the past few days but suddenly I've got full bars. I've been texting people all afternoon. Sharing my near miss and seeking validation for my decision to turn back. But no matter how many people tell me I did the right thing, I still feel like I sorta blew it. Joel offers to rescue me from the slapdash exit where the trail meets Interstate 10 at Red Cloud Mine. He'll bring me groceries and help me formulate a plan B.

In my tent, I flip through pages of my journal and find random messages from a bunch of friends. Katie must have secretly passed it around at my farewell party for folks to write uplifting notes. Like signing a yearbook. "Thanks for sharing your adventures, passion, and energy with our family. You brighten our lives…I know you can do this, no doubt in my mind…You so totally have this!" I also reread my own journal entry from before I started the walk. I wrote, "As the day gets closer, after waiting 25 years, suddenly everything is brighter and more obvious. Like I'm taking it all in for the last time. The big question—what do I want for the second part of my life? My answer—finally accept myself."

I prop the journal on my lap and consider how I might respond to my own words. I still have a lot to work on. I'm still angry. Self-centered. Uncertain. Opinionless. A chameleon. I still need to dig deeper into my heart to better understand why I am out here and why it matters. But one thing that's obvious after today—life is richer when I allow myself to be open. To share and be vulnerable. It's not a sign of weakness. Or of failure.

My friend Michelle sends me a message via social media. "Ask for help, Tom. It's a sign of strength." Someone else writes, "Saying no is as important as saying yes. Well done." Another friend jokes, "You need a donkey to carry that water." The people around me help me get back on the rails. I fall asleep with a full belly and heart.

Day 13

The morning is cool and damp. Wispy clouds slowly swirl and disappear as they move across the sky. An occasional red tail hawk scolds as it circles. I image it's sounding an alert. Announcing the presence of a pasty creature making a racket near an orange rectangle. I've always thought of hawks as my spirit guide and take its presence as a sign that I'm doing the right thing. I'm in no hurry to break camp and do so in parts as I continue to pour water down my throat. I eat a double serving of my instant oats ration then get back on the northbound path toward where I'll meet up with Joel. My pack is a thousand times lighter and I feel great. Which is funny since less than 24 hours ago I was trying to drink rocks.

I reach the exit a couple hours early. The area is stacked with newly whitewashed concrete barriers. Leaning against one heaping pile is a purple-frocked Christmas tree. Someone's discard. I explore the area to confirm I am alone, then snag a shady spot and listen to the incessant hum of traffic. I'm aghast at the smell radiating from my crotch. Even with legs closed, a penetrating bouquet of fermenting gouda gorges my nostrils. It's repulsive, and yet oddly magnetic. I find solace in the tranquilizing pungency of my vile body odors. I breathe in the smell of life. I am finally at ease.

*

Joel's arrival stirs me from a shallow nap. At a nearby rest stop, we reassemble my pack at a shady picnic table and brainstorm what I should do. We decide the electrical line road parallel to the interstate is as good an option as any to propel me safely into Blythe. If things go south again, I'll be close enough to the highway to flag someone down.

Joel and I drive east in search of a place to easily access the service line road. After a week at 4 mph, 80 feels like warp speed. We don't talk much because I'm worried I'm breaking one of my three walking rules. First, make safe decisions. Second, take no rides unless I don't have a choice. And third, be nice. It's rule #2 that's getting to me. I ask Joel if this ride is a cheat. He rubs the back of his neck as he keeps his eyes on the road. Tells me he doesn't like the word cheat. "Because really, who or what are you cheating?" I sit silently with his question. Stare out the window looking south as we glide alongside the Chocolate Mountains. Somewhere out there is the trail I was on yesterday. Now that I am feeling somewhat back to normal, I wonder if I really needed my brother to swoop in like an angel to save me. Or did I just need a pick-me-up? I'm afraid to share these thoughts with him, so I keep them inside. When he takes the exit for Wiley Well where I'll join the service road, I finally answer his question. "Who am I cheating? It's me. I'm only cheating me."

We say goodbye, again, then I start along the path that will take me into the border town. Joel takes a video as I walk away. "This part is going to be boring as hell!" I shout after taking a few strides. The distance increases between us. Each step draws me further into quiet. I turn around for one final wave to Joel, my safekeeper, who's still standing there, watching me disappear.

*

The electrical line road is littered with piles of items. A heap of spent tires, a mountain of refrigerators. A gleaming hillock of scrap metal with branching trails to nowhere paved with purpling glass. There's a beauty in the rambling debris. And also, a loneliness.

These are the details of Americana. Artifacts of a past left behind by modernity. The good ol' days. The picturesque crumblings—like wrinkles on a face—are proof of a life lived.

While taking a break in the winter sun, I throw rocks at a rotten stove until my shoulder is sore. Each time a stone connects with metal, I am overcome by a feeling of satisfaction.

Day 14

I reach hardtop at West Hobsonway and stop to check Apple Maps' suggested route into Blythe. Downtown is just over eight miles away. Should take about two hours or so. I'll make it with plenty of time to grab lunch at a diner before crossing the Colorado River and leaving California. Once in Arizona, I'll duck into the desert and find a place to camp, likely within range of the interstate. Probably follow the electrical line road for a couple more days before jutting northeast on the Arizona 60. Or maybe do an illegal pedestrian stretch on the 10. But I'm getting ahead of myself.

As I pass the Blythe airport, a shooting jolt lurches up from my left heel. Stabs me in the calf and nearly knocks me down. I'm no stranger to mysterious aches resulting from long miles. I've learned that pain likes attention. Usually it comes and goes, moving around from one body part to another. And generally, if I relax and take a few deep breaths, it fizzles. But this grip grabs at me, unyielding. Doesn't fall for my circumvention. If anything, it multiplies, forcing my march to swiftly deteriorate into a biting limp. Making it nearly impossible to put any weight on my foot. My top speed devolves to a creep. Without trekking poles I'd be unable to ambulate. I wince with each step.

I trust the pain's just being stubborn. But if it doesn't relent, the five miles into Blythe will be a slog. I walk a few steps, rest a few steps, walk a few, rest a few. I couldn't go any faster if my life depended on it. My neck burns from the midday sun and I consider my alternatives. I could hitchhike, but I've yet to see a car. The Lyft app shows two vehicles in the vicinity, but the wait time for a ride is 45 minutes. So I sit on a patch of grass near a barren shopping center and seriously consider squatting behind the dumpsters for the night. After my fiasco on the Bradshaw, I've convinced myself that Blythe is the promised land. I've got my heart set on a greasy burger and piles of salty fries. And I want it tonight, not tomorrow.

I lay on the blacktop and raise my foot in the air. Which makes it throb more. I remove my shoe and sock and massage my thumb into the heel. Still no relief. Looks like I'm not crossing the border today. Might not make it to downtown, either. But I can't stop thinking about that juicy goddamned burger. A thick wedge of ground beef, warm and pink in the middle, dripping with hot grease and an excessive whorl of goopy condiments. Crunchy green lettuce holding the thick red tomato in place. Sesame seeds dotting the pillowy, untoasted bun. Thick steak-cut fries on the side, crusted with grains of salt. Barbecue sauce for dip. I ache for this, and my imagined indulgence is enough to motivate me to relent to the sufferfest.

I hobble back to stand, then limp and cringe as I fight the miles to the first somewhat respectable-looking hotel. I call to make sure they have a room, then go directly to the greasy spoon next door and gorge myself. My server calls me sweetie and suggests the cherry pie as I squiggle another pile of ketchup on the plate for the last few bits of burnt fry remnants. I wash it all down with weak coffee, creamed and sugared, because that's what I do in diners like this. But also because something about drinking a cup of coffee with a heavy lunch makes me feel like an outlaw. Like a cowboy. And this matters. Because such fanfare readies me for a thorough triage of my situation. I pay my tab, then limp back to the hotel where I ask the clerk to book me for two nights. I'll rest here. Another day off will do me some good. I'm sure I'll be back on the road in no time.

*

Once in the room I start in on RICE. Rest, ice, compression, and elevation. But it's more like RIE because I don't have anything to truly compress my foot. My years as a runner taught me that many foot issues are actually exacerbated calf issues. I foolishly didn't pack a massage ball, so I improvise and drill my calf with the lip of a coffee mug. Its ceramic edges help me blast one sensitive trigger point after another. The pain makes my stomach churn. I had a track coach back in high school who gave extra praise to athletes who barfed at the finish line. Until right now, I hadn't thought of him in decades.

*

I spend my off day adhering to a self-care circuit. Ice bath, hot tub soak, mug massage, RIE, repeat. I am convinced the pain is decreasing and I visualize my foot coming back to normal. I'm sure I'll wake up tomorrow feeling 100% because that's how it usually plays out. I watch more History Channel garbage. *Pawn Stars* this time. Another marathon of reruns. I've seen them all.

Day 15

Things are worse in the morning. I'm barely able to walk to the bathroom because my injured foot won't allow any stepping weight. There's swelling, but only a little. Also no bruising or redness. In the past I've had undetectable injuries that seem to manifest during times of emotional stress. Maybe this is all psychosomatic? But it can't be—the pain is too intense. It's got to be something. And probably something serious. Like maybe a break? The impossible option keeps popping up, but I pay it no mind. I refuse to entertain the prospect of throwing in the towel. Such thoughts inspire waking nightmares.

Worry stirs my mind into a confused soup. Makes me question my intention to undertake this journey. Is walking across the US something I actually want to do? Or have I simply convinced myself it is? I journal a bit and try to make a list of all the things I want from life. All I come up with is "Good health and enough money to not be homeless." But these answers frighten me. How can I, Tom Griffen, not have a laundry list of specific and attainable wants? Am I not a risk-taker? An adventure-seeker? Don't I have the smarts and know-how to build an impressive personal resume of accomplishments? Don't I have wild and unending aspirations? I flip back to the page with that prewalk question I asked before leaving home. "What do I want from this second half of my life?" And for the life of me I can't tell the difference between my truth and what I'm convinced ought to be true. My thoughts are interrupted by my ringing phone. It's a FaceTime call.

It's my good buddy Dusty. He's facilitated a consultation with Lino, the rare sort of intuitive body worker who's got a knack for naming patients' ailments before they share their complaints. Lino confidently tells me I'm suffering from the effects of severe dehydration. He's certain the conditions on the Bradshaw Trail are to blame—unseasonable heat, an extra-heavy pack, the uneven and sandy footing. Lino's marching orders are not unlike what I've already been doing except for a huge increase in my water intake. Lino also recommends new shoes.

After the call I hydrate so much I need to pee every 10 minutes. I also call Katie and ask her to overnight a new pair of Brooks Cascadias from my home stash. Straight away I feel better, certain I'll be back on the road tomorrow after the shoes arrive. I can't think of a better birthday gift for myself.

Day 16

The first thing I notice when I wake up is pain. Even with fresh kicks on my feet, my walk to the diner is the slowest yet. While downing one of the thick sausages included with the Rancher's Breakfast, I reluctantly text Katie's dad, David, in Phoenix. Before I started, David told me to hit him up at any point between California and New Mexico. I tell him I need a place to stay for a while. "A week, maybe," I write. David doesn't miss a beat. He drives three hours to pick me up.

David delivers me directly to the Phoenix VA hospital where I tell the ER receptionist I may have a stress fracture. A Black man named Charles, also from North Carolina, processes my intake. We bypass standard small talk and dive into a conversation about human connection. He assures me there's a bigger reason I had to stop. One that transcends injury. "You should be open to it, too. Don't question things. Could be you need rest, but could also be this here connection you and I are making right now. You never know." Charles orders an X-ray that shows no evidence of skeletal trauma. "Stress fractures rarely show up, anyhow," the doctor says. "I think it's a bad case of plantar fasciitis." I've had plantar fasciitis tons of times, and when I compare my current symptoms to what I've previously experienced, this is definitely not the same thing. "But what about my limited range of motion?" The doctor says it's sympathetic pain. The irony isn't lost on me.

Back at David's place, he sets up TV trays in the living room so we can eat and watch a Phoenix Suns game. During a commercial break, he excuses himself. Returns with a mini chocolate cake on a saucer. "Happy birthday," he says. "Katie told me you might like this."

Days 17 - 21

Over the next few days I intend to rest but instead I obsessively pack and repack my gear. I borrow David's car and zip around Phoenix, faltering back and forth across town trying to find the perfect long-sleeved shirt and a wide-brimmed hat to keep me protected from the sun. I hope to be back in Blythe by the end of the week, yet I'm plagued by the worst-case scenario.

Between chores I browse flights to Raleigh and send self-absorbed texts to friends. Countless uplifting notes fill my DMs, including two from crossers whose solo journeys I followed last year. Lindsay and Erin separately tell me to hang in there. That this is all part of the experience of the walk.

I scroll thorough photos of their respective trips and consider the gear they used. They both pushed baby joggers to haul their stuff. Kent did it this way, too. Pushing or pulling a wheeled contraption is a common strategy amongst crossers. I knew this before I started, but I didn't want to do it that way. I wanted to lug my load and I longingly fantasized about the suffering it would cause. I figured my accomplishment would be even more impressive if I could do it with everything strapped to my body. I wanted people to notice me. Shit, I still do.

But this unceasing need for external validation has set me up for failure. It's proven, yet again, that I'm not as hardcore as I want to be. Not as impressive as I want to be. Not as accomplished or able or storied or strong as I want to be. As I stuff my face with junk food and watch mindless television on

David's couch, I imagine a different narrative for my life. One in which I honestly don't care what other people think. Where I do what I want to do for my sake alone rather than for others' acceptance of me. This practice resembles thinking with someone else's brain, so I abort it. Refocus on which jogger I should buy so I can get my ass back on the road. Because there's no fucking way I'm doing it with just a pack.

*

After a few hours of online research, I borrow David's car and dive into rush hour traffic. Crawl through Phoenix sprawl to an REI where I find a red Thule Chariot Cougar 2. A stroller built for two children. I unlock the foot brake and gingerly maneuver it around the store. Feel like a new dad must feel. I catch my breath. "Stay focused, Griffen," I say to myself.

I maneuver the double wide jogger around apparel racks and cross the length of the store multiple times. It moves effortlessly. Doesn't weigh a thing. It is also nimble enough to pivot without effort. A red tag identifies it as the floor model. It's priced to sell.

Crosser Erin had previously mentioned getting a four-wheeler rather than a three. "This probably sounds like a really small deal," she wrote. "But four wheels allowed me to straddle rumble strips on the sides of roads, whereas with three you can pretty much expect to be rattling and bumping over them for miles." This Chariot Cougar fits the bill. So I buy it. Erin also urged me to ditch the stock tires and invest in heavier-duty Kevlar options. She recommended I line the tubes with puncture-deterring slime. "And don't forget an air pump!" she wrote. "And a patch kit!" I also purchase a five-gallon water jug that tucks nicely into the cart's main compartment. I'm so excited I won't have to carry my water that I impulse buy a dozen energy bars, too. I tell the checker I'm using the jogger to finish my journey across America. Her blank response is a buzzkill, but another employee hears my story and interrupts. "Man, that's something I've always thought would be cool. Just being out there for so long and not having to worry about a thing except walking." He asks where and when I plan to stop. I tell him about my injury. He hands me a sticker in the shape of Arizona. "For the bumper," he jokes. Tells me he'll be following along on my Instagram.

I shell out a small fortune, then text Katie a photo of my new setup. She insists it needs a name, like Wilson in the Tom Hanks film, *Castaway*. She suggests I name it Little Buddy, which doesn't immediately resonate with me, but it sticks. I assign Little Buddy a masculine gender which, for some unknown reason, feels right. I tell Katie this in a subsequent text message. "It's a boy!" She writes back, "Go LB!"

I mark Little Buddy's panels with neon pink duct tape. In big boxy capital letters on the front I form the words, Walk USA. On the side that will face traffic I write, No Baby, hoping to decrease the chances of anyone thinking I'm pushing an actual infant on the roadside. Maybe keep 911 calls to a minimum.

*

My grandma always says, "Never stay anywhere more than two days, because after two days fish start to stink." I've been at David's for five days now. Broken Gram's rule twice over. Thankfully my foot is responding to the rest. Enough for us to plan a return to Camp Blythe, as David calls it.

I'm desperate to get back on the road. These creature comforts are great, but they're making me soft. I've been kicking myself for being so lazy. For sitting on the couch and eating too much fast food. But maybe that's precisely what I've been needing? My thoughts vacillate between castigation and compassion. I make another note in my journal. "To do this right I need to allow myself to enjoy the down time as much as I enjoy my walking days. Process over product." My words are like prayer. I hope that writing them will help them come true.

Day 22

There's a gem show in Quartzite and I land one of the few remaining hotel rooms in Blythe. Nightly rates are maxed by the event. The woman at the front desk shrugs when I tell her I'm not even here for it. "Me neither," she says. I suck it up and book three nights. A couple more days off should have me game ready again. David insists he's still a phone call away. Before he leaves, I tell him I hope to not see him for a while.

Day 23

I do a video consultation with Dr. Lau, a chiropractor and old friend from my days in Sacramento. He's convinced my talocalcaneal joint is locked up. He gives me more exercises and recommends I continue with the ice and heat regimen. "When you starting up again?" he asks. I tell him the day after tomorrow. "You should consider it a test walk," he says. "So don't push it. But text me as the day progresses, OK?" There's concern in his face, but I blame it on the spotty Wi-Fi.

Day 24

While I'm sitting with my foot in the hotel jacuzzi, an employee strikes up a conversation. I tell him about my walk. About my foot. He passes on advice from his high school football coach. "Drink a gallon of water a day and tape that shit up. Hold it all in place, you know. And if all that don't work, do some of that Mister Miyagi shit." He claps his hands and quickly rubs them together. I tell him I already tried some woo-woo stuff. Herbal remedies and magic tea. "Now I'm waiting for it to start helping," I say. "Oh yeah?" he says. "Well maybe you need to stop waiting for things to happen, bro."

Day 25

I assemble Little Buddy and load him up for the first time. In his hold is a full jug of water weighing about 40 pounds. There's a week's worth of food in a duffle bag, probably another 10 pounds. My backpack is stuffed with all my original camping gear, maybe another 15 pounds. And an assortment of other jogger-related equipment like spare tubes and tires, the air pump and flat kits, adding maybe 5 more pounds. I trashed Little Buddy's user manual back at David's place, but I seem to recall his maximum load-carrying capacity being 100 pounds. I should be fine.

The plan is to cross the California border and enter Ehrenberg, Arizona. Then get on the northbound side of Interstate 10 and follow the electrical line road. Should be a short day. Little Buddy's maiden voyage will test his hard top and off-road capabilities.

*

After an early wake up and my fill of the continental breakfast, I peek outside the hotel window to see if anyone's nearby. All clear. Then I unbolt the door and push Little Buddy onto the breezeway. His bumpers bang the doorjamb, barely fitting through. A stout, white-haired woman crosses the parking lot to her room, then doubles back and introduces herself. She is Leann. Hands me two bottles of water. She and her husband, Minnesota folks, are traveling across the USA in a camper. She offers me money. I tell her I'm good to go. "I'm going to pray for you, OK? People need to take care of each other. They don't do it enough anymore." Leann reaches into her pocket and pulls out two $2 bills. The dark green and red ink is a clue to their age. "Not sure why I have these with me," she says. "They've been in my dresser drawer back home for the past twenty years." She looks at the notes in her hands. "I've always thought $2 bills are good luck, you know?" she says. "But I think you need good luck more than I do right now. So here, please take them." She hands me the bills then asks if she can hug me. Holds on tight for an extra second. I limp across the hotel lot, pushing Little Buddy with ease. Hoping Leann's lucky bills contain some of her good vibes. Or at least some of that Mr. Miyagi shit.

*

I'm a spectacle. Grown ass man pushing a conspicuously signed double-wide cart through town. Drivers brake to rubberneck, honk and wave and shout unintelligible comments out their windows. Pedestrians ask what I'm doing. They marvel at Little Buddy and want to touch his tires and feel the cushioned grip on his handlebar. We are like a vacuum, sucking in the attention of all passersby. And it's all his fault. We can't walk more than a few steps without someone interrupting. This attention agitates me, makes me want to walk faster even though I can't. Makes me curse my new companion and my busted up foot. "This is all your fault," I say, addressing both culprits. I want to get the hell out of Blythe. Cross the Colorado and put a cork in California.

As I near the border, I'm encouraged by my foot's responsiveness. Then pain is static but doesn't seem to be getting worse. I manage sub-20-minute miles past strip malls and RV lots. Before long the bridge spanning the Colorado comes into sight. A separated pedestrian path over the murky water makes it easy to finally exit the sunshine state. Rather than celebrate the accomplishment, I scold myself for not doing this a week ago. "It's about fucking time, Griffen!" Hard to believe that this skinny river is the same one that carved the Grand Canyon. "Oh the things you've seen," I say to it as I unceremoniously pass over it.

*

On Apple Maps, the Ehrenberg service road is obvious. A thin line running parallel to, and south of the interstate. The first mile is hard-packed and effortless for Little Buddy's tires. But when deep sandy patches sporadically appear, I'm forced to pull him backwards to make any sort of headway.

The road slowly devolves, eventually turning into a broken trail littered with volleyball-sized cobbles. Soon it's marked by sharp dips and steep, rugged inclines that tax Little Buddy's axles. I regularly pick angry thorns from his tires and hope I don't have to deal with a flat.

The sections morph into steep ascents. At the bottom of each climb I empty out LB's contents and lug everything separately to the top of the incline. Then I fetch him from the bottom and reload him again. I repeat this same Sisyphean process minutes later at the next climb. My foot is taking a beating. The steady pain from this morning has changed its tune, and now every step hurts more than the last. Even if I were at my physical best, this undertaking would be a chore.

All afternoon my foot screams louder and louder. I stop in the middle of an even plane to reassess. This test walk is proving what I don't want to accept. I am truly injured. And I need more time to rest. How long? I don't know. But I do know I don't have the resources to wait out a full recovery at a hotel in Blythe, or the willingness to do so at David's indefinitely. In the scorch of midday, I text Dr. Lau with an update. "Pain has increased quite a bit as the day progresses. Feeling serious tightness in the Achilles area." I hit send. I already know what he's going to say. Minutes later my phone dings. "I think that's enough testing for today, Tom. This just shows me your foot is not ready. I know it's a tough decision but I think the smartest thing is to go home, let yourself heal up with some proper rest, and try again at a later date. The good thing is now you'll be able to bulletproof your foot and ankle for when you try again. It's gonna make the finish all the sweeter. Looking forward to following your journey when it resumes!"

Dr. Lau's optimism feels good, though it's short-lived. The prospect of being bulletproof, as he says, exists in an alternate universe. I can barely imagine making it to the goddamned gas station five miles ahead, let alone be back out here any time soon. The trip is over, and I never even made it out of California.

*

I call David. Hem and haw before telling him I need to take him up on his offer. His tone tells me he expected as much. He'll meet me on the roadside in a few hours. Before pressing on to where this trail meets the road at Tom Wells exit, I book a flight home. Plan B now in full effect. The cool evening breeze dries my tears before they make it past my sunburned cheeks. I don't want to fucking cry. I want to scream. So I do. Until my throat is out of sound. I text Katie. "I'm coming home. Don't tell anyone."

*

Finally back on an even bit of trail, I adjust my gait and find a semblance of stride. It's broken, but it takes my mind off pain for stretches at a time. I notice something off-trail that seems out of place. A large shape of some sort. I walk past it, then let go of Little Buddy's handle and backtrack for a closer look. I brush past desert scrub and cacti until it's in full view. A large symbol made with rocks. A wide circle with a long, zig-zagging arrow piercing through the center of it. I don't recognize it.

In my raw state I apply the marking's symbolism to my situation. The circle marks my overall journey, and the arrow represents my original plan. The arrow's abrupt shift in direction —the zig-zagging lightning bolt—is what's happening right now. It's the change I didn't anticipate. The fact that it keeps arrowing through the circle implies a new plan is at play. One that will find me back here at some point, continuing along a path unexpected. My heart lifts.

Off the trail, I walk an overpass across the 10 just as the sun sets, making the world glow like everything's brand new. I wave at cars blasting by at the speed of life, a speed I'm not looking forward to rejoining. I park LB in a far corner of a Chevron station and make myself comfortable. It'll be at least two hours before David arrives. The air temperature drops and the cooling air chills me through my sweaty clothes. I scroll through pictures on my phone, already feeling nostalgic for the steps behind me. I look at the group shot on day one, the photo of Derek, Katie, and me in Hollywood, one of Donut Man on Route 66, the waypoints from the goddamned Bradshaw Trail, another of Leann's $2 bills. I inhale a giant burst of air and expect to start bawling, but nothing happens. My arms fall heavy to my sides.

I worry this is the end of my walk across America, but find a morsel of peace in having made it across California. I damn my foot aloud, then search for a positive spin on my predicament. There's got to be a worthwhile lesson in here somewhere, because there always is. But right now I don't see it. Right now everything glows blue under the humming station lights and I feel hopeless. Like I blew it. And now I have to return home and deal with the outcome.

*

Our ride back to Phoenix is quiet. We make small talk about dinner and grab takeout that we eat on TV trays in his living room. Later, as I lay in bed, I open my social media and post a photo of the symbol I found at the moment the trip ended. I'm worried its connotations may be negative. Nick, an old friend who's been following my journey, immediately identifies it and posts his findings. "I just looked it up," he writes. "It's the international squat symbol taken from the American hobo sign language. It means you're on the right track." I am relieved. Thankful it wasn't some white power or Nazi bullshit. I do some more research and learn that it's also called a *kraakteken*. In Dutch, *kraak* means crack or heist. *Teken* means sign. The right path, the keeping on, something that's split, a theft of sorts. It's all relatable. Hope flickers. Though barely.

Day 26 - 42

I'm asleep before we take off. Wake up at 30,000 feet as a flight attendant hands over a bag of peanuts and asks if I want something to drink. I shake my head and go back to sleep, and don't wake up again until the wheels hit the tarmac. As we taxi to the terminal, I book an appointment with Brian, a physical therapist I've worked with in the past. When the seatbelt light goes off with a ding, everyone scrambles. I follow the herd, and take my walk of shame up the jetway, down the glowing hallway, and out to the curb where Katie is waiting.

*

My PT appointment is more a counseling session than anything. Brian wants to know my *why* before I even take my shoes off. My answer starts with a sigh and is as clunky as ever. "A lifelong dream…to push the limits…to see America at a walking pace… because I can…and why the hell not?" But Brian isn't satisfied. He prods more. Articulates my stuck foot as he pushes his inquiry deeper. "Yes Tom, I get it. But really, why are you doing this? Why are you doing this to yourself? This stuck foot, energetically, has a lot to do with whatever else is stuck in your life. The physical is always connected to the mental."

Brian confirms what Lino suggested back in Blythe. My injury is the result of dehydration, excessive pronation, some pretty major navicular drop, and a fatigue-compromised gait cycle. It's all the stuff I used to regularly deal with when I was a distance runner. But unlike in those days, I haven't been accommodating my wonky foot biomechanics with any sort of shoe orthotics. I purposely started the walk without them because I didn't want to have to worry about replacing them—a strategy that's now backfiring. Brian assures me my prognosis is good. "But there's nothing anyone can do that will speed up the repair of soft tissue." He figures I'll need at least a few weeks. Says it's all going to depend on how I frame it. "Are you prepared to scrap this journey if you have to? What will it mean if you can't finish what you started?" His question fills the space between us as his next client walks in. Brian introduces us and tells her what I'm doing. "This guy is in the middle of walking across the U S of A!" She steps back and asks why. Brian laughs. Looks at me with wide eyes. "See Tom. You need to rethink what this thing's all about before you can expect any sort of lasting progress." I leave the office feeling like a puppy whose snout just got mashed in a puddle of its own piss. How many times do I need to consider my reason for walking before I understand it?

*

My inspiration for this walk hit me in 1994 when I was fresh out of the Army. The crystallizing moment happened in, of all places, a barbershop, while I waited for my turn with Hassan. I'd been going to him for years. He sculpted my high school mullet and later maintained my high and tight when I was home on leave. Hassan was Iranian. When I first met him he went by Hussein. But some point early in the Gulf War, he changed his name. My mom included the news in a letter while I was stationed in Germany.

Hassan spoke with a thick accent. I had to pay closer attention to understand his words. Whenever we crossed paths, he'd ask about my family. I'd assure him everyone was well. At which time he'd hold his comb and scissors skyward, raise his gaze toward the ceiling and announce "Thanks God, thanks God!" He always seemed relieved by my news. Then he'd bring his large hands together, close his eyes, and mutter a silent prayer. I'd watch his lips move without a sound. Something in

Hassan's vocal upswing and subsequent calm made me feel a certain devoutness missing from my Catholic upbringing. But rather than credit a higher power for this sign of something heavenly, I ascribed the magic to Hassan himself. When I was with him I felt something. Something for which I had no words. These moments always made me want to hug him. But truth be told, I never had the guts to do so.

Growing long hair was the sort of civilian fantasy all soon-to-be-discharged troops bragged about. But upon my return home, I backpedaled on my plan and held onto my military persona. When I hit up Hassan's shop for a clean-up, the place was bonkers. The line maybe four or five deep. So I grabbed a couple tattered magazines off a banged-up rack and settled into a wobbly wooden chair. I flipped through a dog-eared Thrasher, pages soft as toilet paper, and a *National Geographic* from April 1977. The cover—a portrait of a smiling Nepalese child, floppy fur hat playfully tilted atop his head. A closed-mouth grin suggested an inside joke. The magazine's main headline was "Pilgrimage to Nepal's Crystal Mountain." Another title just below it asked "One Canada—Or Two?" The third headline didn't make sense. I had to read it a few times before it sunk in. It said, "A Walk Across America." A *what*? A walk *where*?

I raced to find the article within and inspected the opening photo of a young, bearded man sitting on the ground, his back against a roadside shack. A tall, aluminum-framed backpack leaned next to him. The snapshot captured him chatting with an Alabama state trooper who sat nearby, a Smokey the Bear hat atop his head and big smile on his face. Another man, who seemed to be the shop proprietor, stood laughing in the narrow doorway with a newspaper between his fingers. The article's subtitle: "Confused by our turbulent times, a young Connecticut Yankee sets out to span the continent in search of his country and himself." This is where I was first introduced to Peter Jenkins, transcontinental walker. I nosed in.

On October 15, 1973, Jenkins and his malamute Cooper set out afoot from New York en route to the Pacific. He figured the journey would take nine months. But four years later, when the *National Geographic* article was published, he was still going at it.

As I read the piece, my hands shook. My heart raced. Nothing made sense and yet everything did. I examined the intricate details of the photo essay. The wrinkles on a grizzled face. The strong back of a foundry worker. A woman in a fur coat smoking a cigarette while posing near her 240Z. I stroked the glossy pages. Admired the font and italicized captions. Read the 33-page spread as I breathed in the muscular smell of lemony aftershave. I finished the story with two thoughts. *Holy shit, you can walk across America?* And, *Someday I'm going to do it, too.*

Hassan called my name, startling me. I jumped up with the magazine still in hand and asked him if I could keep it. He shrugged yes, brushed off the chair, shook out the cape, and told me to take a seat. Once settled in, I asked Hassan what he thought about walking from the Atlantic to the Pacific. "Too much far," he said, shaking his head. He blew on the clipper blades, then dabbed a drop of oil onto them. "Too much dangerous. Too, too much." His words only made me want to do it even more.

For 25 years I've been telling myself and others that someday I will walk across the US. The thought has become a mental groove. Like a notch in a record player from which my life's narrative needle never deviates. It's the sort of psychological imprint that subsequently formed who I am and what I've done through the years. When I ask myself if I actually want to walk across America, there is no answer besides *of course*. Now, in my middle age, I have a sense of why walking across America was so appealing on that day in the barber shop. Back then, I was still trying to name myself. Still trying to create an identity that I could get my claws into. I figured the more head-turning things I did, the more likely I was to earn positive attention. From peers, from love interests, from employers. And I was right. My life has subsequently been a series of big things in my quest to prove that I am interesting. And now, a quarter century later, I fear this insecurity remains true. It scares me to think that all I've become with age and maturity is a less physically nimble version of my wildly uncertain younger self. Still unable to truly name why I'm embarking on a big thing. Unable to put into words why such a massive undertaking even matters.

*

Barely a month ago I gathered for beers and farewells with my local supporters and figured I wouldn't see them again for at least six months. Now I'm home way sooner than anyone imagined. I sit on my blue plaid couch, reluctant to leave the house except to retrieve a couple pieces of daily junk mail or play fetch with Pepper, the neighbor's dog. I don't dare go downtown. No way. Last thing I want to do is tell my failure story over and over. I feel like I let folks down. And even though Katie is helping me remain optimistic, her presence complicates everything. We're supposed to be breaking up. And now that I've failed the walk, I also have a daily reminder of my relationship failure, too. Nothing feels right, nothing tastes right, nothing sounds right. I start and interrupt countless movies on Netflix. I can't settle on any background music from my playlist. And I put off responding to texts or phone calls or emails or social media comments because what the heck am I going to say? I'm stuck. And all I want to do is sleep.

My friends Scotty and TR plan a coffee meet-up. I'm terrified of going anywhere beyond my front yard, but at Katie's prodding I join them. Familiar faces at the cafe smile and wave, while others stop by our table to offer encouraging words. "Thanks for doing what you've done! You gave it your best shot." Some ask for hugs, and each time they do my throat tightens. One woman, more an acquaintance than a friend, asks if she can interrupt us for a second. "What you did was enough. It got us all thinking about what's really important." She says something about there being only one journey. "When you realize everything you do is all part of the experience, you'll see failure is impossible. Stopping is simply a detail. But it's all in the way you look at it."

At a yoga class the same night, my instructor Scott stops by my mat to welcome me home. "There's no shame in making the right decision, Tom." His heavy hand on my shoulder accentuates his words. At some point during the class I catch a reflection of myself in a mirror. Me and everyone moving together through poses in varied ways. Some folks superflexible, others stiff as logs. But still, all of us together uniquely expressing ourselves.

I fall asleep during savasana and wake up disoriented. As I leave class in a haze I inexplicably recall a random encounter with a man I met a few weeks back while walking down Foothills Boulevard in Pomona, California. As I waited at a crosswalk for the pedestrian light to change, he rolled up alongside me in his wheelchair, gave me a once-over, then asked what I was doing. "What, for charity or something?" he said. When I told him no, his brows raised. We crossed the street together and he introduced himself. His name was Art. "So why the hell you doing it then?" he asked. My answer sounded more selfish and privileged than usual. "Well, why not?" I said. "Life's too short not to do cool things, isn't it? I'd hate to be that old guy who looks back on life with regrets knowing I could have done something but didn't. I can, so I am." My answer was not a dishonest answer, but even in the moment I was acutely aware of how crass my words must sound. But this awareness didn't stop me as spewed my all-about-me narrative.

Art listened carefully. Squinted toward me to make sure he took it in just right. When I finally stopped, he let the silence hang for a few harrowing seconds before responding. "You know what, man?" he said. "What you are doing is cool—really, really cool." He stopped his chair's momentum, then pivoted it to face me. "Setting out to accomplish a long-time goal is an important thing. But let me tell you this, Tom. This walk you're doing—it's not about you at all. You may be the one walking, but you're walking for me. For people like me. For folks who want to do it but can't. Folks who'd give anything to do something like this.

You're doing this walk for all the people who think you're nuts." Art outstretched his arms. "Brother, you're walking for all of us. Make sure you don't forget it."

That day, Art's words made an impact on me—enough for me to detail our exchange in my journal. But as soon as I wrote it down, I forgot all about it. Until now. Back home after the yoga class, I dig out my notebook and relive my exchange with Art. Suddenly I'm inspired to make a drastic shift in my mental stride. I formulate a new answer to the most common question. Why? Then I frame my response in a way that takes Art's words to heart. Why am I walking across America? *I'm walking to connect with others so I might better connect with myself.* I test my words for truth by saying them aloud until they roll naturally off my tongue. Art's right. This walk isn't about me. Shoot, nothing is. It's about us. All of us.

Over the next three weeks, I repeat Art's words like a mantra and notice gradual progress in my recovery. Then, 30 days after wobbling off the Bradshaw Trail, I'm back in the car with David as we make the trip from Phoenix to where I stuck a flag in the sand. If all goes well with my foot, I'll see him in a week or so. Walk up to his door and proudly announce, "I walked here from Santa Monica!" Again he insists I let him know if I get in another pickle, but this time I sense his shuttling services won't be necessary. "I'm going to slow down this time." And I don't just mean my pace.

Day 43

Little Buddy's tires are still shiny and clean when I find a place to camp next to a single-armed saguaro. I eat chili from a can. Before long there's dust on my pants and under my nails. I'm happy to be dirty again. I can't believe I'm finally back out here and feel grateful for all that happened to make it so. My outlook has transformed. Zigged and zagged just like the hobo sign. My skin perks up under the cooling air and my hairs stand on end as I lay out my walk's new rules. I promise to take my time. To stop rushing. I promise I'll abandon any destination agenda and engage fully with others who cross my path. I promise to stay open. I promise to camp as much as possible. To limit hotel stays. To do some yoga and meditation before walking every day. I promise to never forget that this trip isn't about me. I promise to let go of expectations.

I have a cell signal so I call Katie. Tell her I'm settled into camp and back at it. She asks about my intention for tomorrow's restart. I sum up the promises I just made. "To chill the fuck out," I say. "Shit, that ought to be my intention for the rest of my life!"

We hang up just in time for me to enjoy the winter sunset as it silences the landscape. I take a few photos and debate sending one to Katie. This Arizona desert is her favorite place. Wouldn't she want to see it aglow, too? I watch as the orange mass sinks slowly and listen to the ghostly yip of waking coyotes. There's a plummet in temperature, so I nestle into my tent cave and scroll through the unimpressive photos I just took. I choose the prettiest one and type out a text. "Wish you were here." I press send and immediately wish I hadn't been so quick to reach back. I look again at the photos. They're a good reminder of what was, but nothing compared to what's actually happening right now. They're nothing compared to what's to come, I hope. I put my phone away. Squeeze into my sleeping bag. "I got this," I say. A slight breeze bellows on the nylon walls and I swear I can hear the stars.

3

Against a background of the familiar,
we recognize with astonishment a new pattern.

- Barry Lopez
Crossing Open Ground

Day 44

SINCE DAY ONE I'VE HAD THREE

laminated signs stashed in my backpack: I Need Water, Help, and Walking Across America. I wore the Walking sign for a few hours in LA, but promptly packed it away when it drew more attention than I could handle. Today, in an effort to more readily advertise my intentions to drivers who regularly blast horns and shake fists, I pin it to the back of my dayglow construction vest. The shift in perception is immediate. Drivers mash brakes and flash thumbs-up. Their honks are infused with encouraging energy. I hope the other two signs will elicit a similarly positive response if I ever need to bust them out.

*

Every hour I stop to take off my shoe and elevate my injured foot for a few minutes. The pain doesn't seem to be getting worse, which is probably attributed to my new pace, less than three miles per hour. The wide shoulder and light traffic make it easy to find a steady stride. I take in the empty desert without worrying about the solid white line.

The roadside represents the people who traverse it. Highway 60 is littered with tire scraps, fast food waste, and water bottles filled to the brim with dark yellow urine. But the path is also marked by an abundance of empty booze containers. Twisted Tea, a drink I've never tried, seems most prevalent. I'm fascinated by the presence of random curios. A John Deere pocket knife, a pipe made from a NyQuil bottle, the severed hind leg of a goat, and a green, ribbed vibrator with three button settings: +, -, and FUN.

Day 45

I wake to find Little Buddy's night tarp a dozen feet away. I wish I had a bungee cord to brace it down. Hours later I find one on the roadside. I also want something to hold my ball cap on the handlebar. I promptly find a scratched up but functioning carabiner. I'm starting to believe I can muster anything I need by simply wishing for it.

During breaks I regularly bounce from Instagram to Facebook for an emotional boost. Likes and comments are my leash to the outside world. My need for external kudos is one of my empty buckets. A veteran crosser left a response to my post about deviating from the Bradshaw. He wrote, "Glad to see you got smart and off those sandy trails." I type a knee-jerk response and immediately delete it. Then I write something about how I'm an idiot to have considered that route in the first place. I delete that, too. Next I try something snarky. "Thanks for the support, dude." Which doesn't stick either. I stare at the blank box, wanting to say something that makes it clear I'm not OK with his chiding. That I'm not a pushover. But I can't find the right combination of words. But also, something is telling me to keep it blank. I tuck my phone away and try to ignore my brewing anger.

Multiple times each hour I retrieve my phone and defensively read and reread the man's comment. I want to scold him for questioning my intelligence. And in a public forum, no less. *Who is this guy, anyhow? He doesn't know me! What gall to say such condescending things to a total stranger.* More hours pass as my rage stokes itself.

*

In the shade of a broken-down truck, I relax my foot on a rock. A hawk circles overhead. I shade the sun with my hand and watch as the raptor's underwings turn black in silhouette. It dives, then pulls up before making a kill.

I pull out my phone again and scroll to the comment. I read it out loud. "Glad to see you got smart and off the sandy trails." The words are not snide or disparaging. In fact, the comment can easily be read as neutral, even kind and supportive. I set my phone in the dirt and think about why the words bugged me so much. I come up with three things and write them all in my journal: "1) I like to be in control. 2) I want to be perceived as having my shit together. 3) It's hard for me to stay humble when my limitations are exposed." I read my words and shake my head. Because these are all things I struggle with on a regular basis.

How I responded to this man is how I often respond to people in my life. Though I desperately want to trust their good intentions, I don't. I want to believe folks are being authentic. That they aren't judging me, or talking down to me, or saying one thing but meaning another. But typically I absorb advice or kudos or kindness through a lens of suspicion. One that stems from a deep-rooted assumption that I don't deserve good things. That I don't deserve things akin to love. I know this is an irrational remnant of my childhood, but there's no denying it still has a strong grip on my adult impulses, especially when I am under stress.

Adjacent movement catches my eye and I look up as the hawk reappears. I squint at the empty blue then close my eyes and listen to its distant call. The breeze is warm and cool at the same time. I imagine it blowing away my fury in exchange for gratitude. I place my hands over my chest and feel my slow and strong heartbeat. Then aloud I thank the man for his comment. "It forced me to face a part of me I don't like," I say. I open my eyes and scan the sky above. The hawk circles a couple times, then soars upward until I can make it out no longer.

Day 47

I need a grocery stop. And as much as I'd like to eat good food every chance I get, doing so is not easy. I'm on a limited budget. And the abundance of cheap markets I pass on my way in and out of town makes bad food an easier option. I've settled comfortably into a habit of canned meat and syrupy fruit that won't go bad or attract animals. And honestly, I don't particularly mind this low-nutrition, high-calorie fare. It's the crap I grew up on, after all.

While I'm taking a break in a hint of rare shade a few miles out of Aguila, two cyclists pull onto the shoulder to join me. Abby and Bart are soloing the Southern Tier, a commonly ridden bike touring route from California to Florida. They just met a few hours ago. "You folks are the first bikers I've seen," I say. My comment seems to surprise them.

In real life, Abby is a hiking guide in Yosemite. She's attempted a bike crossing before, but quit midway through. This trip is her redemption. Bart is Dutch. Newly unemployed and fresh out of a long-term relationship. He's riding to get his head straight. He offers some advice. "If today seems so hard that you want to quit, make the decision to quit tomorrow. Because your tomorrows will lead you all the way to the finish." Watching them ride away is cinematic. They pedal off into the long horizon, turning their bodies in unison for a final wave goodbye. Our brief visit reminds me how lonely I am.

*

In Aguila I beeline to the first market I see. It doubles as a gas station. I park LB on the side of the building, then swap my floppy sunshade hat for my LA ball cap and make myself presentable. An old bearded guy with a carved wooden cane approaches. He asks me in Spanish how I'm doing. "Estoy bien, gracias," I say. He introduces himself as Leo. We shake hands and make small talk. He uses a mixture of English and Spanish and asks where I learned the little bit I know. I tell him I learned the basics in school. But jobs and travel have given me a chance to practice. "Es importante to speak another language," he says. "Sí pero necesito practicar," I say. Leo asks for a few centavos. I hand over four bucks. We enter the store together and he heads straight for the back fridge and pulls out a 40 oz. King Cobra. He pays for it with the money I just gave him. I wander the short aisles, shocked by the snowbird prices. No way I can afford to stock up on three dollar cans of beans. I'll feel bad leaving empty-handed, so I buy a single stick of beef jerky. Outside, I catch up with Leo walking away with his bottle under an arm. "Leo! Necesita carne con su cerveza, amigo!" I hand over the jerky, then watch as he disappears into a crop of tall bushes along the train tracks.

As I prep Little Buddy to leave, a guy leans on his Camaro as he fills his tank. His arms fold across his broad chest. His stereo is so loud it vibrates the entire place. Classic big-hair metal. He yells at other patrons, telling them to tune their radio to the same station as his. "Let's rock this motherfucker out!" he shouts. But nobody pays attention. An older couple topping off their RV is too kind to completely ignore him. They acknowledge him with smiles, but don't mess with their radio. The old man seems relieved when the loud guy's attention shifts to me and LB. "Yo! Come here for a minute!" he says. I do, and he leans into the driver's side window and pulls out a roll of money. Peels off a twenty and hands it to me. "Woah! Really?" I say. His face widens and he asks what I'm doing. Then he shakes his head and tells me to be careful. "You better be carrying a knife or a gun," he says. "You don't know what's out there, brother. I do." I thank him for the money. My biggest roadside donation so far. "It's all good, bro," he says. "This is how we do it around here."

The loud man's attention returns to the song on the radio, an oldie by Def Leppard, then tries again to rally other customers into syncing their radios. Someone takes him up on it. "Fuck yeah!" he cheers. "That's what I'm talking about!" When the man's friends exit the market, he tells them I'm walking across the US. "For real?" one asks, shifting a grocery bag to his other hand. I nod as "Pour Some Sugar on Me" fills the space. "This motherfucker's crazy," the friend says. The loud guy shrugs and tells me to remember what he said. They peel out of the lot in a wake of dust. I walk through it as the song fades. His $20 covers all my groceries at the Dollar Store on the eastern outskirts of town.

Day 48

I walk against traffic. Figure if a car's going to take me out, I want to see it coming. I brace myself for the pressing wall of wind that follows each speeding 18-wheeler. Gratefully anticipate the subsequent rush of air as it slices through the stale heat and temporarily cools my skin.

I make it to a shady park in Wickenburg. Ask a long-haired and leather-clad man if he's using the empty picnic table. He's not. I depress Little Buddy's parking brake and dig into my food stash. Pull out a pack of tortillas, peanut butter, and an apple. The man's black and white Boston terrier is off-leash. I'm leery of petting it when it flops onto its back at my feet. "Troubles," the man says, taking a step toward me. "Sorry?" I say. With his hands in his pockets, he tips his head toward the dog. "That's his name. Troubles. He's the park ambassador." I ask if he worries about Troubles running away. "Oh no. He's got nowhere to go. The law says he's supposed to be on a leash but he likes his freedom. So I'm like, fuck it. Let him have it. Plus, all the cops here know me. And they love Troubles." I give the dog's chin a scratch. "I'm Anthony, by the way. What's this all about?" He motions to LB. "I figured you were one of those shopping cart guys. And we already got too many of them around here."

We watch Troubles bounce back and forth between us. "Hey," Anthony whispers. "You wanna get high?" I decline. Tell him that weed will only put me to sleep. Anthony says he's a wake and bake. "Pretty much high all the time," he says. "Been smoking every day for the past fifty years." I do the math. "You must have started young." Anthony lights a joint and takes a hit. Holds it in before lifting his chin and exhaling out the side of this mouth. "This is what keeps me young."

Long ago, Anthony met a guy who was wandering across America. He picked him up and they got stoned together. "I asked if there was anything he needed," he says. "Then I introduced him to a couple chicks I was living with. He left pretty happy the next day, if you know what I mean." Anthony never heard from him again.

"This thing you're doing, it's not a bad life," he says. "Unless you're running from something. But that ain't none of my business." Anthony flicks out his joint, wishes me luck, and walks away. Troubles stays for one more quick pet. When Anthony shouts, "Come on, Troubles!" the dog bounds after him.

The skunky smell of Anthony's smoke lingers and I kick myself for not saying yes to his offer. I imagine impulsively trading my big-mile afternoon for a chill party back at Anthony's place. I'm constantly setting myself up for opportunities to live more spontaneously, but then I chicken out when things arise. "Sometimes I'm such a square," I say to LB. I tell him if this happens again, I'll say yes.

Day 49

After a week of peaceful camp spots on Bureau of Land Management (BLM) land and untouched wide open spaces, the road swells to accommodate a sudden increase in traffic. The nightly glow in eastern skies confirms I'm nearing Phoenix. As shipping trucks roar past me at top speeds, their tires kick up bullets of highway shrapnel. A piece hits my cheek like a dart. It breaks the skin. I let it bleed and hope it leaves a scar.

*

My entry into the biggest city since LA is marked by a mountainous sand storm. From earth to sky a blob of brown nears the highway like a massive slug. I inhale dust so fine I imagine my lungs will dry up. Any sip from a water bottle includes a sandy mouthful of dirt, too. Soon the gusts are enough to knock me over. Occasionally the gales shift and Little Buddy goes into sailboat mode. Once, for fun, I let go of the handlebars and he shoots straight and true down the wide shoulder, gaining speed so quickly I have to run him down. Even with a tight grip on the bar I need to double time to keep up. We're both feeling a magnetic pull toward Phoenix. Which is no surprise since it's taken forever to get here.

My arrival reminds me of the problems that come with being a pedestrian in a city. Shoulders disappear, sidewalks become inconsistent, motorists are more distracted. And there's also the noise. The sonorous and never-ending peal of a megalopolis. My ears wince to the deafening shrill of the city's million moving parts.

*

I tune in to the feeling coursing through my body and identify it as fear. The traffic and busyness doesn't help, but most of my anxiety stems from being so conspicuous. Out here in my stupid hat, wearing a boasting sign that advertises my novelty, while pushing, of all things, a goddamn baby jogger on the side of the highway. I am ridiculous. I yearn for the anonymous quiet of a blank shoulder. For the anonymity of one hour ago. I dither between excitement and embarrassment and feel fully exposed. This is all my doing. My choice. I need to accept it, to own it, and

I give myself these orders. The words hit me harder than the next wall of wind. Accept it. Own it.

Soon the shoulder turns to sidewalk. I wait for lights to turn green and ease LB across wide streets stacked with anxious drivers. People crane their necks. Squint for a better view. Set their phones down. I keep my eyes forward. Put my blinders up. I whisper Art's words until my shoulders relax. "This isn't about me. This isn't about me. This isn't about me."

*

I'm barely into my week-long foray across the Phoenix sprawl and I already miss the expanse of the desert. There will be plenty more cavernous miles, that's for sure, but in the meantime I'll be hanging out with David again. Using his place as my home base. He meets me at my stopping points and returns me each morning to where I ended the previous day. When I finally make it to his house on foot, I knock on his door and announce, "I walked here from California!" My words feel impossible.

Day 51

Following David's recommendation, I walk the canal trail to bisect the city. It keeps me off busy roads for the eastern portion of the urban crossing. I share the dirt path with runners, walkers, cyclists, and people strolling the waterway as it courses through the cityscape.

The canal is stocked with White Amur fish. Native to Siberia, these two-foot-long, herbivorous fish were introduced to keep the canals clean. I watch as they swim in place against the current as if walking the opposite direction on an escalator. Every few seconds they flip their tails to hold their spot and stay aligned. Occasionally they allow their dorsal edges to poke through the water's surface, bringing their scaly bodies a touch closer to the sun.

Day 53

The next day along the canal near Scottsdale, a tall Black man runs across the street, waving me down. He has a piece of cardboard in his hand. His accent is thick. Jamaican, I presume. A knit hat contains his dreadlocks. Wide, dark sunglasses cover his eyes. "Hey! I saw you back there," he says. "You really walking across America?" When I say yes, he spreads his arms and engulfs me in a hug. Then he shakes my hand in four movements: normal shake, cool guy shake, claw shake, and fist bump. His hand envelops mine like a catcher's mitt. "My name is Lion. I'm a Rasta. I'm homeless. Been sitting right over there for fifteen years asking folks for spare change." Over the years he's saved enough to buy a car. "Just bought one in November," he says. "It doesn't run, but it's a place where I can safely sleep."

Lion takes off his sunglasses and puts his heavy hand on my narrow shoulder. He leans down to lock eyes with me. "Tom. I've always thought I'd do something big someday. But I'm starting to think it's never going to happen. As much as I'd like to join you on this walk, it's not for me. Not now, anyhow. Instead, I'd like to help you out." I assure Lion that by taking a moment to talk he's become part of it. He shakes his head. "No, no, no. You see, I want to help you. In fact, I'd like to give you some money. Is that OK?" I say nothing. Because what the hell am I supposed to say to a homeless man offering me cash? Because really, I'm good. I've got ample funds in my account and an abundance of resources at my disposal. I budgeted for this. I definitely don't want to take any handouts from someone who has it way tougher than me. I step back and hold up my hands. I tell Lion I'm all set. That I've been planning for a while and I'm financially square. None of my words come out eloquently as I refuse his offer.

Lion pauses. Holds his deep gaze and I want to look away. He presses his lips together. "Tom. Listen. If you say no to kindness today, you're more likely to say no to it tomorrow. And later, when kindness comes around again, you won't even recognize it because you've been pushing it away it for so long. Then down the road you'll be one of those sad and fearful people who think the world is a bad place—a painful and violent place. But know what? It's not. But you'll think it is because you've been rejecting kindness for so long." Lion's eyes pierce mine. "So, let me ask you again, Tom. Can I give you some money?" I look at my feet. Then back up at Lion. I say yes. Then Lion pulls a one dollar bill from his pocket and holds it between us. "Tom. Someone gave this to me, and now I would like to give it to you." As soon as I accept it, he wraps his arms around me like a father would his son. "Always say yes to kindness," Lion says before letting go. Lion asks for my contact information and assures me he'll reach out. "I want to check in on you."

I return to the canal trail. When I'm out of sight of Lion and the busy intersection, I sit on a bench and cry. Then I pull out my phone and look closely at the selfie Lion and I took together. I zoom in on his sunglasses and try to see his eyes behind them. I notice his braided beard that I didn't notice when we were talking. My head tilted toward him. His draped arm. The clear sky above us. We interacted for no more than five minutes but it's like we've known each other forever.

I close the photo and open up my phone's settings. For the first time in as long as I can remember, I turn on the ringer.

Day 54

After my final night at David's place, we drive to BoSa Donuts in Mesa where I ended yesterday. There's no telling when I'll see him again, if ever. He doesn't know that my relationship with his daughter is on the fritz, or if he does, it doesn't affect his outpouring of support. Over these past few weeks, he and I have developed a strong bond. He's not just my girlfriend's dad. He's my friend.

*

I walk a short 10 miles to Gilbert where my sister, Kim, and her family live. Gilbert is part of the Phoenix metropolitan area, but it's a far cry from the urban bustlings of the Valley of the Sun. Neighborhoods are a mix of front yard horse ranches, vast spans between sprawling developments, and tons of raised trucks and minivans. Besides fields of agriculture, the most common sight seems to be roadside taquerias.

Kim and her husband Chris live in a modest home nestled in a cul-de-sac on the Mormon side of town. They, however, are not Mormon. Kim homeschools their two sets of identical twins. Chris is an electrical engineer. They rarely get away, and I arrive in town in the midst of their no-kids staycation at Estrella War, where event-goers dress up in medieval garb and live for a week in an altered version of reality. Kim scoops me up and hauls me to the festival grounds. I'm not allowed to walk around in regular clothes—*naked* in war speak—so Chris lets me borrow a cloak. He's nearly a foot taller than me so the tunic fits like a parachute.

The gathering of thousands is divided into myriad encampments. Kim and Chris's camp is known for their raucous tavern. "We are a drinking society with a cos-play problem," someone says. I haven't touched alcohol since New Year's so I'm a quick mess. I decline a late round of Irish car bombs and stumble back to my tent. I slowly fade to the crackle of a campfire. Bursts of laughter roar around me and become part of my dreams. I wake at sunrise with a headache just as everyone else is just getting to bed.

Day 56

Kim and her boys return me to where I left off in Apache Junction. Superstition Mountain looms in the background as does my jittery interest in the upcoming stretch of Highway 60. A local guy heightens my unease as he warns of the Queen Creek Tunnel.

"It's deadly for people in cars. I can't imagine how it would be for a pedestrian." On an outdated biking blog, I read about the now defunct Superior to Miami Highway, a possible solution to sidestep the distressing quarter-mile pass through the mountain. I find it as described and give it a go.

Trail conditions are not ideal for Little Buddy. Broken hard top, lots of loose cobbles and deep indents. As we enter the narrow trail, I ask a group of day hikers about conditions ahead. "It's rough," says a woman as she inspects LB. "Not sure that thing's gonna make it." Nobody saw the bypass tunnel I'm hoping to find.

*

The Superior to Miami Highway opened in 1922 and connected the region's prosperous mining districts with agricultural centers in Phoenix. Prior to construction, a trip into the city would take all day. The new road drastically shortened the commute and became known for its breathtaking views and steep grades. Wasn't until the early 1950s that it was replaced by the more modern Highway 60, the exact one I'm trying to avoid. Nature is now reclaiming the old road. Giant boulders sit where they've fallen, scrub fills cracks and dark corners, and the thoroughfare's original surface is ravaged by decades of water and heat damage. The broken path is cumbersome for an overloaded baby jogger. Up and over each obstacle, my breath is heavier than it's been the whole trip. I may be in pretty good walking shape, but my climbing game could use some work.

Roads like this make me wistful. I think of old-timey cars kicking up dust. Of touring families with heavy metal coolers filled with cold cut sandwiches wrapped in wax paper. I imagine mid-century Americans looking to satisfy an innate need for adventure, discovery, togetherness. There's a unique beauty, an undeath in this old highway. Its long ago energy and ghosts remain.

*

After more steep grades, the tunnel I read about in the blog suddenly appears. A black dot in the near distance. As I near, it gapes into the mountainside, wide enough for one car. Before I enter, I gauge its length. A quarter mile, maybe? The cool air within makes me want to take a nap.

Walls inside are covered with modern day graffiti. Large red letters proclaim "I love Destiny." I breather the smell of stale piss. A distant pinprick of light creates an optical illusion that makes me feel like I'm walking downhill. It lures me deeper as the walls thin and the end draws further and further away. When I reach an approximated midpoint, both ends of the tunnel look the same. I close my eyes and spin, challenging my ability to directionally orient myself. I fantasize about this being a time portal. Maybe I'll exit into somewhere else. Into a world where I can start everything from scratch. But as I step back into the light, I hear the familiar scream of mining trucks. Bummer. The tunnel isn't a wormhole after all. It's just a tunnel.

*

When the old road spits me back onto the new highway, I'm beyond the shoulderless passage I'd been warned about. Still, this section of the 60, riddled with mines, presents a gamut of nerve-racking challenges. Narrow shoulders, blind curves, reckless traffic, and overworked miners. Drivers in these parts have a reputation for aggressive speeds and risky maneuvering. Any of these details is enough to make me think twice about walking along the road, but at this point I don't have a choice.

I find a pullout just east of the main tunnel and step on Little Buddy's emergency brake. I don every piece of reflective clothing I have, then attach blinky lights and day glow bands to anywhere they'll hold. I tie two pilfered orange construction flags to LB's top bar and add extra swatches of neon material to his front and sides. We are fit for a parade.

For a while I study the flow of traffic. Meditate on its patterns and visualize myself moving within it. My mind plays out all sorts of sticky scenarios. What I'll do if a car swerves into the shoulder. What if I need to walk around a stalled vehicle. How I'll negotiate a blind curve or get away from an angry, stray dog. I trust that imagining these undesirable contexts will help me take quicker action. Because odds are I won't have the luxury of time to wonder what to do next.

As a rule, I always walk against traffic. But after a quick analysis of Highway 60, I decide to walk on whichever side of the road seems safer. So I frogger from one side of the highway to the other. Do everything I can to put me and Little Buddy in clear view of drivers. It's a dangerous dance moving back and forth across the lanes. I do everything I can to keep from being an unintended target at 80 mph.

*

On the steep grade, cars ride their brakes as I white knuckle the handlebar and sweat my ass off. I melt with exertion and fear. The weather turns windy as I climb higher, and soon the sky is filled with thick, surging clouds. Thunderheads. The air smells like sweet tea and the temperature tumbles. Rather than press on and risk walking through difficult conditions in inclement weather, I begin the search for a stealth camping spot hours earlier than usual. I swiftly investigate a couple options, but they're too close to the highway to offer ample solitude. For miles it's nothing but blacktop and safety barriers. No pull-outs, no trails into the brush, not even more questionable options like the ones I've already passed up. The later it gets, the faster I walk. When a possible opportunity appears on the opposite side, I wait for a break in dusk traffic then race across to inspect. It's a turn out. Not much of one, but deeper than others. On the far side of the highway rail is a trail that winds out of the road's sight. It'll do. There's no way to wheel Little Buddy around or over the barrier, so I'm forced to completely empty his contents and hoist him across the three-foot threshold. It's a hassle, but I feel a thousand times safer on opposite side.

My nose assures me I'm not the first person to stop here. Seems I've chosen a makeshift roadside toilet for drivers who can't wait. I steer Little Buddy through a field of shit landmines. Beyond the turds, the trail peters out. This'll be home tonight. The cliff behind me shields the spot from increasing gusts. Shifts in wind fill me with the smell of waste as I make camp in the lingering sunglow.

I scarf a can of chili without bothering to use a bowl. Debate opening another. Down three tortillas swathed in crunchy Jif. Kill a squishy apple and an extra large Snickers. But I taste nothing as I chew and hold my breath. I think this spot might be my worst sleeping location, ever. There was that garbage beach in southern Baja. The spider nest hostel in Cambodia. And the ox-patty plain in western Mongolia where, in the absence of wood, we boiled water using mounds of dry animal feces as fire fuel. But nothing before this has ever been quite so toxic and disgusting at the same time. Awarding it this title changes my perspective. It creates an unlikely bond between me and this gross little nook that will be my home for the night. I can only hope it remains undisputed. Untested. Because I'd hate to find myself in a place that might nudge this literal shithole into second place.

Day 58

I wake to tinny drumming on the tree canopy. It sounds like uncooked rice spilling onto a linoleum floor. Snug in my sleeping bag, I wear my puffy jacket. My warmest piece of clothing. Yet still I wish I had more layers. The white noise escalates. The patter now a pummeling. My usual departure time comes and goes as hail surges and the air temperature plummets. During a pause in the deluge I break camp in record time. Pack everything away wet. I dig out my winter hat and gloves and put on my raincoat for the first time of the trip.

I repeat the annoying process to get over the highway guardrails and I'm back on the road just as the first snowflakes fall. Big, sticky flurries. The kind of snow that makes really good snowballs. The world is a gray shade for a solid hour before accumulation stops. There's maybe an inch on the ground. Traffic is light so the view is accompanied by a rare quiet. Hearty desert blooms peek out from the white blanket as if they have a secret. In the hush I'm aware that I'm thinking of nothing. I enjoy the sound of my feet crunching the bits of fresh ice. I enjoy the footprints and wheel marks I'm leaving behind me.

*

After a long and sweeping curve, a police cruiser slows to a stop on the opposite side of the road. "Hey buddy," the officer hollers. "Got a minute?" I laugh at his question and wonder how he would respond if I said I was sort of busy right now. I ask if he wants me to cross over to his side. He tells me he'll come to me.

I pull over into a snowy ditch and lock the parking brake. The cop stands with his hands on his hips looking both ways, then jogwalks across the highway to my side. He shakes my hand. "I'm just responding to a 911 call. Someone told dispatch there was a guy walking down the middle of the road." I blow air through my teeth. Say something about people making up stories to make their world make sense. The cop's face doesn't break. "We take these calls seriously, Mr. Griffen. This isn't the best setup for pedestrians." The cop tells me safety is his number one concern, and I say it's mine, too. But his half smile clues me in to how he's actually reading me. "Look, there's a bridge ahead with no shoulder. It's going to be hairy. Why don't I meet you there and drive you across?" He asks if I'll take a ride. "Under these circumstances, yes, I say." I do the trail math and agree to meet him in three hours. He drives away and I press on.

The flurries swell into whiteout conditions. I can barely see oncoming vehicles so I'm damn sure they can't see me. I pull Little Buddy into the next turnout and make a temporary shelter with my blue tarp. I sit in the cave and listen as the snow lands on it. Watch my warm breath heave out of me. Figure I'll just wait it out. I crack up at the irony of being in an Arizona snowstorm and wonder if there will be more of this in other places. I compose a text to Katie, then erase it all and put my phone away, figuring maybe I should conserve my battery.

When I hear a vehicle pull into the turnout, I poke my head out of the shell to investigate. It's the cop again. I give him a wave. He flips on his red and blue lights and hollers at me from his window. "Hey! My boss isn't going to let you go any further," he says. "We can't in good faith allow you to keep walking in this mess. It's way too dangerous." I tell him I'm happy to wait it out and get back on the road when the snow mellows. "Sorry, but I can't let you walk anymore. Not this stretch, anyhow. How about I drive you over the pass into Miami? Drop you at a gas station?" I ask if I have an option. He shakes his head. "Well, OK then," I say. "Let's get on with it."

In order to fit Little Buddy into the cruiser's trunk, I have to completely empty the hold and break down his removable parts. I then settle in the front passenger seat and lean my face into the heater vent. The cop asks me again about my route. His eyebrows raise when I mention the Apache reservation ahead. "Well, you're going to want to take extra care. Lots of riff-raff out there," he says. I stare over the dash and consider his words. He turns his head to look at me. "You know what I mean, right." His statement is not a question.

*

Would that cop have been as cordial with me if I were a woman or a person of color? I'm a white, middle-aged male so I'll never truly know the answer. But there's no denying that my experience is privileged.

Today, 59 days after leaving Santa Monica, this privilege is heavy on my mind. I imagine walking as someone other than a white male. Because when I interacted with that cop, my only concern was crossing the icy bridge without incident. Not once did I worry about being alone in the cruiser with him. If anything, I had a chip on my shoulder as I always do with men in positions of power. I didn't feel threatened or worried that he might rummage through my stuff or give me a hard time. I didn't have to revert to any sort of script to prove my willingness to cooperate. And I damn sure never considered how close his hand came to his sidearm. Or if I'd make it home alive. This absence of worry is a privilege afforded to me by how I look.

Back on the road I can't stop thinking about my life of relative ease. I live in a bubble of assumed safety. Truly believe that I can do pretty much anything I set my mind to. I have seemingly unlimited access to helpful resources and likely will for the duration of this trip and my entire life. I rarely am afraid. I take for granted these basic details of life and often find myself making grand statements about what it's like to walk across America. "People are so nice! They come out of the woodwork all the time to say hi and do nice things!" But these statements are *my* truth. And though I want them to be universal, they aren't. I don't want to forget this. I don't want to forget how easy I've got it.

*

The longer I'm out here, the more common it is for people to offer cautionary advice about destinations on my route. I can't help but notice a pattern: So far, the people issuing these warnings have all looked like me. White, and mostly male. Their concerns are always regarding areas where white people are scarce. I can't help but wonder how many of these protective white strangers have actually spent time in the places they are so quick to admonish.

Day 59

As I enter the San Carlos Apache Reservation, I regularly look over my shoulder. I'm worried about each approaching vehicle and what I'll say when I meet people who live here. I'm afraid to make contact—but I'm also ashamed of this fear because I know it's not mine. The various exhortations of the past few days have injected my body with others' aversions and disquietude. I want to purge their poison from my present, but no matter what I do or think my heart races abnormally. If there was an alternate route, I'd take it.

I grip Little Buddy's bar more tightly than usual and stiffen at any hint of an oncoming car. The first honking horn makes me jump and I assume they're giving me the vehicular version of the middle finger. I've heard that single-note song plenty of times before. But on the reservation, where it's arguable if I should even be here, it seems more poignant. I want to scream, "Yes, yes, you're right! Fuck ME!" Because if white guilt is deserved in any place, a reservation is a top qualifier.

More honks follow. I'm beeped at by as many vehicles in an hour as I have been during this entire trip. But folks are not only honking, they're also slowing down to shout words of encouragement, too. Some stop in the middle of the road to ask for my story. I tell it and feel like a braggart. Yet they drive away cheering me on.

*

Modest homes sit surrounded by stacks of scrap wood. Tarps blow like flags. Ribbons of smoke rise from aluminum chimneys. The stretches between homes are dotted with scattered trailers and toppling RVs with flat tires. Tall horses graze in cloud shadows behind fences. Dogs off-leash bark aggressively at me. I'm more self conscious than ever. I constantly straighten my straw hat. Make sure my sleeves are rolled up nice and my shirt tails aren't tangled within my safety vest. More people stop. High-fives and fist bumps. Good lucks and prayers. But I can't shake my embarrassment. There's part of me that wants to apologize for my self-serving ordeal and all the luxuries making it happen. I also want to say sorry for everything my forbearers have done, and for my making it to middle age without giving their plight a second thought. I'm guilty of normalizing, if not romanticizing their history. I played cowboys and Indians. And the cowboys always won.

There's also a part of me who wants to join the parade of supportive strangers. To allow myself to be accepted, albeit briefly, by people I've been programmed to avoid. I take a deep breath and force my body to relax. Release my two-handed clamp on Little Buddy's handlebar. I loosen my face, wiggle my jaw around to soften my teeth, and unclinch my buttocks. I return to my natural gait and arm swing. I don't want to be afraid. Or feel shameful. I don't want fear to replicate itself using me as its medium. I choose to put trust in what's unknown. Choose to let go of control. Of what could be. I choose to eschew expectations and allow to happen what needs to happen.

*

As I roll into Peridot, an unincorporated community on the Apache reservation, a young couple is hanging out at an outdoor grill under a pop-up. The guy asks me where I'm going then introduces himself. "I'm Mike and this is Yasmina," he says. "Order something. I'm paying." We sit on the ground and eat burgers together. He points to the market, the gas station, the school. Tells me the circuit of drug runners in the adjacent mountains sends signals via telescopes and mirrors. "They've probably been watching you ever since you set foot on the rez," he says. "They'll watch you until you leave." He asks about my burger. Wants to buy me another one.

"It bothers me people come from all over the world to visit the reservation to see a real Indian," Mike says. "But I understand their misunderstanding. I mean, look at all the TV shows. People call us Indians but they don't realize it's an insult. But we're not from India. Calling us Native Americans is OK, but saying Native is better." Mike takes a bite of his burger and we sit chewing for a few moments. "But really," Mike says. "All of us out here—we are Apache."

*

An older man walks up his dirt driveway toward the road. "I saw you way back there," he says. "I want to give you this." He hands me a bottle of water, a Gatorade, and some money. "I'm Apache, but I'm a cowboy. Name's Curtis. I made a living riding bulls back in the eighties. Got a few of these here things to show for it." He angles his silver belt buckle to point it upward. It reflects the sun. I bend down to read it. "Bull Rider Classic 1970-1980." His inscribed name in silver borders a brass bull and rider.

Curtis and his family have lived on the reservation their entire lives. "But our people have been on this land forever before that," he says. I lock on his word choice, "forever." As in, before the white people came. As in, before we took this land. When it was truly free. Curtis looks toward the mountains. "This is the view that's always existed," he says. We shake hands. "Every morning my wife and I do a traditional prayer ceremony in the old way," he says. "Tomorrow we will start praying for you."

Day 61

I shorten my second day in the reservation so I can camp another night within its boundaries. I choose a spot away from buildings and traffic and set up my tent. A familiar shape on the ground catches my attention. A broken piece of a stone tool. My eye now trained to the stone's color and composition, I start finding them everywhere. Pieces and parts of all sorts of items used by Apaches in days past. I collect handfuls of them and examine the best ones. Admire their chips and cuts, their angles and sharp edges. Normally I'd ignore the rules I learned during my anthropology undergrad and put the artifacts in my pocket. But here I do the opposite. Before leaving the site, I hurl them all back into the scrub. "Thank you for letting me find you," I say. I repeat the same words as I finally leave the reservation in Bylas. Continue on past the bones of abandoned homes. One with a rusty cross hanging above the front door and graffiti across its boarded windows. Someone has written "Help your soul. Free your mind" in white spray paint. All of a sudden there are fences again.

Day 63

The cheaper the hotel, the better the complimentary breakfast. And though it's always an assortment of overprocessed and empty-calorie foods, I always look forward to the opportunity to fill both my belly and my pockets. Given my increasing appetite, I probably split the nightly rate 50/50 between a roof over my head and the morning foodstuffs.

This morning in Safford, I walk into the dining area and am greeted by the usual smells. Oily sausage, acrid coffee, and burnt toast. I've come to appreciate this combination because it means I'll be full soon. My appetite is insatiable, but every day my belt pulls a little tighter.

Today's spread is the hotel standard and divided into typical sections. Refrigerated things, hot things, dry goods, and beverages. Everything I touch is sticky. Pastry case handles and pancake batter ladles, fake marble countertops, and mealy red apples. Looming over the space is an outdated, wall-mounted TV with its volume turned up too loud. I don't look at it. A crop of strangers sit too close to each other, yet somehow they manage to maintain an impressive amount of personal space. Like nobody else exists.

Day 65

There are themes of roadside rubbish along stretches of highway sections. Early on I encountered an abundance of toys—broken boogie boards, deflated soccer balls, and countless Nerf bullets. The Twisted Tea empties from earlier have recently given way to Fireball Cinnamon Whiskey. The slogan on the drink's website is "Tastes Like Heaven, Burns Like Hell." I've tried it, and it's a far cry from heavenly. But obviously some local motorists might disagree.

I've also come across items wedged into the blacktop. Today I found a tin of chewing tobacco that had somehow been pressed into the tar and become part of the highway. It's now flush enough not to get crushed by cars, yet sturdy enough to defy the elements. A modern fossil. These are the sorts of things I find on an hourly basis. Like a scavenger hunt to help pass the time.

As I think about all the things that needed to happen in order for that dip can to get permanently embedded into the highway, a cyclist appears on the opposite side of the road. Unlike the others I've met, his bike carries no saddle bags or gear. Just rider and a water bottle. Chester tells me he's a Duncan local out for a ride. He's also the owner of Apex Cyclez, the only bike shop in town.

Chester crosses the highway to ride alongside me. The shoulder is wide and fits both of us comfortably. Still, I have to pick up the pace a bit so he can stay balanced in the saddle at 4 mph. It's nice to have company for more than a few minutes. Gives the conversation a chance to deepen. "I used to live in the mountains overlooking downtown LA," he says. "I'd ride my horse to a viewpoint where I'd sit and watch everyone crawling all over everyone else." When his car was stolen, he left and came here. Now he's a retired school district employee. Spends time volunteering and riding his bike. "Lately I've been supervising prison work crews," he says. "When I first meet these guys, they act all hard. I always encourage them to relax. But it takes a while for them to do so." Not too long ago an ex-inmate tracked Chester down to say thanks for treating him with dignity. For creating a space where everyone could be themselves. "It boils down to empathy," Chester says. "These days too many people are wrapped up in their own lives to worry about others. But you know what? People need each other more than they realize. I'm just trying to do my part to make it so."

Chester rides six miles with me until the New Mexico border. I leave Arizona with him at my side. "You're really going to be alone out there," he says. "Like, if you happen to get run over by a truck, nobody'll know. So you may as well live it up before you become a grease spot." I've never heard that turn of phrase before and ask what he means. He laughs. "It's the mark you leave on the highway when you get run over, man!" he says. He then gives me a big hug and rides away.

*

So much has happened in a short couple months. The start, the injury, the trip home, the delay, the question about whether or not I'd be able to return, followed by a conservative restart with a compromised foot. Now my foot is fine. A non-issue. And all seems to be working out. But as I cross into New Mexico, I suddenly realize I've passed beyond the range of David's safety net. "Call me with any problems, Tom—from the start to the New Mexico border," he said. "Reach out and I'll come find you." But now, two steps in to a new state, I'm officially on my own. For a brief second I want to turn around.

I pull out my phone for a jolt of virtual connection. I've been keeping up with my daily posts and have a few new comments on Instagram. One from James, a writer buddy from

Seattle. "Hey Tom—thinking of you, pal—here's a dash of Neruda—All paths lead to the same goal: to convey to others what we are. And we must pass though solitude and difficulty, isolation and silence in order to reach forth to the enchanted place where we can dance our clumsy dance and sing our sorrowful song." I dig into Little Buddy's hold and retrieve the Arizona sticker I got from the REI employee in Phoenix. Peel off the back and stick it to LB's side panel, then step clumsily into my third state.

4

We attract forces according to our being.

- George Gurdjieff

Day 65

THE ROAD RIPS through high desert rock before opening up to a misty silhouette of distant mountains. Everything far away is colorless and lost in haze. An occasional big rig shreds past and kicks up bits of detritus, but mostly it's just locals who cruise by, craning their necks to give the weird guy on the roadside a closer look.

An eastbound tractor trailer brakes hard and snakes onto the shoulder about a quarter mile ahead. Throws on its safety flashers. Seems like an emergency stop, and from afar I intently watch as the monotony of walking is briefly interrupted. I pick up my pace, hoping to catch a better view of the unfolding drama.

The driver's door opens and a large man climbs out. When his feet make contact with the highway, he looks in my direction. Then he reaches back to the cab and grabs something. A box, maybe? A flash of sunlight blinks from it as he heaves the container into his arms. He walks toward the rear of the truck and just stands there, arms full, looking my way again. Then he walks to the other side of the road and sets the box down on a guardrail post. He faces me again, raises one arm in the air, and points at the box. I wave back and turn up my cadence. "Thanks!" I yell as loud as I can. But he can't hear me. He's still too far away. He recrosses the highway back to his truck, gives his sagging pants a tug, climbs back into the cab, and drives away blowing the horn. He's long gone when I reach the box—a six of mini Gatorades and a case of peanut butter crackers. Enough snacks to last a couple days.

Later that day I tell this story on social media. My good buddy, Big John, sends a personal message in response. "Basically most people are great. In a mad rush today only three miles from my house, I blew a radiator hose towing a huge tractor. Some dude pulled over, drove me home where I could get some water, and a huge problem was solved. Got a new friend. Keep plugging away. You're a boost to the common man. Your adventure gives us all hope."

Day 66

Lordsburg is a minor detour off the Southern Tier cycling route. It's often used by cyclists as a place to rest and restock. They then backtrack to join Highway 90 toward Silver City, climbing steep ascents while enduring cooler temperatures and possibly snow. The route crosses the Continental Divide then climbs into the Gila National Forest, at times gaining and losing significant elevation over short stretches. This upcoming leg of the Southern Tier scares the shit out of me. I've encountered a handful of westbound riders who've expressed their concern as they consider my predicament. "I can barely imagine walking it, let alone doing so with that cart you've got," one guy said. At the Lordsburg fork, I give into my fear and bypass the bike route altogether. Instead I'll illegally walk on Interstate 10 for the next 120 miles.

Walking or biking on national interstates is generally prohibited. But on this stretch of the 10, bikes are allowed. And since Little Buddy is sort of a bicycle, a wheeled machine at least, I use him to justify my unlawful decision. Worst thing that could happen besides becoming a grease spot—as Chester called it—is a highway patrol officer disallows my forward progress and hauls me off the highway. At which time I'll come up with a plan B. I commit to this idea even though everything about it makes me uneasy.

*

I stash my gear in the hotel room then head over to Kranberry's Chatterbox where I order breakfast for dinner. Between sips of weak coffee I text Katie to share my apprehension for the interstate walk. "Let go of what you are afraid of," she texts back. Her simple words crush my face like a peach and I hide it behind my sunburnt hands. I'm suddenly aware how stressed out I am. But I should have already known since a nagging hemorrhoid— my body's regular response to anxiety—has been ever-present the past few days. At times the discomfort has been so severe I could think of nothing else.

Another tell of the all-encompassing strain is my recent apprehension to social interaction. For the past few days I've mostly wanted to crawl into a hole and say nothing. Don't want to explain my journey. Don't want to shoot the shit. Just want to walk and be alone. Earlier today I sat on the edge of my bed trying to muster up the gumption to ask the hotel clerk for change for the laundry machine. All these symptoms trace back to the real problem—I'm terrified by the prospect of walking on the interstate. Both it and the mountain route are monsters waiting to devour me. And either choice feels like it could be my last.

Day 67

Most of the hotels I stay at are one- or two-star dumps. Old motor lodges with outside facing doors. They want payment in advance and don't require a credit card for incidentals. I've learned it doesn't take much haggling to secure a reduced rate. My requests for a "walking across America" discount generally amount to a 10% shave. Basically the senior citizen markdown.

As much as I appreciate sleeping indoors, I'm growing increasingly opposed to being inside. I've started leaving my door wide open whenever possible, allowing in fresh air and sunlight. A symbolic best-of-both-worlds scenario: I want in, but I also want out.

Sometimes while I'm inside doing upkeep on LB, messing with social media, or starting blankly at the tube, I notice people looking in as they walk past. An occasional brave soul says hello through the shadowy threshold. My fantasy is that someone actually comes in to chat. Sits down on my bed and watches TV with me. Maybe we even sit close enough to feel each other's warmth. This is not a sexual daydream, just me longing for an interaction that's more intimate than what I experience on the road.

I have a lot of profound and unforgettable exchanges with humans while walking. But even with these amazing interactions, I feel empty. It's made me think a lot about the source of happiness. I guess I've always assumed it comes from something external, but I am mistaken. My contentment should come from inside. From me. Which is tricky because I'm still trying to figure out how to fit into my own skin—a truth I find humiliating.

*

I lay on the bed and stare at the water-stained ceiling as a delicate breeze whispers in through the door. I get a message from another crosser whose acquaintance I recently made online. "I hope you don't get kicked off of I-10. I don't understand why people insist on taking that route knowing it is illegal." This guy has walked across America multiple times and knows what he's talking about. But again I am bothered by a well-intentioned message. I don't want to believe I might be blowing it again. I don't want to acknowledge that my decision may be misguided. It's like he's shaking a finger at me, which makes me feel like a failure.

*

I look out the open door. The sky is a soft and empty blue. One solitary cloud alone in its center. A woman in the parking lot walks slowly in my direction, her hand shielding her eyes from the sun. Maybe she's looking in my room. At me. Trying to make out shapes and lines in the silhouetted cave contrasted to the glaring brightness outside. Maybe she's wondering why my door is open and what I'm watching on TV. Maybe, like me, she's lonely, too. I sit up and gather myself. Watch as she veers away. I stand up and gently close the door. Turn the bolt. Latch the chain.

Day 68

I empty an array of individually-wrapped sweet breads into Little Buddy's food bag. Cheese and berry danishes, a cinnamon roll, a bear claw. I fill water bottles from the bathtub nozzle. There's a chill in the air. A slight breeze cools things further. Today might be a hat and glove kind of day. I give thought to my layering plan —I'll start with less so there's less to peel off. I swathe myself in sunblock. Put some anti-chafing lubricant between my thighs, on my nipples, and between my toes. The day off has made my feet good as new. My body, too. Except for that hemorrhoid. It still burns, but not that bad. From the room, the distant hum from the interstate sounds dim. Like I'm hearing it though a wall of cotton.

I inspect the scab formed over a new tattoo I got while recovering back home. It's of the hobo sign I stumbled upon that day I called it quits. I pick at the bisecting arrow. Then stop, knowing it won't heal right if I mess with it. I recall Katie's text from the diner and check myself. I'm still afraid. "Let go, Luke," I say out loud in my best Obi-Wan voice.

I walk outside and listen to the roar of cars on the 10. I shake my head. "Fuck it," I say. "I ain't doing it. I ain't walking on the motherfucking interstate." When I hear these words escape my mouth, I know I've settled on the right plan. I'll backtrack this detour and return to the Southern Tier.

*

Back in the room, I stand with my hands on my hips. "Alright, LB, what do you think?" Then I spend an extra half hour tweezing minuscule thorns from his wearing tires. I dampen a flimsy towel and wipe the fine dust from his rims and sidewalls. "Looking good, LB. Looking goddamn good." I double-check my provisions. My maps. Ensure I've got enough snacks handy. I wire the USB cord to my solar charger. I scarf an extra two danishes before locking the oversized key in the dank room behind me.

I leave the hotel parking lot with one thing on my mind—everything is scary from afar. The brutal climbs to come will undoubtedly present a challenge, as will the weather, most likely. But nothing is certain until I'm facing it. Nothing at all. For the first time in a while, I am excited by what's unknown. I'll face what's to come when it comes. I'm not going to sweat anything until I absolutely need to.

As I walk past the interstate on-ramp, I punch my fist into my hand and clap a few times. I know for certain I'm going in the right direction. Takes about a mile before I realize the pain from my hemorrhoid is gone.

*

As the 90 grades upward, my view of desert emptiness is broken by the conifer line. Been a while since I've seen trees, and they throw me off a bit. Like when clouds break over a jutting mountain and put its elusive peak into rare view. My brain needs a moment to remember what they are. *Trees! Oh yes! I remember those things!*

I anticipate the Continental Divide like there's a large cheese pizza there, then approach the lackluster sign without fanfare. "Continental Divide: 6,355 Feet." I wish the elevation was higher because then I could justify my labored breathing. "That's it? Damn." I pause for a moment to determine if I need to mark this milestone with a phone call or video or something. Nope. So I take a token selfie, post it on Instagram, and keep on charging.

*

Social media is a strategy I obsessively employ in an attempt to put all eyes on me. It's easy to connect this compulsion to my unmet childhood need for attention. My upbringing was largely hands-off. One in which I was allowed to do pretty much anything. Though my youthful freedoms gave me bragging rights amongst my peers, such leeway was not ideal for my personality type. I craved guidance, rules, expectations, and consequences. But my parents treated everything with the same neutral filter. My behavior, good or bad, was rarely celebrated or punished. I came to resent their parenting style, and looked elsewhere for ways to place myself in the limelight.

This yearning for external validation is an impossible request from the universe, but even in my middle age I remain under its spell. I fully realize that I'm the only one who can truly satisfy these innate needs, but this understanding doesn't stop me from seeking kudos when I need them. And a quick post on Instagram or Facebook usually does the trick.

Climbing the miles into the mountains has been lonely. I've had no interactions with strangers, no toothy waves from drivers, no truckers' fists in the air. Doesn't take long for the quiet isolation to morph into a dull and constant heartache. It sits like a weight on my chest. I've heard that solitude is the biggest challenge of this sort of undertaking, but until now I've not felt its torment. I reach for my phone, seeking texts or voicemails or icons with red shields. Anything to click on, really. Anything announcing that someone is thinking about me. But my phone has no service so there's nothing. Just me and this emptiness.

About the time I start looking for a place to camp, I see two people ahead on the roadside. Two leathered bikers hang out near a Continental Divide trailhead. One guy is tall and broad, like a quarterback. His bike is devil red. The other guy more like a lineman. Or maybe a Viking. Long beard and all. His bike is a weld of rust and chrome. Both men lean against their bikes with cans of Bud Light. They stop their conversation as I near. I'm tempted to say, "*what's up*" and keep on, but they're curious what I'm up to so I hit LB's parking brake. "I'm Darren," says the taller guy. "And I'm Paul. Actually, Little Paul." I'd put Little Paul at about six feet four. "You want a beer?" Darren asks. I decline, and immediately kick myself. No is always my default answer. I make a mental note to work on that.

Darren and Paul offer to hook Little Buddy up to one of their bikes and haul me into town so we can grab a bite. They're only half-kidding. "You retired?" Darren asks. I shake my head. Tell him I just figured out how to make it work. "Shit, that's the difference right there. Folks who figure shit out and folks who don't." Darren jokes this is my midlife crisis. "But it's better than showing up one day with a Corvette," he says before taking another slug. Paul raises his can and takes a pull, too.

On Darren and Paul's black leather jackets are bright yellow New Mexico flags topped by the stars and stripes. Paul's has a smaller patch on a lower panel that says, "I Don't Like Me Either." Both men are initiates for the Vaqueros Motorcycle Club. I contain my budding curiosity after sensing that fielding questions about the club is not permitted. Paul sips his beer, then asks how I manage to stay warm at night. He opens up a saddle bag and gives me a stack of hand warmers. Tells me his boss at the fishery passes them out like candy. Paul is headed into Silver City where I'm planning to take a couple days off. He insists we plan to meet again. "I want you to meet my girlfriend," he says.

As I shake their hands farewell, Darren offers me a beer. I start to say no, then reach out to accept it. "Give him two," Paul says. Darren hands me the icy cans and says he'll keep an eye out for me over the next few days. He works in a mine just east of town and I'll walk right past it. They heel into their kickstands and fire their engines. Darren peels off first, flying away with his gloved hand in the air. Paul fist bumps me. "See you tomorrow," he says. Then he guns it and quickly overtakes Darren. I still hear them racing away even after they both disappear.

*

Near the CDT trailhead, I find a secluded spot away from popular trails. I set up camp and hang my wet clothes on tree branches hoping they might catch some final rays of sun. All night I hear voices in the distance. Either ghosts or fellow campers. I'm too tired to be concerned and they are too far away to matter. I check my phone for messages. There's still no signal, but one text from Katie snuck through at some point. It's a simple note: "Good morning. Hope you have a good day." Her words irk me. They seem so impersonal. I put my phone in the tent's hanging pocket and listen to rising voices in the distance. They seem to be getting closer. It sort of sounds like laughter, but it could just as easily be crying.

Day 69

No way I'll beat the deluge, but I try. I clock 15-minute miles on the unrelenting uphills, and solid 11s in a braking jog as Little Buddy drags me down the steep descents. The forecasted rain commences with an earsplitting thunderclap and instantly everything is soaked. I'm afraid to stop since momentum is all that's keeping me from exposure to bitter cold and headstrong winds. If only the rain would turn to snow. But the incessant torrent pounds like it's got something to prove. I repeatedly curse the swirling sky with the name of my Patagonia rain shell. "H2-NO! H-2-NO-fucking way!" The pricey coat keeps water from soaking through, but exertion drowns my layers in sog until sweat drips out my sleeves in a steady stream. I chug up the steep and foggy shoulder, poised like Superman as I push Little Buddy up the sharp grades. My fingers are numb. Visibility nearly zero. There are plenty of reasons to worry, but I don't have time for any of them.

For no apparent reason, the front of my left shin begins to scream. A pulled muscle, maybe. But the sudden pain is so acute I'm forced to halt my roll and grab LB's handlebar to stay upright with all my weight on the right foot. Any attempt to bear weight on the left is met with agony. From one moment to the next, I've gone from fine to feeble. In an effort to stretch my lower leg, I press my toe into the blacktop and maneuver my ankle in circles. But the motion increases the soreness and decreases my range of motion. I'm in a pickle— I'm seven miles out of Silver City, caught in a goddamn rainblizzard, my teeth are chattering, and now I'm barely able to stand upright, let alone walk.

With my pant leg rolled up, it's easy to locate the affected area with my frozen fingers. There's a protruding lump rising from my lower tibia. When I point my toes up and down, I see and feel an obvious gap in the muscles sliding under the skin. The movement makes an audible squeaking sound. My body shivers, and not because I am cold. "What the fuck!" I scream at my foot. "Fucking again?" I wrack my brain trying to determine the cause. The climbing, maybe. Or my increased pace from trying to beat the storm. Possibly the pounding from the ferocious downhills. There's no doubt I am injured again. And on the same side as my other sideliner. But this one is completely different than the injury I sustained in California. I tell myself it's an extreme case of shin splints. I blame the shitty conditions. There's nowhere to stop, and nobody to call. So, using LB as a crutch, I press on as the rain finally turns to snow.

*

My walk of shame into Blythe was a mere three miles. It's twice that to Silver City. I suffer my thoughts as much as I do the injured limb. With each step I worry my body had failed me. But I also know I need to take action. So I become my own rescue team and bark loudly at myself. "Alright Griffen, here's what's going to happen. You'll walk for 10 minutes then rest for a few. Walk 10 more and rest again." I tell myself I'll keep warm, stay extra-hydrated, and eat every 15 minutes, hungry or not. I follow my directions. Constantly tell myself all's going to be just fine. "You're good. Suck it up and move on. You got this!" My words take hold and propel me into a painful, yet steady crawl.

I clamber along and formulate a plan. I'll find a hotel and relax. Book a room for a few extra days. Eat lots and lots of breakfasts. I don't like this plan, not one bit, but I'm learning that liking the plan isn't always part of the deal. Thoughts of food draw the home stretch closer. Runny yellow yolks and syrupy stacks of pancakes. Greasy, spicy sausage links and buttered sugared grits. Slabs of sourdough toast swathed with strawberry jelly and honeybutter. Hours later I plod into Silver City. Fractured, frustrated, and ravenous.

*

I crank up the heat in the room and hang everything up to dry. My tent and blue tarp drape across lamps while soaked clothing envelops the television and chairs. Everything else is laid out on the queen bed. Little Buddy drips in the corner. I make a mental note to oil his axles before we cut out again.

When I'm finally settled in, I get a text from Little Paul. I hobble across the street to meet him at a Denny's. We both order coffee, but I'm the only one eating. "You know, the timing of you walking up on us was uncanny," Little Paul says. He assures me a year ago he'd have blown me off. "I wasn't happy back then," he says. "But this year I've decided to change how I see things. Be more mindful about the way I move through the world." He asks about my tattoos. He's especially interested in the one on my left forearm that says, *be nice*. "It ought to say *to yourself* in parenthesis below it," I say. "Because that's what I need a daily reminder of." Paul nods. "But people read it and apply it to their own lives," he says. "And I think that's cool."

We say goodbye in the parking lot and Little Paul sends me off with two more beers—a couple bottles of microbrew. Back at the room I promptly down them both, which not only makes me sleepy drunk, but also kills my foot pain. I mash a pile of my drying gear to one side of the bed and snuggle up to it. Spoon my duffel of foodstuffs as I drift off.

Day 71

Little Paul arranges for me to meet his girlfriend, Christine. She's the editor of the Silver City Daily Press. "You'll love her—she's the nicest person you'll ever meet." And Paul is right, her energy is downright joyful. "You ought to give that foot a soak in the hot springs," she says. "I'm going tomorrow. Want to join me?" I do, but first I text Little Paul to make sure he's OK with me accompanying his girlfriend to the hot springs. "I don't have a bathing suit," I tell him. He says it's no big deal.

Christine and I soak together under pink clouds. We drink IPAs and eat pretzels and berries. We watch the sun sink into the earth while we marvel at the sky catching fire.

Day 73

After four days in Silver City, I've had enough. Enough bad food, enough of my cramped and dingy hotel room, enough sitting around waiting for things to get perfect. My braced foot is definitely progressing, but it's still not 100%. To test my ability to ambulate, I've done a few walks to the post office. I manage with a limp and minimal pain, and my gut tells me more movement is probably a good thing. I hit the Drifter Pancake House for a final breakfast where the server greets me by name. "Come on and take a seat, hon." She takes my order and I tell her I'm leaving town for good. "Wish I was, too," she says.

I sip creamy coffee and study my maps. Figure I'll veer off the Southern Tier again, this time to avoid Emory Pass, an 8,300 ft. ascent on Highway 152. My route will nudge me south, back toward the interstate. I'll zig and zag on secondary roads toward Las Cruces, en route to the Texas border. With a piece of thick toast in my hand, I sit back and gnaw a mouthful of greasy bacon. My choice feels good in my body. I scarf what's left of my huevos rancheros and pay the bill. Head back to the room and prep LB for departure.

*

The doorway of my room is too narrow to wheel Little Buddy out, so I disassemble him and carry my gear, piece by piece, into the hotel parking lot where other travelers are loading up rental cars and RVs. My pile of gear makes me a little self-conscious, and I'm a little scattered when two women walk up as I'm snapping LB's wheels back on. "The folks at the front desk told us about you!" they say. I introduce myself to Sue and Anica, mother and daughter from Minnesota. They're on their annual trip together. A week away from families and kids. "If we see you on the road, we'll honk the horn!" An hour later that's exactly what they do. I smell perfume in the wake of their car and my spirits lift.

Day 74

An occasional blast of intense wind knocks me off balance. I free a few tumbleweeds trapped in a barbed wire fence and they roll away. Their oblong shapes jump and bounce as they carelessly navigate broken paths. I stop to take a leak, and a sudden gust catches my stream and sprays it up and into my face. I hurry to finish then catch my skin in the teeth of my zipper. Leave a line of dribble down the front of my pants.

Another windy burst pelts LB's side panels with sand, and I cover my face with my arm. But I don't do it in time and my eyes fill with a fine talc. I close my face and wait it out. When the air calms, a dust devil dances away, then loses energy and disappears.

A solitary cricket sings from within a tall patch of grass. Its voice is accompanied by another, then another, and soon I can't count how many have joined in song. I imagine they're doing a headcount, making sure all are present and accounted for after the brief tornado.

Day 75

I arrive in Deming, New Mexico and consult Apple Maps. One main drag with an abundance of hotels. I walk past the pricier options near the interstate. Further down the strip, I'm bugged by advertising marquees announcing "American Owned and Operated." Sounds like code to me. A stand-in for *owned by white people.*

*

It's not uncommon for a song to pop into my head while I'm walking. Often its beat coincides with my cadence. But today that wasn't the case. Today it was just a random song, or so it seemed. Bob Marley's "Three Little Birds." Until I Googled the lyrics, I had always assumed it was called Don't Worry About a Thing. And after reading the lyrics, it's obvious why it's been in my head. Funny how the brain sends subconscious clues in all sorts of packaging.

As I'm humming along, my phone dings. It's an email from Pete, a buddy in Florida with a background in sports medicine.

"Simply *resting* is amazing therapy." Then a similar message from Jay, a friend from back home who owns a record store. "Be kind to yourself. This is a journey, not a race." These back-to-back sentiments make me question my current mindset. They make me look beyond what I want, and instead tune into what my body actually needs.

*

Is Deming a one-night stop, or will I continue my Silver City foot recovery here? It doesn't seem like a tough question, but I fight the answer. Taking extended breaks is tricky. They entail either long and expensive hotel stays, or find me parked in a campsite for multiple nights, which isn't ideal if I'm trying to give my feet a rest. I lay on the stale bedspread and try to imagine the advice I'd give to someone in my shoes. *Look here, Griffen. The second phase of this journey has definitely been marked by a different perspective than the first. So, good on you. You also haven't been pushing the mileage for the sake of pushing mileage, and you are no longer as obsessed with the Atlantic as you were before. But can you honestly say you're truly taking care of your body? Because, if you never fully recover, you'll never be fully recovered.*

I dig into these thoughts. Try to take them in without judgment. I'm right—I definitely have not been giving my body the TLC it needs as I ask it to cover these ridiculous distances. It's no wonder I'm always teetering on injury. "What do you think, LB?" I say. Then, after a long pause, I change my plans. I'll stop here in Deming for two nights, rest, and honor the needs of my body. I'll do everything I can to ensure that every little thing's gonna be alright.

*

Just as I make the decision to spend an extra night in town, I get another message. This time from one of my mom's oldest childhood friends, Pamela. I've never met Pamela, but she's been following my journey on social media. She offers to cover a third night at my hotel so I can get some additional rest. I want to tell her no. That I've got this. That two days off will do it. I also don't want to say yes because it proves I need help. I write a text to Katie asking for her guidance. But I know what she's going to say so I delete it without sending.

*

Back in Scottsdale, Arizona, Lion hugged his wisdom into me after schooling me on what it means to accept kindness. If I say no to it today, I won't recognize it as readily tomorrow. And someday I'll think it no longer exists. Saying no to kindness allows fear and isolation to take over. Keeps me from achieving what I'm seeking—genuine connection. And not only with others, but also with myself.

I read Pamela's note and think of Lion. Wonder what he's doing today. Maybe sitting on his corner accepting alms from passersby. Adding another day to his 15 years on the streets. Fifteen years that have done what I'd never expect homelessness to do to a human being—open a heart and create space for selflessness. I am selfish. I think mostly of me. I desperately needed his reminder to consider others, to say yes to the kindness they offer me.

I text Pamela back and accept her offer. She writes back, "Rest easy, buddy. I am so in awe of you. You have a good mama...she raised a courageous and thoughtful son. Frankly it made me feel good to do something for someone who is a huge inspiration in my life right now. Sooooo....thank you."

This, I am learning, is how kindness works. We take it, we give it, and we pass it on.

Day 77

I settle into the flat recliner and tune into some midday basketball. March Madness. My foot is elevated atop a dunk bag stuffed with freshly laundered clothes. My entire stash. The room phone rings and I pick up. Nobody's there. A few minutes later it rings again. Nothing. The third time I ignore it. Figure something must be wrong with the hotel's system.

A minute later, I'm startled by a soft knocking at the door. I hit mute on the remote and listen, but there's only silence before more gentle tapping. I tiptoe to the peephole and peer one-eyed at indecipherable movement in the hallway. A woman with long hair. I crack the door to a tender voice rising almost in question. "Surprise?" It's Becca. One of my oldest friends. My face opens and I start to swing the door wider. "Uh…hold on a sec! I'm in my underwear!" Becca giggles. Her kids do, too.

The heavy door slams and I tear into my dunk bag. Trip while trying to get my legs into my only pair of pants. Wrinkled and still warm from the dryer. I grumble at my reflection in the bathroom mirror. Ruddy, fatigue-swollen cheeks and eyes. I'm ragged. I reopen the door and swoop in for hugs. Becca and her two young children, Enzo and Ociee, come inside and look around. "We were in the neighborhood!" Becca says as the kids swarm my legs. "Jeff's outside reorganizing the truck." I scramble to find something to say. Becca says she read about my foot situation on social media. When she learned of my plan to hole up in Deming for a few extra days, she and Jeff added a minor detour to their family vacation. "I can't believe you drove all the way from Little Rock for such a short visit!" I say. Enzo announces, "Oh trust me. The extra driving time has been terrible!"

Becca and I met in 1993 while we were both in the Army and stationed at Fort Myer in Arlington, Virginia. Fresh off tours in Germany, we got acquainted while sitting in an office awaiting job assignments. We shared a quirky sense of humor and soon became inseparable. After work we'd hit up dance clubs downtown, watch up-and-coming bands at the 9:30 Club, and wander Georgetown's M Street to mix ourselves with the academic kids. We often lingered in musty bookstores, lying across aisles reading erotic excerpts aloud from Henry Miller or Anaïs Nin's books. At some point the barracks reached capacity, and single soldiers were offered stipends to live off-post in a low-rent complex. We accepted and moved in together. I felt grown up in my own place. Even more grown up having Becca for a roommate.

Most folks thought we were a couple, but we weren't. Maybe it could have been more than it was, but neither of us ever pushed for that. And though our friendship was deep, it was brief. Within a year of meeting Becca, I became smitten with a woman I met at a gas station, fell foolishly in love, and abandoned my dear friend. I left Becca with half the rent and a new, disastrous roommate who made her life a living hell. Outwardly I showed no remorse, but inside I battled my poor decisions until convincing myself I had done nothing wrong. Before long I was too caught up in my new and dysfunctional relationship to iron things out with Becca. So we became estranged. Over time we completely lost touch.

Years later, Becca reached out, and I was finally able to apologize. I rediscovered what brought us together in the first place—a friendship based on genuine connection. Which, I've come to realize, is exactly what I've spent my entire life seeking. Ironically, it's also something I have a long and repeated history of sabotaging, too. When things get good, I often make them bad.

Day 78

I meet Becca in the hotel lobby at sunrise. We drive downtown to the Rise-N-Shine cafe where the owner, Dennis, says everything is made in-house. His wife and kids do the baking. "We're Mennonites. Came here a year ago from Pennsylvania to open a place where we could interact with the community." As Dennis rings us up, he shows me his pedometer that's logging all the miles he walks at work. Behind the register, a red line extends through a map of the United States and marks his virtual distance covered. "In a year I've made it from San Francisco to Denver," he says. He slowly traces his finger between the cities. "Not bad, huh?"

Becca and I sip fancy espresso drinks just like we did in the old days. We could sit and talk all day at Dennis's cafe, but we both need to get going. We take the long way back to the hotel where Jeff offers to haul me back to my turnoff. Since the drive is all a backtrack, I agree to the short shuttle. Takes longer to strap LB to the roof of their truck than to drive the distance. I'm grateful for any extra time with these friends. Love is a hard thing to walk away from.

*

By the end of the day my foot feels so-so. I illegally camp on the far side of a railway paralleling the road. I hunch over as I set up my tent on a gradual grade, then lay back on a rock and eat a can of chili. Slight movement beyond the fence catches my eye. A lone coyote glides across the empty space. Its mouth is closed, its haunches are lean, whiteish swatches dot its feet. I wave and it freezes. Our eyes lock as the sky turns orange, then pink. I whisper to it as if it can hear me, as if it might understand my words. "Hello coyote. You. Are. Beautiful." When I hear a truck downshift, my muscles clench, and I peek over the raised track behind me to see if it stops. But it rolls past. I return my attention to the desert and scan the emptiness hoping to lock onto the coyote again. But it's gone, too.

Day 79

By 6:30 a.m. Little Buddy is loaded up and ready to go. I'm standing on the roadside near the railroad tracks when a rail police truck stops along the shoulder, kicking up a cloud of dust. A large white man in a badged uniform leans out the window. His red goatee looks perfectly round on his swollen face. "The fuck you doing out here?" he barks. I tell him I slept along the tracks. That I didn't have any other options. He lashes into reprimand and I dismiss his scolding with a snarky toned-response. "Yes sir, I know it's illegal," I say. "Yes sir, I know it's dangerous."

The officer may just be doing his job, but I project my loaded assumptions onto him. That he lives for moments like this. That he's exploiting a chance to flex his power. My mouth shifts and I chew my lip as I emit my veiled disdain.

The man's tone reminds me of all the white, male, authority figures I've ever had: Boy Scout leaders, priests, military superiors, bosses. I sarcastically tell him I appreciate his concern as my self-control wanes. This man represents one of my ongoing triggers—when confronted by what I perceive to be power-hungry men, I become the angry kid I've tried to leave behind. Moments like this prove I've still got a lot of work to do.

Spittle flies from the officer's mouth as he issues a warning. "Catch you out here again and you're gonna be in trouble." I nod, cavalier. I want him to leave and am confident he will, and soon. Then, somewhere in the throes of the cop's ramblings about railroad legalities, I recall Art's words. "This isn't about you, Tom. It's about all of us." And suddenly my perspective shifts.

The officer's mouth continues to move but I hear nothing. Instead, I wonder about him. About how he feels right now. Is he scared? Or frustrated? Is he considering the gun and taser that are attached to his belt? I'm thinking about how this situation might shake out if I were not me. Like, if I were a woman or a person of color. Or a non-English speaker. Or if I were waving a rainbow flag. This badged man, to me, is no more than a minor inconvenience. I'm not worried he'll cite me or cuff me or take me to jail. I don't consider the possibility of him inflicting any physical harm. My biggest problem with him is the memories he's stirring up. Which, frankly, aren't his fault.

This moment is yet another example of my white privilege. I may be a weirdo walking along the roadside pushing a baby jogger full of food and water, but I still easily beat the system. Why? Because the system is built precisely for people who look like me.

All day I am haunted by my interaction with the rail cop. I walk and stew for hours afterwards, unable to shake our exchange. It was a disturbing reminder of how easy I've got it. Not just out here, but in life.

*

A man on a trailered bike rolls up on the opposite side of the road. Cracks up at the signs on LB's flank. He asks where I'm heading, then advises me to get through El Paso as fast as possible. "People aren't nice there," he says. "Lots of Mexicans." His name is John. He raises his voice when he tells me he's not homeless. He's retired from his job as a freelance fabricator and has been pedaling back and forth across the US ever since. "I'm out here by choice," he hollers across the lanes.

For three hours we walk and talk. Him walking his bike on the eastbound side and me against traffic, per usual. Mostly I listen as he informs me how to go weeks without spending money. "Man, I hate staying in hotels," he says. "They bring out the worst in me. All I do is watch TV and stay up too late." When I stop for lunch in a pullout near a wash, John crosses the street and joins me.

I offer John what I have. An apple, carrots, crackers, some rubbery cheddar. He declines it all. Opens a jar of Jif and says that's all he eats. Between spoonfuls, he explains how to be a successful hobo. "You know what hobo means, don't you?" he says. "Homeward bound. We're all heading home whether we realize it or not."

John describes the process of boiling water in a milk carton. How to shower in any public restroom with a floor drain. How to never again pay for a campsite. "And never pick up anything smaller than a quarter," he says. "Banks won't change it for you if it's all scratched up. And those little coins usually are." As John packs away his peanut butter, he says he's got something for me. He rummages through his pannier and hands me a small, solar-powered lantern. Says he doesn't like artificial light and has no use for it. I hang it from the carabiner on LB's handlebar.

We finish lunch and continue walking. Get a couple miles up the road before John realizes he forgot his sunglasses at our lunch spot. He hops on his bike, turns around and rides away. Something tells me he's not coming back.

Once he's out of sight, I wonder if he was even real. Maybe he was a hallucination. I consider my water intake. The pounding heat. John's image fades into the rippling horizon and I grab the lantern. Fiddle with the switch. It works fine, but I don't really want it, either. Right now, however, I notice its weight in my hands and take it as proof that John wasn't a figment of my imagination, after all.

Hours later I stop on a dime to pick up a scratched token that says "Always With You" on one side and has a rough image of an angel on the reverse. I dust it off and put it in my pocket.

*

The long stretches of fencing on BLM land have occasional gate access. Each is a chance to exit the highway and disappear into nowhere. No matter the time of day, at each unlocked barrier I consider stopping. The opportunity feels empowering.

When I notch these gates behind me and take my first few steps toward an unknown campsite, I'm always overcome by a sense of lightness. There's joy in knowing the day's work is done, but it's more than that. The trails softly crunch—a soothing sound —as I distance myself from the road's lumber and roar. Quiet is always louder and more obvious in desolation and I fantasize about plunging deeper and deeper into it. I dream of making my permanent home in the hidden areas beyond.

*

A few miles from Hatch, I find a wide gate that funnels into a narrow trail. I pass through it and tromp another half mile before landing on a hidden clearing. I get down on all fours, put my cheek to the ground, and eyeball a flat spot for my bedroll. Once the tent is up, I place dinner fixings on my mildewed tarp. Then I remove all my clothes and hike naked around the campsite, occasionally stopping to pick up a fragment of an arrowhead, reddish-yellow and razor-sharp.

Day 80

I reach the Rio Grande. The great river. The first major body of water I've seen since the Pacific. For miles I've known it was on my left, but it remained hidden by desert brush and rock formations. Then all of a sudden, with a gasp, here it is. I first see it between a rusty shed and a trampoline. I want to take a token photo, but children are playing in the yard and I don't want to be mistaken for some kind of weirdo. I lock the image in my mind instead.

For the rest of the day, we walk together. The river, Little Buddy, and me. I pay attention to it as I would a running or hiking partner. Make sure we're keeping a similar pace. Together we wind gracefully through cranberry canyons, pass homes built feet from the bank. We border lush valleys and endless acres of farmland and flooded nut orchards with signs announcing that "Pecan Thieves Will Be Prosecuted."

The river offers refuge from the heat. It cools the air. It's proof that soon I'll cross into another state. The river makes me think of chocolate milk. Which makes me dream of my next big meal. Which won't be tonight. Tonight, like usual, it'll be tortillas and beans. Which, right now, sounds delicious.

*

Later, after the sun sets, I read a comment left on yesterday's Instagram post. It's from Leslie, a man I met a few years back while I was writing my master's thesis on the deceased poet, Larry Levis. When I learned that Leslie had interviewed Levis in 1989, I reached out to start a conversation. We connected on Facebook and now he's following me on social media.

Leslie shares an excerpt from Gary Snyder's book of essays, *The Practice of the Wild*. Snyder's words: "I think many of us would consider it quite marvelous if we could set out on foot again…to travel across a landscape. That's the way to see the world in our own bodies." Leslie continues with his own thoughts, "In other words, Tom, your journey, moving on foot, on our land, is a kind of pilgrimage. I find it beautiful! Keep it loose, wild, and sweet." These three words—loose, wild, and sweet—churn through my head like a lullaby as the hard ground swallows my aching body.

Day 81

Highway 185 into Las Cruces offers nothing but chain restaurants. And though I'd prefer something local, hunger calls and I settle for a Subway that smells like Pine Sol. I nearly slip on the floor when I walk in, which triggers the two teenage staffers behind the counter to tuck away their cell phones and focus on me. I make an attempt to strike up a conversation, but the banter is one-sided. I mention I'm walking across America. They couldn't care less.

I let the Subway staffers upsell me the value meal. And though I'm hungry enough to devour it on the spot, I want to dine while enjoying some creature comforts, too. In the parking lot I make a couple calls to nearby hotels and am floored by the nightly rates. Turns out the Bataan Memorial Death March is happening in a couple days. An annual commemoration of the 1942 marching transport of POWs in the Philippines. Coincidentally, it's an event I've always wanted to do. My last-second request for a comped late entry goes unanswered.

I find a place willing to extend the walking across America discount. They upgrade me to a first-floor suite where I promptly wash my rank clothes in the sink using shampoo as laundry detergent. I eat my footlong, cold cut sandwich stacked with veggies doused in olive oil, then hit Golden Corral's all-you-can-eat buffet for meal number two. I don't count calories, but I think I'm consuming more than 6,000 per day. Which my increasingly baggy clothes prove is still not enough.

Day 82

The next morning I wheel LB through the breakfast crowd in the lobby. I've already filled up on my share of pancakes and coffee, but the smell of maple syrup and warm toast makes me consider a second round. I pass. Mostly because I don't want to deal with the crowd. I exit through the automatic doors and am blasted with the spicy smell of creosote. "Make a hole!" someone shouts. A group of preteen boys wearing fatigues shifts to the side to clear a space for me to pass. A man with them looks me up and down. He wears a big smile. "Where ya headed?" he asks. The boys surround me as I answer his question.

The boys and Chip, their leader, are the Tornado Alley Young Marines from Wichita, Kansas. Like the rest of the crowd, they are here for tomorrow's Death March at the White Sands

Missile Range. "Today we're off to do a little acclimating," Chip says. One boy asks if he has to keep his boots on this time, which seems like some sort of inside joke. There's sideline conversation about snakes, but I miss the punchline. I ask if any of them have done the marathon-length march before. Two of the older boys raise their hands. "Any advice for these newbies?" I ask. One older boy speaks up. "Yes sir," he belts. "Don't give blood the day before the march." I ask if he has personal experience with this kind of situation. "Maybe, sir," he says. The older boys laugh knowingly.

These young boys are tomorrow's American military. They already look more squared away than plenty of the soldiers I served with, which is both impressive and a little disturbing. I want to tell them to just be kids. Go collect frogs and play video games or something. Don't waste your childhood preparing to fight wars. But I don't say anything because really, what do I know? They are here as kid Marines, playing a role, which is not much different than being in the band or on a basketball team. Right now they are amped for their long march tomorrow. I tell them I wish I could join them.

I ask for a group photo, and they happily comply. I walk off, waving to these young men while hoping for their safety. Tomorrow, sure. But also in their unfolding lives as inevitable American soldiers.

5

Confront the dark parts of yourself
and work to banish them
with illumination and forgiveness.
Your willingness to wrestle your demons
will cause your angels to sing.

- August Wilson

Day 82

I'M FAR LESS LIKELY TO DIE walking in Texas. In New Mexico, one out of every 25,000 pedestrians is killed in a traffic-related accident. This rate is more than twice the national average. I celebrate my rainy arrival to Anthony, Texas, population 5,000, with a sigh of relief and a blurry photo of the unremarkable welcome sign.

The area is largely industrial. Shoulders, though wide, are a patchwork of rutted dirt lots. As Little Buddy and I approach a gated junkyard, three rottweilers and two Doberman pinschers race to the cyclone and issue noxious warnings. They track us as we walk past, barking and growling while lunging at the wire barrier. When we reach the edge of the property line, the pack trots back to a shady spot with tails wagging. We are nothing but an amusement. "I think they're barking at you," I say to LB.

*

I'm hours into my approach to El Paso when I reach a roadblock. Beyond the barricade is a raised highway, still under construction. It's so new that my GPS doesn't know it exists. All traffic is detoured from this point. My maps show an alternate route but it adds miles to the day and I'd rather stick as close as possible to my original plan. Since it's Sunday and the site is empty, I wheel past the NO TRESPASSING signs and push LB up the fresh on-ramp onto the elevated roadway. His wheels track into the fresh grooves of the thoroughfare. I kneel down to feel the roadruts and wonder if mine will be the only fingers to ever touch this spot.

It's like I've warped into a post-apocalyptic version of the El Paso outskirts. I intently watch the fleet of heavy equipment for any sign of movement—like a blur moving between giant tires or a human shape in a cockpit. The quiet here is more profound than usual. I savor the familiar and soothing sound of LB's tread. Then take an exit adjacent to a main avenue into the heart of the city.

*

I stop at Crazy Cat Cyclery to get a new light for LB. There I meet Amédée, a cross-country cyclist from France who's stopped for a new inner tube. Neither of us speak the other's native tongue, so we use an app on his phone to communicate. He goes first. Speaks into his phone's mic then shows me the transcription on the screen. "I'm cycling around the world," the app says. "I'll finish in San Diego and maybe go to China next." He reaches his phone toward me. I do my best to summarize the last 80 days in a couple sentences, but I can't complete a thought. He resets the app and I start over, keep it simple this time. "Right now is most important," I say. Amédée reads the screen, nods slowly, then responds. "I think we are similar," he says. Then he speaks into it again. "I heal with my hands. If ever you have a problem, contact me and I'll work on you from wherever I am." I perk up. Point to my leg. "Right now, if possible," I say. But Amédée insists the healing is best done at night. "It's very strong," he says nodding. I ask how long he's been a healer. "Since I was a child," he says. "But I ignored it for years because I was afraid. But it's who I am so now I embrace it." I give a thumbs up and he shrugs.

"You're right about this moment being the most important part," he says, touching his finger to my chest. We stand without speaking for a few minutes while he admires LB. Then I ask for his phone again. "Love attracts love," I say, and watch as the screen translates my words into French. He reads it aloud. "L'amour attire l'amour." Amédée then says "one minute" in English and runs over to his bike. He removes a small antler bungeed to the back of his trailer and hands it to me. Talks into the app. "I want to share some of me with you. I found this on my journey." The smooth gray shed fits perfectly into my fist. Three weathered points and a broken skull attachment. "For you," Amédée says. We exchange information and continue our journeys.

*

Some crossers map out the details of their entire walk across America before they've even started. Not me. With the exception of planning day one's clunky route from Santa Monica pier to my brother's house, I've pretty much been winging it.

Every morning after breakfast, I take a look on Apple Maps to determine what's due east. Then I concoct a loose agenda that takes a couple things into consideration: access to food and water replenishment, and the options for a safe place to sleep. But my ambling isn't completely random—I have made tentative plans to see folks along the way. I'll probably stop in Phoenix and Austin to visit siblings. A colleague in Dallas has offered a homestay. Maybe Little Rock to spend more time with Becca and her family. Possibly Nashville to see friends and past clients. And maybe Asheville, too, because I love it there. But I've also imagined bolting north at some point to visit my parents in upstate New York. I'm doing my best to take this trip a few days at a time and have no clue where I'll finally hit the Atlantic.

*

Crossing borders makes it easy to suddenly think I'm farther along than I actually am. Sure, 83 days and 887 total miles is a nice chunk. But really, I'm still in the trip's infancy. Barely in Texas. The Lone Star will ultimately represent a third of my total miles and time spent on the journey. When I consider what needs to happen before I reach another state's border, I get a sinking feeling in my gut. Worry about what all those miles are going to do to my feet. I've barely started and already sustained two pretty significant injuries. Will there be others? All I want to think about is what's in the near distance. And right now that's a couple days rest in El Paso. A comfortable bed, a hot shower, and some bad TV. For a few days I'll trade my nightly can of beans for authentic Mexican cuisine. I'll replace my Nescafé instant coffee with specialty espresso. Right now, these simple pleasures are all I want.

Day 84

I get a call from my sister Lisa, the oldest of five. By a stroke of serendipity, she's arriving in El Paso tonight on a work trip. How is it we rarely see each other in real life and now we're going to be able to hang out here? We capitalize on our unlikely convergence.

Lisa suggests a fancy restaurant for dinner. I'd be happy with a pizza or burgers but that's not how my sis rolls. She chooses a swanky joint where I feel totally out of place in my off-day Crocs, salty pants, and pink accessorizing neck buff.

At the bar, Lisa raises her martini glass. I cheers it with my bottle of Stella. Once our order is placed, she fills me in on her local work, gives me the skinny on her recent divorce, and gets all giddy describing a new love interest. She mentions the books she's currently writing, strategizes the future of her business, and correctly deciphers the spices used in her entrée. My sister is a 1,000 mph non stop fireball. I barely get any words in, which is fine. Because it's a delight spending this unexpected time with her.

It's barely 8:00 p.m. when she drops me at my hotel and I'm already yawning. I apologize and explain that lately I conk out when the sun goes down. She assures me the timing is perfect—she's got an early flight the next morning. We say our goodbyes and I watch her drive off until the red lights of her rental car fade into the distance. Back in my room, I feel more alone than I have for the entire trip.

Day 86

Tufts of raw cotton snagged on roadside bramble are the sky's missing clouds. The cellulose fluffs shiver in the cooling gusts that press them deeper into their thorny stopping place. I park LB and snap off a boll. A blanched, milky ball of fibrous snow. I brush it on my sunburnt cheek. Pass it over my chapped lips where it catches burrs of peeling skin. I get chills. It smells like nothing and carries no heft. I let it sit in my palm until the wind takes it.

Barely 50 miles into Texas and the geography has already transformed. There's a small grouping of mountains in the eastern distance, far enough away to be my imagination, and everything is suddenly green. And though it has been hot lately, over 90°F on a handful of days, this Texan heat feels more harsh. Like the sun is closer. I like the heat. I pride myself in my ability to muscle through it. But here it saps me.

*

By lunch I want a nap—one of my dehydration tells. And just as I find a spot for a quick siesta, a minivan pulls up and rolls down its window. One person inside. A man, probably older than me, with thick black glasses and a sharp part down one side of his head. "Hi. I work at the elementary school, and we had a few extra lunches," he says. He hands me two brown bags. "There's a sandwich, a juice box, and some carrots in each. Good luck with whatever you are doing."

Directly behind him comes another vehicle. And one behind that. They line up like a drive-thru as I accept their handouts. The driver of the final car is an old woman with a shock of white hair. Tan face and thin eyes. There's a child in the passenger seat, and more kids in the back. "I saw you back there, way back there," she says. The three youngsters peer at me. The two in the back grip the headrests with dirty hands, pulling in for a closer look. "The children want to know if you are tired," the old woman says. I ask them if I look tired. They all nod.

The woman says she'd like to give me something. Digs in her purse and hands me two dollars. "It's not much, but we'd like to help you out," she says. I take the money and place my hands together in prayer. "Thank you," I say. The old lady smiles. "Guess what?" the little girl says. "I am six!" "Awesome!" I say. "Being six is the best! Wanna know how old I am?" She does. "I'm forty-six," I say. The old woman turns around to look at the kids in the back, then gives me a smirk. "Oh yeah?" she says. "I got you all beat. I'm eighty-five. How about that?"

Another car pulls up behind her and she tells the kids to say goodbye. As the electronic windows roll up, the children wave and smash their faces against the glass. By the time the line of cars clears out, I have enough water and snacks for at least a couple days. Couple extra bucks in my pocket, too.

Day 87

Between blasts of West Texas wind I hear a whine. A meow, maybe? It grows louder and I'm certain it's a cat. A crying cat. I can't quite place it, so I stop walking. I suck tiny bursts of air through my pursed lips and make the sound my childhood cat, Lucy, always responded to. It works. The meow increases in volume and frequency and leads me to a storm drain. The cat's call weeps out from behind a steel grate blocked by an overgrowth of weeds. I pause. This is the perfect place to encounter a rattlesnake. I use a stick to poke around in the brush before stepping closer to the moaning.

I make out the shape of the cat's head. Its desperate cries announce, *Help me,* over and over. I pull out branches that block the cover until there's enough space for the cat to come out. But it doesn't budge. Its meows only become louder. I run back to Little Buddy and dig out a pack of tuna from my food duffle. I pour some of the packaging water near the drain. The cat stops meowing, reaches out its paw to touch the tiny puddle, then cranes its neck for a lap. I pour the rest, drop a few flakes of pink fishmeat. The cat speaks nonstop as it scarfs every drop and morsel within reach, occasionally choking. When it's done it looks up at me and demands more.

As I drop more wedges of tuna, the animal's body comes into view. The creature moves at a crawl, and its handicap is obvious once it's completely in view. The animal's rear body drags uselessly behind it, its hind legs unnaturally twisted and contorted. Injury or birth defect, God only knows. But my gut says this cat was struck by a car and somehow managed to survive. I scoop out bigger portions of tuna until the pouch is empty. While the cat devours the last of it, I fetch another packet from my stash.

The animal continues meowing, though the tone is less troubled. More like a normal cat than one in need. I refrain from touching it. I'm allergic to cat dander and don't want to expose myself to fleas or some sort of zoonotic disease. I'm also afraid to hurt it even more. If I were in its shoes, however, I'd want to be touched. To be handled in a way that proves I'm finally rescued. But I don't. I just watch it ravage the second pack. And when it's done, it wants more still.

When I leave to grab the third and final pouch in LB, the cat bleats a frenzied plea, as if begging me to stay. *No! No! Don't go!* When I return it stops carrying on. I open the pack and dump the contents under its yearning mouth and suddenly regret interfering. Because what am I supposed to do I do now that I've ruined its refuge? The blocked drain has likely been responsible for keeping the cat from becoming coyote food. And now, thanks to me, the drain is wide open. And worse yet, the broken cat is outside of it, lured by me and a meal. Unless I further interfere, like somehow get it help, the cat will surely die. And soon.

But what more can I possibly do? I'm in the middle of nowhere with no phone signal or internet. No way to reach out for immediate assistance. I'm a day's walk away from any place where someone might be able to fix a messed-up cat. Shoot, I don't even have any more tuna. I don't want to leave it out here, fully exposed to the elements and hungry predators, but I also don't know how to care for this mangled creature.

I tell the cat how sorry I am for fucking up its shelter. I apologize for not being the sort of person who'll take the risk to scoop up its shattered body. I want to be the one who says, *I got you. Take it easy there, little one*, but that's not happening. I apologize to it for not doing all within my power to save its life. For being selfish and self-centered. For making this all about me. I don't want to accept responsibility for this creature's life. I don't want to be its caretaker. I should never have stopped or cleared the drain or busted out three pouches of what was supposed to be my lunch for the next few days. I should have minded my own damn business. I don't want to think more about what I'm doing. I just want it done.

So I walk back to LB, and just like when I set off for the last pack of tuna, the cat howls bloody murder. *Don't leave! Please, please don't leave!* Its loudest yet. But I keep going. Since the wind has died down, I can clearly hear everything as it begs me to return. I know I'm not the only thing who hears it. Coyotes and birds of prey have, without a doubt, tuned into the keen sound of an animal in agony. And once I'm gone, they'll swoop in. I pray this happens quickly. I do not wish the cat a slow death. But now, because of me, its death is inevitable.

Immediately my decision haunts me. I question why walking away was even an option. There's no way to dance around the fact that I abandoned a life when I had a chance to help save it. I killed this creature by ignoring it. Does this make me a bad person? I think it does. And what if something similar were to happen to me? What if I get hurt and someone finds me but leaves me out here to die anyhow? I'd hate them for it.

I'm such a hypocrite. I make like I'm living up to Art's advice—that this trip isn't about me. I accept an abundance of kindness from strangers because Lion told me to. But now I wonder if my adherence to their wisdom is nothing but a pretty wrapping around a self-serving endeavor. A way to help me justify my need to control how I am perceived. I can't shake my regret and a few miles later I consider turning back. But I don't. I tell myself the cat has already met its end. I plod eastward, away from the forlorn animal.

*

Long into the night I dream of how things could have been. I consider the possible alternatives. I could have swathed the cat in a spare T-shirt and carefully put it somewhere in LB's belly. I could have figured out a way to make the cat cozy, set up bowls of food and water. I could have told it that everything was going to be alright. I could have stopped at the next veterinarian and paid a couple hundred bucks to make sure it was on the mend. I could have provided it a less traumatic ending.

Maybe the cat would have made a full recovery. Maybe it could have become my travel companion. My two-legged cat who had endured far more than most living creatures could. Struck by a car only to suffer nightly raids by desert predators and then live to tell about it. I'd be that guy on the road with the special needs cat and we'd travel all the way to the Atlantic Ocean together. I even come up with a name for it, Tornillo, the name of the closest town. Tom and Tornillo. Got a nice ring to it.

Afterwards, I'd bring the cat home and maybe get it outfitted with a set of wheels so its useless rear half could ambulate like a wheelbarrow. I'd be lucky to have such a life force on my side. Shit, anyone would. But no, I took the easy way out and left it behind. Blatantly ignored it even as it cried for me to stop. *No, don't go! Please Tom, please! Pleeeeease!* I may as well have walked away whistling as I pretended to hear nothing. Shit. I wish I could go back and do it all over again.

Tonight I camp on the edge of Plainview Lake and watch the sky bleed red. When morning comes I lay in my tent as the sun warms the air. I break camp, then wheel Little Buddy along the crust of the crumbling shore. A gaggle of Canada geese perched nearby honk their alarms then aggressively give chase. One catches me and nips at my thigh with a wrenching pinch. They hiss and flap their wings as their long, black necks shoot at me like arrows. They know what I did and banish me back to the highway. *Don't let us ever see you again, cat killer!*

Day 88

The news claims America's southern boundary is a war zone. The current administration makes it sound like people are violently flooding over the borders. But here all is serene. People on both sides of the dividing wall look up at the same aquamarine sky, feel the same breeze, inhale the same toxic smoke snaking up from smoldering trash piles.

I spend the day within view and earshot of northern Mexico. A fence line and narrow section of the Rio Grande divide us. The highway winds so close to the border that I see a village beyond the tall fence separating the US and Mexico. Boxy architecture painted with colorful advertisements. A church spire reaches toward the heavens. At one point I hear a siren. I stop to listen as the vehicle races toward an emergency. I feel compelled to pray.

*

It's Good Friday. In Fort Hancock I stop at an elementary school playground for a calorie break. I down a pack of mini chocolate donuts, a small bag of cool ranch Doritos, and a stick of teriyaki jerky. I watch a procession of people led by a man bearing a wooden cross on his shoulder. The group stops, says a few prayers together, then moves on. The Catholic ritual is an anchor to my childhood.

Witnessing the stations of the cross in a language other than English makes it seem more solemn. I watch intently from the playground's wobbly picnic table until the small crowd is out of sight. I recall my elementary days at St. John's, moving alongside classmates from station to station along the perimeter of the church, hoping to reposition myself next to Cecilia, my classmate crush. The thrill of our shoulders touching. The smell of her perfume. The class half-listening to Fr. Dollen drone on about Jesus' condemnation, crucifixion, and death. This thought makes me wonder if any of my classmates were molested by the litany of priests who shuffled in and out of our parish. I have no such stories, thank God.

Day 89

I hustle through a giant day. Twenty-seven miles of frontage road and an illegal bit on Interstate 10. The goal was to get to Sierra Blanca in time for some Final Four basketball. When I make it to town, I'm wrangled by Leti who passes me in a convertible then U-turns to talk. She's the owner of The Lodge, a vintage motor inn. "My husband Chuck is there," she says. "I'll call and tell him you're coming."

The door chimes as I walk in. The room is painted purple and smells like fried food. Chuck sits at a table and insists I join him for some KFC. "Leti said you'd be here any minute," he says. "Good timing." Behind Chuck, the front desk area is adorned with varnished wood panels covered in ranch brands. The JJ, 3A, the Lazy S. "You must be parched," Chuck says, dabbing his mouth with a paper napkin. "Please eat. No way I can put it all away by myself."

Chuck is an ex-NASA employee. A safety engineer. He also spent 12 years in the Army and was once stationed in

Babenhausen, a short drive from where I was based during my German tour. Chuck is a Sacramento transplant who's suffered multiple heart attacks. But these days he's feeling better than ever. "I have a 23-year-old's heart in my chest," he says. "And recently I've started taking on some of the donor's traits. Like food cravings. I want things I've never even had before." He wags a chicken wing in the air. Chuck says The Lodge has an interesting history. Apparently General Patton took it over during WWII. "He was here with the Third Army doing tank training exercises," Chuck says. "Also, there are tunnels underneath us that run for miles. Probably go across the border." But Chuck's not sure who made them. "Could have been the Chinese or maybe the Mexicans," he says. "But whatever the case, nobody talks about them."

Chuck scoots the containers of mashed potatoes and gravy closer to me after I clean my plate. Offers me a soda from the cooler then asks if I know anything about volcanoes. Says he foresees a doomsday event in the not too distant future. "Don't know about you, " he says, "but I think if there's gonna be any sort of apocalypse, it'll be natural. If the volcano near Tahoe erupts, Sacramento will turn into a lake. And if Yellowstone goes, well shoot, there will be another ice age."

Chuck bites into a chicken leg and shifts the conversation to politics. "I gotta admit I firmly believe in our president," he says. "I truly think there's hope for the future." Chuck says Trump is a good manager of people. Says he's exactly what America needs. "He gives it to ya straight, you know. Isn't afraid to fire folks who aren't doing a good job."

Chuck looks at my plate again. "Here Tom, eat more. There's plenty." He motions toward the red and white bucket. I end up eating two big plates of chicken, a couple big helpings of gravy potatoes, and a heaping scoop of coleslaw before excusing myself to my room. "Thanks for the hospitality," I say. "I appreciate the food more than you know. But hey—I'm sorry about my appetite." Chuck shakes my hand. "It's our pleasure," he says. "Now go enjoy the peace and quiet. But heads up, there's no TV in any of the rooms. We're in phase two of our refurb. Hope that's not a problem." Damn. No basketball.

Day 90

The next morning I join Chuck for breakfast in the lobby. He tells me about when he worked as an independent hazmat remover. I stir hot water into a couple packs of instant oatmeal, a combination of maple brown sugar and cinnamon apple, then follow it with a couple Svenhard's cherry danishes. I eat while Chuck describes how to clean brains and skull fragments off walls, and how tricky it is to get blood out of a rug. "Folks called me because I was good at it, you know?" he says. "Cleaning up those messes. You'd be surprised how many people kill themselves in a hotel room. Some are really thoughtful and lay out plastic bags to catch the fallout." I ask if his experience had any lasting effects. Chuck shakes his head. Says it's like any other job. "The more you do it, the more you get used to it."

*

Around late morning, the support vehicle for a cycling tour stops to give me a cold orange and a couple cans of Coke. The driver tells me his 11 riders will pass me at some point during the day. His unexpected news gives me something to look forward to. I start knocking out sub-15-minute miles on the frontage road. Challenge myself to see how far I can get before the first rider appears.

Two hours and about 10 miles later, Emilio rolls up. Neon green jersey and tan cheeks splotched with salt. "Some guy at a gas station told me about you like a hundred fifty miles ago!" he says. I ask where everyone else is and he motions behind him. "I like to ride alone. It's my meditation."

Emilio tells me that at the end of each day he likes to clean everyone's bikes. "Most folks feel like they have to give me something in return," he says. "But I expect nothing." When he first moved to the states from Uruguay, he was struck by Americans' attachment to giving and receiving. "Everything here is transactional," he says. "Even this." He motions with his hand back and forth between us. "It's as if being nice is an investment with an assumed payoff." Emilio believes this is detrimental. That gifts ought to come from the heart with no expectation for anything in return. "We should do good things because it's the right thing to do," he says.

I tell him I get it, even though I tend to keep meticulous track of what I owe others and what's owed to me. I manage kind gestures and gifts like debts. Even worse, I pass judgment based on how well others adhere to my social banking system, and I'm irrationally quick to hold grudges when folks don't live up to my expectations. This personality trait of mine is a source of conflict in my relationship with Katie. She's not a giver of material objects. Not one to organize a surprise party or acknowledge an achievement with much beyond a celebratory beer. I spent years allowing this to frustrate me, constantly wishing she would give me what I needed. I wanted her to nourish me, and resented her when she didn't.

I tell Emilio that one day I'd like to be selfless in giving and gracious in receiving. I'd like to figure out how to nurture myself so that others' responses didn't matter as much. "I want to genuinely relinquish my need to control things," I say. "These days I'm consciously trying not to make my life all about me." Emilio listens. he allows a pause to linger before responding. "Tom, we are merely eddies of energy," he says. "We give and borrow from each other. No more, no less. I wash people's bikes because I want to. Because it feels right. I think life can be that simple."

*

For the rest of the afternoon, a massive whitewashed structure ahead is my beacon. Mile after mile I train my eye on it knowing eventually I'll get there. From far off it looks like a Mormon church. I walk toward it for hours but it never seems to change. Never gets closer, never comes into full detail. It remains forever away as I seem to make zero progress.

At some point I stop paying attention to it. I play Rush's *Moving Pictures* on my phone and ponder Emilio's words. In a blink the massive structure is suddenly before me. And go figure, it's not as big or white or interesting as I thought it would be. Not some kind of megachurch or architectural curiosity. Just a regular old factory building made stark against the fallow desert backdrop. The difference between my expectation and reality is amusing.

*

Agent Lim, a stout Asian man with dark sunglasses, stands rigid with a hand on his radio. His Border Patrol uniform is snug on his muscular arms and chest. He hands me back my ID and explains that this dirt road jutting toward the mountains is a well-known smuggler's route into the US from Mexico. People often hide out along its periphery, like I'm doing. "You picked a weird place to stop," he says. "I guarantee you aren't alone. In fact, a few people have already called to report you." I ask him if it's OK for me to stay. He shifts his face, turns down the chatter on his radio. "Mr. Griffen, this is a high patrol area." I understand what he's telling me, but mostly I want to know if I have to break camp. "This is the perfect site," I say. "I mean, look at the sky. It's like it's purple. But that's probably just the sunset at work." Agent Lim ignores my comment and paces around my gear. Keeps looking off into the southern distance like he's waiting for something to happen. "Mr. Griffen, you're out here in the middle of the desert," Agent Lim says. "The middle of total nowhere. There are coyotes and stuff out here. Snakes, you know? It's dangerous for a lot of reasons." I tell him that wild animals don't want anything to do with me or anyone else. "And actually, I love listening to coyotes," I say. "They are like my nightly lullaby."

Agen Lim's brows scrunch. My words don't compute. He leans his ear toward the crackling radio attached to his chest. "Roger that," he says into it. Takes a deep breath and puts his hands on his hips. "Well, I guess you're cool to stay," he says. "But don't be surprised if other officers pay you a visit." He then looks toward the mountains, now scarlet, and shakes his head. Looks back at me and tips his hat. Within seconds, his olive-drab fatigues blend into the ocotillo maze. I know he's there, but I can't see him.

Day 92

As I leave my cheap hotel in Van Horn, I stop to admire tricked-out cars showcased in a front yard lot. A faded red '80s era convertible Mustang, lifted like a 4x4. Asking price $2,650. For $200 more, a hot-pink Volkswagen Rabbit stretched into the length of a limousine. I leave the main strip and join Highway 90 where white, yellow, and periwinkle wildflowers line the shoulder. A few bees bounce around the thick carcass of a rattlesnake in a flat and permanent coil. I inspect its head, wider than my fist. A few curious horses trot toward a fence line to meet me as I approach. One lets me scratch her muzzle.

Day 93

A black highway patrol car with a brush guard eases to a stop on the opposite side of the road. A trooper climbs out, puts on his cowboy hat, and motions to me that he's coming over. He looks both ways, then takes long strides across the lanes. Tips his hat. "Morning. I'm Officer Schlaudt. Nice to meet you, sir." His white skin is tan. Eyes hidden behind mirrors. He's probably half my age and has an extra firm handshake. A kind smile. "You must have a story," he says. Rests his thumbs on his belt buckle.

Schlaudt asks if I the saw three guys about a mile back. I didn't. "Yes sir, just a mile or so backaways," he says. "Three illegals. The Border Patrol had to chase them down." The word "illegals" makes me cringe. It's a slur I've heard a lot as I've neared the Mexican border. "Nope. I didn't see anything," I say.

This is a tricky stretch of highway. Between the endless boundaries of private property and paralleling railroad, I am left with few, if any, options for overnight cover. I tell Officer Schlaudt I expect a challenge come nightfall. "Given what I'm working with out here," I say, "do you have any suggestions for where I might safely make camp?" Officer Schlaudt shifts his weight and looks up the road. "This area is all government property," he says. "Whatever you do, make sure you stay away from the train tracks. You got a tent, right Because then you won't be mistaken for an illegal."

He asks to see my ID. Also asks permission to take my photo. I'm leery. "I want to put a notice out for law enforcement along this way," he says. "If they know you're out here, they're less likely to give you a hassle." I don't believe his intentions. Figure he's collecting data in case I turn out to be trouble. But I do as I'm asked, then pose with a shit-eating grin behind LB. Signed warnings and a tall blue sky fill the backdrop. Hidden families concealed behind bushes. The cop counts down, "One...two...three," then gives me a thumbs up.

*

The culvert is dark and rocky. Opposite it and along the train tracks is a bare spot to accommodate my bedroll. But there's a problem—it's barely 20 feet from the tracks. I haven't seen a train all day, so I cross my fingers and set up camp.

My spot is opposite a gated road leading to a TARS station. A tethered aerostat radar system—basically a small blimp on a long leash—monitors human movement along the southern border. Miles earlier I saw a weird thing above the horizon and excitedly snapped photos thinking it was a UFO. But now I see it for what it really is—a cartoonish submarine in the sky. It hovers above as I set up my tent. I imagine someone in the control room watching as I lay out my ground cloth, hammer in the stakes, then walk downwind to do my business. *Hey Martha, come look at this shit*, they say with a snicker. *Another bonehead on the tracks.* With my pants around my ankles, I look up and wave.

*

As I lie down on my sleeping bag, I'm overcome with vertigo. Like I'm managing a bad hangover. Whether it's from dehydration or the uneven ground, I can't be sure. Takes me forever to relax, and a few times I catch myself jolting awake as if crashing down from above. I once read this sensation happens when the soul departs the corporeal space and we begin to have an out-of-body experience. But then it gets tugged back, like someone yanked the tethered leash.

I finally fall asleep, but soon wake to the ground quaking as a train's horn blasts in the near distance. A brightening spotlight illuminates everything inside the tent and casts long, moving shadows. As the engine gets closer, the noise grows deafening. I press my hands over my ears, duck my head, and curl into a ball. But it does nothing. I brace myself and scream as it reaches me. A thunderous horn sounds and my organs reverberate. The rhythmic crush of passing boxcars on ties sends undulating ripples beneath my tent. I fully expect the train to derail. I wait to be crushed by a mountain of hot steel. Or bulleted by shrapnel. I cannot think or move.

When the final car passes and the rumble fades west toward Marfa, I breathe. Unclench my muscles and melt back onto my sleeping bag as echoes ring in my ears. Eventually I fall asleep again, but through the night three more trains roar past. But each one gets easier than the one before it and I nearly sleep through the last one.

Day 94

Thorny plants have ingenious mechanisms for survival. Roadside plants transform dewdrops into a brilliant cluster of bloom strong enough to sustain windstorms that curb 18-wheelers. Here, the landscape goes on forever. Puts all 103 train cars into view at once.

Most of us take this in through a windshield, chilled by AC. Or we marvel at its vastness from above, glancing from our window seat. In the velocity of our lives, we miss the overwhelming breadth of the desert.

*

Architectural skeletons assure me I'm nearing a town, so I walk faster. A billboard advertises services ahead. In a blink there's more traffic—an energetic buzz of people and a wake of cigarette smoke and car air fresheners. I inhale these human ingredients and wonder if it's possible to know things by simply breathing their essence.

A car pulls over ahead of me. A tall man exits and walks in my direction. When we're a few paces away from each other, he waves. Hollers to introduce himself. He's Richard from the Netherlands. He's solo-crossing the US on a bike. Today, however, he rented a car to backtrack to the Trinity site in New Mexico where the first nuclear bomb was detonated in 1945. Twice a year they open it up to the public. "I met another one of you crazy walking guys when I rode across America last time," Richard says.

He's following the Southern Tier route, too. We figure we'll meet up again.

*

I stop for the night in Marfa at El Cosmico, an eccentric trailer park close to downtown that offers tent camping. I park Little Buddy in full view of restored Airstreams, Mongolian yurts, and tall teepees. Glampers come and go as I shell out motel rates for my measly patch of grass and a picnic table. But I'm fine with it because I'm smitten by the novelties—open-air showers, live nightly music, and an abundance of cold local beers in the communal fridge. El Cosmico is a West Texas hipster oasis where postcards cost two bucks. I fucking adore it.

*

A couple walks hand-in-hand past my site and I catch a whiff of patchouli, a scent that brings to mind deep blues and shades of purple. "One of you smells really good," I say. They stop. "It's definitely her," the guy says, motioning with his thumb. He looks at Little Buddy. "You really doing that?" They look at each other and crack up.

Caleb and Dakota are here to celebrate their one-year wedding anniversary. Both are grad students. Caleb studies architecture and Dakota's area, she says, "falls somewhere between ecology and psychology." Their wide eyes reflect an earnest joy, an insatiable curiosity. I find their social authenticity refreshing. They ask a bunch of questions but I keep my answers short because I sense they are off to watch the sunset. They offer recommendations for my off day tomorrow. We make hopeful plans to chat later.

The next evening we cross paths again. "So glad we caught you," Caleb says. "I made you something!" He digs into his backpack and pulls out a drawing. "He drew it while we were at a cafe," Dakota says. Caleb hands me a sheet of white paper creased in half. I hold a corner as I gently unfold it. From edge to edge the page is filled with pencilled lines, perfect circles, and stark marks made with rulered exactitude. Every angle of view offers a different visual experience. It's terribly simple, yet amazingly complex. "Wow! How'd you do this?" I ask. "Oh, he always carries around his drawing tools," Dakota says like it's no big deal. Caleb fishes a compass from his pack. He also pulls out a straight edge with no markings on it. He catches me admiring it. "This is my edge," he says. "One day I needed a ruler and didn't have one, so I made it." Caleb describes the artwork. "All day we've been talking about your journey and, to me, this drawing represents your plan," he says. "The lines and circles represent you letting everything happen organically." I look closely at the page. The stylized lines and loops seem too perfect. My eyes follow the paths like a maze. "I love it," I say. "Everything is connected to everything else." I tell Caleb and Dakota that this sort of togetherness has become an unexpected theme of my walk. Dakota moves us all in for a long group hug. Then they walk shoulder to shoulder to the hammocks, never letting go of each other's hands.

Day 96

"You must be Tom!" the cyclist says as he stops his recumbent bike. I first notice the beige noseguard attached to his dark sunglasses, then the bright helmet that matches his saddlebags. A Texas flag windsock flutters from a pole fixed to his rear fork. He's the sort of crosser who takes safety to the next level.

I ask how he knows my name. "You're famous!" he says. "Guy at a gas station way back told me about you. I figured I'd run into you today. I'm Elroy Whitworth." Elroy is riding his bike from Austin to the Pacific Ocean. I tell Elroy that Whitworth is my mom's maiden name. "Oh yeah? Where's your family from?" he asks. My grandfather, Tom Whitworth, was from St. Louis. "Ha! We're probably cousins!" he says. "My family hails from Cave Pump. Small town in the center of the state." Elroy tells me he owns a bed and breakfast just south of Austin. Whitworth Farms. Says I'm welcome to stay in his Airstream any time.

I ask Elroy how he got into long-distance cycling. "Oh, who knows! I ran ultramarathons back in the old days," he says. "Did Leadville when it had only a hundred fifty runners. But running took a toll on these bones, so cycling was a natural transition, I guess." He says just last week he was looking at his finisher's buckles. "I once got the trophy for being the last ass up the pass," he says. "A bronze donkey's backside." He wipes the sweat from behind his sunglasses. "Back then things were different. There was no fancy sports nutrition, no gels, none of the weird stuff that's out there today," he says. "Ann Trason used to eat Spam and mayonnaise to stay fueled. The military types drank olive oil. That's how we did things." I tell Elroy that all these years I figured my athleticism came from my dad's side. "But maybe I have the Whitworths to thank," I say. Elroy's raucous laughter fills the highway. He scratches under his nose protector. "You got that right," he says. "We got us some good genes. Now you be careful on this road. It's scary enough out here being on this bike. I can't even imagine walking it."

Once Elroy is out of sight, I Google his name and find 13 race results on *Ultrarunning*'s website. Included are multiple 144-hour races, a sub-24-hour finish at the Vermont 100 when he was in his 50s, and an official last place finish at the Leadville 100 in 2002. Elroy is a hellman.

*

Just east of Alpine on Highway 90, I stop at the fake Target store, a public art installation, where I meet George and Heather, a young couple on a road trip to Pennsylvania. "He found a job up there and we're leaving Texas," Heather says. "But not soon enough," adds George, who promptly offers me a beer. He's curious about the walk, but also about the people I've met. "It's nice to know people still do nice things. I wouldn't have predicted it," George says.

Back on the road, I start falling asleep. My eyes close mid-stride and I pop awake just as my knees begin to buckle. Damn beer. I stop for an early lunch in a wide turnout on the eastbound side. Take in the roadside geography offering impressive evidence of geothermal flux. An ancient lakebed shifted into vertical strata. The vista triggers thoughts of time. Its irrelevance. I watch my hands as they unpack my meal. They work alone, as if driven by a force that doesn't include me. My dirty nails could use a clipping. My stomach grumbles. I down the same fare as always. Three tortillas wiped with peanut butter, a sun-warmed can of Beanie Weenies in barbecue sauce, a few handfuls of salted mixed nuts, and a fleshy apple that's been in my duffle since Arizona. Food is fuel. A lucky bonus if it tastes good.

*

An orange bicycle appears in the western horizon. The rider waves from a distance. It's Richard, the guy who stopped to chat a few days ago. He rides alongside me for the final eight miles into Marathon. As soon as we enter the city limits, I hear someone calling my name. It's a cyclist from a touring group who passed me this morning. He hollers through the fence at an RV park. "Come camp with us! No charge!" he says. "And free food, too!" He doesn't invite Richard, which makes me feel bad. But Richard insists it's fine. He already has a reservation for a private room at the park's motel. "I'm sure I'll catch you again tomorrow."

*

During dinner with the cyclists, an older white woman with red painted nails wants to know more about my walk. In a loud voice she asks the questions most folks ask. Where did you start? Where are you going? How many miles per day? Where do you sleep? What happens if you need to use the bathroom? She raises her brows at all my responses, which strikes me as odd since I assume this group attracts like-minded endurance junkies. She looks around at her fellow riders, trying to get them involved in the conversation. "OK, Tom. I have a question for you," she says.

"What would you do if someone in a late-model Mercedes pulled up and offered you an all-expenses paid ride to Maine? Would you take it?" The look on her face tells me she thinks this is a tricky question. It's not. "Nope," I say. "Wouldn't even cross my mind." I tell her I get offered rides all the time, and my answer is always the same. I'm walking by choice. And though I appreciate the offers, I'm not simply trying to get across the country. "Sure, I could hop in a car and make it to the coast in a matter of days," I say. "But what would be the point? I'm doing my best to enjoy the journey." Folks sip their drinks and nod, but the woman shakes her head. The palms of her hands lay flat on her lap. "Well," she says with a huff. "I'd damn sure take that ride."

Someone looks up and comments on the stars. It's already clear enough to see the cloudy edge of the Milky Way. Another person says something about their big day tomorrow. I take their comments as a cue and excuse myself. They graciously welcomed me in, but I feel like an intruder. Making my private side public, as I did tonight and as I'm doing every day on this walk, is a challenge. It forces me to claim my life as my own.

Day 98

I break camp early, thank the touring group for their hospitality, and am back on the 90 as planned. I can't shake a sensation of regret, as if I said or did something wrong. The first few hours of the day I replay the previous evening's conversation with the woman. Worry that I was rude and dismissive. Even if I was a jerk, it's done now. Still, I carry an unbalanced weight of lingering melancholy. Wish I could redo the night.

*

My thoughts turn to Katie and further compound my grief. Her morning text, like all her texts lately, is an acronym. Which, to me, is lazy and empty of meaning. "GM SP. IWYAGD." *Good morning, sugar pie. I wish you a good day.* She sends similar messages morning after morning. Tonight she'll write a predictable repeat of what she wrote the past few nights. "GN SP. ILY." Copy and paste. Mindless and generic. Would it be so hard for her to spell it out?

Lately when we talk on the phone, it's just me gabbing away then waiting for her to share too. But she has nothing to say. No comments about her life nor any curiosity about mine. Inevitably the call ends after I ask, "So...anything else?" And there never is. So we hang up and I feel sick. Like it's just me out here alone. But I don't want to be alone. I want her here, too. Participating. Even if from afar. And I guess she is, kind of, but obviously not to the level I'm needing. Shit, I'm not even aware of what this need actually is. But I do know that enduring our gray space much longer will lead to regret. Or worse, resentment.

*

A large red truck, extended cab, crawls to a stop in the westbound lane. Passenger window slides down. A white-haired man in the driver's seat leans over the console. His clip-on sunglasses flipped up. His squinting eyes. A blue cap rides tall atop his head. "I saw your vest from a mile back," he says. "Just about the same time I saw a herd of wild antelope. Mind if I pull over for a minute?" He eases his truck onto the wide shoulder. Grips the top of the door as he steps out. Hobbles over to me as he flattens out his shirt. Reaches into his chest pocket and pulls out a business card. "I'm Ron," he says. "Or, like it says there, *Retired Ron.* From Katy, Texas." We shake hands. "I imagine you could use some water." I tell him I won't turn down any handouts.

Ron asks if I've seen any Border Patrol. I describe my interaction with the cop who took my photo to pass around. "And it seems that's exactly what he did because every officer since then has mentioned it," I say. Ron is happy I'm on their radar. "It can be dangerous out here, you know," he says. "People come across the border all the time and some are desperate. Probably a good idea to watch your back." Ron asks what I think about the proposed border wall. Before I have a chance to respond he addresses his own question. "If Trump goes ahead and builds that wall it'll be the dumbest expenditure the US has ever made," he says. "Rather than spend billions on the wall, we ought to use the money to help people. That would be the right thing to do."

Ron remembers the water and returns to his truck. He comes back with two bottles and a white bag. "Brought you my lunch," he says. "Some sugar-free chocolate pudding and a breakfast burrito from Laredo Taco. Mind if I give it to you?" The smell of warm eggs and bacon fills me. "As long as you let me give you a hug," I say. "Well…sure. I mean…if you want to," Ron says. I wrap my arms around him. He smells like Aqua Velva.

*

Richard rolls up on his unmistakable orange bike. We discuss how to say goodbye after our brief road connection. "But do you think we'll ever meet again?" Richard asks. I pause. Look at him and shrug. "Probably not," I say. We both crack up.

Richard rides alongside me again as we contemplate nuances of American vernacular. "Americans say *See you later* as if they will actually see you later," he says. "But do they really mean it?" He questions other common greetings like *How's it going* and *What's up*, and doubts their authenticity. "I know these sayings are just combinations of words," he says. "But they have meaning, too, you know."

We stop to watch a lone antelope bound across the rolling desert, snout down into the wind. As it disappears into the waiting herd, I think out loud. "The American language is meant to prove our independence. It keeps us at a distance and away from what we all innately want—togetherness." Richard suggests we snap a few photos. Back on the road, he restarts the topic. "OK," he says. "But what about calling something *badass*? I've met maybe five people on the road who've told me that riding my bike across the USA is badass. That word is funny. It's like a joke. What does it even mean?" We share a laugh at the literal meaning. *Your ass is not good. Your ass has misbehaved.* Yet somehow it translates to *What you are doing is wildly impressive.*

"Well, if what I am doing is badass," Richard says, "then what you are doing is even more badass." I assure him we occupy this badass space together. "I'm not sure if there are various degrees of badassery," I say. "Maybe it's more in how the word is said. Tone and intonation."

Richard rides off, and for the rest of the day sends me texts describing everything as badass. "Check out these mountains. Aren't they badass?"

Day 99

I'm happier on the side of the road than I am in real life. I don't stress about money or bills and I don't sweat the small stuff like I normally do. I want to be able to feel this way all the time, and I wonder if it's possible. Because if my most genuine self only exists on the roadside, then I can never stop walking. And shoot, maybe I won't.

*

At the Budget Inn in Sanderson, the two Indian proprietors, Danny and Sunny, let me choose my price as long as I give them something memorable for their blessing wall—a section of the lobby plastered with notes from satisfied guests. "Plus, you are the walking man!" Danny says. "We heard about you from the tall man on an orange bike."

I sign their register and they present me with a silver tray holding a fresh cup of creamed coffee and two packs of mini donuts. Chocolate and powdered. I shake Danny's hand. When I reach for Sunny's, he extends his pinky instead, so I do the same.

Then he hooks his finger onto mine and shakes his hips back and forth. I mirror that, too. "Yeah, boss man!" he says.

After doing a load of dusty laundry in the sink, I text Richard two photos. One of the decaying room, another of me and the hotel proprietors giving the camera thumbs up. "Badass is right!" I write, hoping that wherever Richard is in the belly of Texas, it lifts his spirits.

Day 101

I wake up with precipitous certainty that I'm going to finish this walk. And though such thoughts are dangerous, they fill my being. I've made it to my guesstimated halfway point and all remnants of any foot injuries are long gone. I feel bulletproof, just as Dr. Lau said I would. I'm throwing down crazy big mileages. Hitting triple digits in three days.

But I'm spending way too much time pondering how it'll feel to dive into the cool ocean at the finish. Imagining how it'll be to finally say *I did it*. Thinking about rolling LB down a sandy beach and making a wild scene as saltwater baptizes our completion.

But I've still got 2,000 miles to go. And though my thoughts pep me up, they also distract me from what's before me—like the West Texan primordial lava fields and the artful design of bullet scars on steel signs. Enmeshed in a dreamy future, I mindlessly pass ideal camping spots and forget to drink enough water. I visualize Katie at the finish. Then us driving home with LB folded up in the trunk. What will we talk about? What will we decide to do about us?

A honking car shocks me from my daydream and I realize that I'm straddling the solid white line. Directly in harm's way. I lose my breath and shake it off. "Fucking close call," I say to LB. Then to myself, "Come on, Griffen. Get your head back in the game."

*

The air cools and the sun gives way to an early moon. I'm in a pickle. I need a campsite, stat. Something safe and off the road and easily accessible. After failed deliberations in a handful of exposed turnouts, I settle for the far side of an electrical generator. I set my tent on angled ground that butts up against a cyclone fence. Throw all my gear inside and crawl in. I'm out of sight from the road, but at the cost of comfort.

Finally on my back after 31 miles on my feet, everything spins. I'm seasick. Adrift and barfy. Don't want to eat. Don't want to drink. I sit up and break into a cold sweat. Start to shiver. It takes all the energy I have to reach for my food duffel. I pull the top off a can of Chef Boyardee spaghetti and shovel it in my mouth. Don't stop to enjoy the weird texture of the meatballs like I usually do. Between bites I take massive slugs of impossible water. Turn the lid off a jar of Skippy and chew spoonfuls of peanut butter. My jaw cramps. Whisper voices surround me and my head jerks, trying to place them. But it's just me. The hard ground. The hum of the generator outside.

Replenished, I remain unfocused. Pull out my sleeping bag and crash. I sleep fitfully. Dream of water. Of waves. Of swimming until my legs give out and I sink. I keep expecting to hit bottom, but I don't. Just sink down, down, down, until I wake up after what seems like minutes. Disoriented.

I unzip the door. Breathe in the cool air. My hands are swollen. My face, too. I retrieve my phone and snap a photo of the morning glow. I flip the camera view and look into it like a mirror. Examine myself. My face is a red, unshaven skull. Shadows hang on my cheeks. More gray in my beard. I never realized how green my eyes are.

Day 102

The two Border Patrol officers look like a cover of *Soldier of Fortune*. One's got an M16 draped across his chest, muzzle pointed down. The other's rifle is slung against his back, his sidearm tucked in a shiny black holster. Armed teenagers. They tell me I should drink as much as possible. It's going to be more than 100° today and the same the rest of the week.

It isn't long before the heat gets me. I doze off then snap awake as Little Buddy's frame weaves from the shoulder to the lane, making us an easy target for oncoming traffic. Curling into a ball on the roadside seems like the best idea I've had in weeks. "Just five minutes," I tell myself, fully aware of the similarity between this and my slow Bradshaw Trail disintegration. "Just a quick minute to take the edge off." But as soon as I position myself in a tiny bit of LB shade, I'm interrupted by two cyclists. Bill and Tim are older white guys heading west on the Southern Tier. I jump up to greet them. Our lively banter brings me back to life.

Bill and Tim's transcontinental ride started as an item on Tim's bucket list. He planned to ride while Bill drove the support vehicle. At some point Tim asked Bill to join him on a bike, so they ditched the car and have been pedaling together since. Long ago, Bill was an employee at Tim's whitewater rafting business on the James River in Virginia. "Lots of life has happened since then," Bill says. "Now we're both retired. For years we were out of touch. But we circled back to do this adventure." Like me, Bill and Tim are planning to stop at the Vashti Skiles Community Center in Langtry. On wheels they'll be there in less than two hours. I should make it in six if I can keep some kind of normal pace. We make a hobo dinner date and off they go.

*

I walk in an oven. I take short, strategic breaks in any patch of shade I come across. I guzzle extra water knowing there's a spigot in Langtry. I'm fixated on the needs of my bodily engine and my repeated cycle of rest, water, and calories nourishes my effort. Focus prods me forward, but my thoughts stray.

I'm consumed with worry. Fretting about what comes next. I wonder if walking across the country will make me a better person. Less self-conscious. Less reactive. More confident. I wonder if I'll be less likely to meet conflict with frustration. Less apt to roll over when conversing with someone who is more informed than me. More likely to accept contrary opinions with an open mind, rather than with anger and disdain.

My life is a giant gray area. I'm most comfortable sitting on a fence. I'm neither here nor there. My tendency is to blend. Like a chameleon. To mold into crowds to keep the peace. I want people to notice me. And I want people to like me. But this sort of existence often makes me feel like an imposter, or worse, a hypocrite. Because it's not the real me I am drawing attention to. And I don't like that one bit.

I keep thinking that what I need are stronger opinions— something to help me establish a more solid personal foundation. But this isn't accurate. What I really need, at root, is to accept myself for who I am. Because right now I don't.

*

The child inside of me desperately craves validation and acceptance. This need remains an empty chasm in my adult life. Walking across America, like all noteworthy things I've done, serves to fill this void, even though I know it can't.

After pouring a liter of water over my head during a woozy break, a face from my past pops into my consciousness. It's Kathryn, my first therapist. I haven't thought of her in years. Back in the early 2000s, she helped me connect my adult tendencies to childhood deficiencies. I routinely scoffed at her recommendation to engage my younger self in conversation. But sitting in the dust on the roadside, I finally give in to her suggestion. I imagine putting my arm around little Tommy to tell him what he needs to hear. *I see you. You are marvelous. I got you.* I tell him that everything's going to be OK and hold him against my chest as a father might. I put my adult hand atop his soft head. I admire his red hair, his rosy cheeks. Gently put my crooked finger beneath his little chin and look into his worrisome eyes. *Little one, I will always be here for you. You are just right, as is. I so dearly love you.* And since I know he doesn't believe me, not yet anyhow, I tell him these words over and over and will do so until they become him. Until he knows, in skin and marrow, that they are true. That I've got him. That he's alright. That he—I—am enough, as is.

6

Change is the measure of time,
and I discovered that in order to see change
you had to be slower than it.

- Rebecca Solnit
Recollections of My Nonexistence

Day 102

I VEER FROM TEXAS HIGHWAY 90 toward Langtry and easily find the community center. I don't see any bikes so I assume Bill and Tim rode beyond it. A woman stops to greet me. "So you're the walker, huh?" she says. "A couple bikers said you'd be coming along at some point. I'm Patricia. You can sleep anywhere you want behind this building. Water faucet back there, too." She says the center was once the area's only school. All grades under one roof. When another opened in nearby Pumpville, this one closed its doors. But the building, named for one of the school's long-time teachers, is still used for community gatherings. "I'm here today getting the place cleaned up for next week's kid fry," she says, then reads my quizzical expression. "You know, goats. But it'll be quiet around back, so make yourself at home." I thank her for the hospitality. "It's nothing, honey," she says. "And oh, if you need to poo, just go into the field and hide it."

I wheel LB to the rear of the building and find Bill and Tim lounging in some shade against the building. Their warm greetings fill me. Bill hands me a partially consumed can of Natural Light. "Some fellow just brought these to us," he says. "Tim doesn't want his so I got two. You got here just in time to finish what's left of Tim's." We spend the evening getting better acquainted and comparing journey notes. "I could never do what you're doing," Tim says. "Too much solitude. I need to be around people or else I go crazy."

After dinner, Bill prepares three cups of air-pressed coffee while Tim and I watch a sandstorm brewing in the distance. "Seems to be moving our way pretty fast," he says. And it does.

Just after Bill hands out the coffees, we're in the thick of a swirling dust cloud. We press our backs against the community center and bow our heads as the whistling wind bends trees like twigs. Gusts whip the chains of a mid-century swing set, giving flight to empty seats as if being ridden by rodeo ghosts. I cover my cup between quick, delectable sips, but my hand is no match for the fine powder filling the air. "Earthy notes!" I shout to Bill. "Cheers!" Even with the grit, it's the best cup of coffee I've ever had. Bill makes us a second round after the storm passes. The bruised sky glows a purple pink apocalypse. Soon stars appear in full view.

*

We decide to forego tents and roll out our bedstuffs under the Milky Way clouds. I'm acutely aware of the noises around me. Nylon fabric and downy fill, a sliding zipper, the pops of crepitus as well-used bodies lower to the ground, the crush of grass, a sigh of relief. It's all just right. With Bill and Tim nearby, I feel safe. I tell them as much before saying goodnight. "Just don't ask for a cuddle," someone says. Followed by the comforting poof of a muffled fart.

Day 103

By midday it's 100°F and I'm only halfway to Comstock, today's endpoint. Exhaustion holds me. I keep falling asleep. A blurry mound ahead is enough of an unknown to perk me up until I reach it. It's a scattering of bleached bones. "Poor bastards," I say aloud as I examine what's left of multiple animals. This spot's some kind of wildlife death trap. I navigate LB around the shattered bits sharp enough to puncture his Kevlar tires. I pick up an intact deer skull with leathered chunks of fur still affixed to the cheekbone. The small antlers hint of youth. I set it on LB's solar panel and get back to walking. Consider using a spare bungee to attach it to the top of my floppy hat. Just the thought of the looks on Bill and Tim's faces when I roll into Comstock with a deerskull on my head keeps me wide awake for the final blistering miles into town.

*

At the Comstock Motel, Alton, a bowlegged old cowboy with a sweat-stained hat and a wide white mustache, checks me in. His deep drawl is definitively Texan. "I run this here town. Own this motel and others in the area. When it came up for sale I bought it before any goddamn outsider could." His wife Lois wears a faded denim sweatshirt and stands behind the registration counter. She listens intently. Watches her husband as he talks, nods at his every word. "Here you got one place to sleep and one place to eat," Alton says. "So hurry and go eat so later we can have a beer." I ask about Tim and Bill. "Yup," he says. "Third room down."

*

The door is cracked but I knock anyhow. "Housekeeping!" I say in a falsetto. They greet me like an old friend. Tim marvels at the distance I covered. "At least you got to lounge in this five-star resort," I say. "You ready to eat?" Bill asks. He already knows the answer.

We hit J&P Bar and Grill. I order a Shiner Bock and tell a story about tending bar at the Cat's Cradle, a music venue back home. Any time a band from the Lone Star would play, we'd inevitably run through our inventory of Texas's favorite brew. "I don't know if it's any good, but it's definitely Texan," I say. "I suppose now's the perfect time to give it a try." Bill orders one too.

We devour heaps of heavy food under the glow and clamor of a wall-mounted TV. Occasionally we take a minute to chat, gathering more information about each other's lives and trip timelines, but mostly we just sit together. We plan to meet again for a rest day in Del Rio, the next big town. "It'll be fun to hang out some more," we all say in our own way.

*

Back at the motel, Alton's shooting the breeze with a couple other patrons. We join in. Alton hands me a can of beer, another Shiner. I pop the top as Red—a middle-aged white guy with a bushy beard—drones on about all the snakes and lizards he encountered while hiking today. He shows us a photo of a baby rattler he wrangled with an engine dipstick. Alton lets out a burst of air, catches my eye and raises his brows. Bill and Tim turn in for the night and I hang for a few more yarns. Put another beer away. When it's gone, I crush the can in my hand and name the bewitching hour. I thank Alton and Red for the stories. "Be safe out there, walker man," Alton says. Red offers me a ride to Del Rio. "Man, can't you hear?" Alton says. "The boy said he's walking. Sheeeeit." Red tells me to *wait one* and excuses himself to his room. A peaceful quiet briefly lingers. Cool air kicks up. Alton faces the open desert. "It's like this every night," he says. "Never gets old."

Red returns with an armful of packaged snacks. Danishes, muffins, granola bars. "Here, take these," he says. "I bought way too much for this trip. I'm even gonna give you my favorite cinnamon roll. But you'd better go now or else I'll take take it back." Once back in my room I tear into a blueberry muffin and two toasted almond fruit bars. I save the cinnamon roll for morning.

Day 104

The next day I reunite with Bill and Tim in Del Rio. For two days we share nearly every meal together. I give voice to my struggling relationship with Katie, and hearing my words makes the inevitable outcome feel manageable. "These things happen," Tim says. "You never know what the future will bring." Bill talks about being homesick and missing his wife, Lucy. In his tone is a lingering melancholy. Something to write a song about.

As we follow our noses to a nearby barbecue joint, I learn more about my new friends. Bill is a retired dentist. He started playing the guitar at age 52 after his first wife passed. Now he builds guitars and is talented enough to riff with bluegrass musicians in his local jam circles. Met his new wife at one. I tell him I've been dabbling for years. "Stick with it and I'll build you one," he says. Tim spent his career in the water industry and divides time between Florida and Ottawa, Canada. He's a bachelor. A great listener. Talking with him makes me feel relaxed. His curiosity is something I yearn for when I talk with my own father. I tell him so. "He's listening, Tom," Tim says. "Make no mistake."

I ask Tim about his fresh haircut. "It's the Walmart special," he says. "You can get anything there. But don't expect much. A buzz is hard to mess up." Bill insists Tim goes to Walmart hoping to find a girlfriend. Tim throws his hands up. Doesn't deny it.

Day 106

I decide to take a third off day. My schedule can afford it, and my body could definitely use it. Still, I wake at sunrise to have breakfast with Bill and Tim before they rejoin the trail. After my numerous brief interactions with countless strangers, I'd forgotten how rich it can be to spend extended time with kind people. The three of us have become quick friends. Tim scoots his eggs around on his plate. "I'm feeling kind of sad this morning," he says. I assure him the feeling is mutual.

They both insist I get in touch if I pass through their necks of the woods. Then they ride off into the thick Del Rio traffic. When they are out of sight, I meander back to my room and flip TV channels. I check my phone every few minutes. No calls, no texts, nothing to read on social media. I send Bill and Tim a message telling them how much I enjoyed our visit, then I rest my head on my pillow and wonder what I'll do with the rest of the day. Maybe I'll go for a walk?

*

Come evening I call Katie. I rehash my days with Bill and Tim, share my myriad interactions with various strangers, mention the rapidly changing landscape and new routes east I'm considering. Our banter today represents how we've been communicating for the past decade—me talking and her listening. I've always wished for more of a balanced back and forth. And today it bothers me more than usual.

My resentment escapes volcanically. I bitingly ask her why we are even talking. Because call after call she never has anything to say, anyway. Katie responds with silence. Doesn't even make any sounds. Not a huff or a sigh. Nothing. I want her to tell me she enjoys hearing my voice. I want to know our calls matter. I want to know that she actually does look forward to our phone time together. But instead she remains quiet. Which makes me angrier. And though I'm well-aware that anger is how I disguise other difficult emotions, I hold onto it and lash out more. "Well fine then. I don't think we should talk any more during this trip," I say. "Probably better for us both to get used to it anyhow."

I want her to argue. To put up a fight. To tell me to chill the fuck out. I want her to say that she's got me. I want her to tell me all the things I'm unable to tell myself. Like, *I know you're feeling sad and lonely. You knew these feelings would take a toll. But if you let them pass through you, you'll feel better. Because everything's going to be just fine.* I want Katie to be everything I can't be for myself.

Long after we've hung up, I recognize my frustration isn't about her at all. I badly want to call her back and her as much, but I'm stopped by our bigger picture. We've let our indecision drag on for too long. Neither of us are brave enough to cut the final threads. We're probably trying to protect each other, but all we're doing is making our lives way more difficult than they ought to be.

Day 107

I check out of the motel and enter the thick of Del Rio. I project my mental strife onto the cluttered urban landscape. Shout and curse the city planners who obviously don't want citizens to walk anywhere. I make ridiculous and self-righteous promises to become an advocate for pedestrians. "I'm fighting for sidewalks in every American town!" I soapbox to commuters like I've lost my mind, spewing meandering tirades about the nation's obesity problem, unfair access to resources, and Trump's selfish political agendas. I curl my nose, point and snarl at drivers on their cell phones. I disregard curbs and allow Little Buddy's wheels to take a beating. My stomping wrenches my Achilles and I scream, "Fuck it, I'm fine!"

This fuming is comfortable. I fit perfectly into it. I spent the majority of my life masked with similar venom, always looking for reasons to hold grudges and spew torment. I easily fall back into a vitriolic stride. I walk and pout and whine and let aggression guide my enraged breakdown. I do everything I can to distract myself from the frustration I'm feeling—and not just about Katie, but with my life.

*

Escape has long been my go-to coping mechanism. Which explains why I never stuck around long enough to grow a job into a career, or turn a love interest into a committed relationship. The closer I get to putting down roots, the stronger my impulse is to *get the fuck out.*

But I'm sick of this lifelong pattern. I want to hold fast in one place alongside a partner. Work a job into which I can evolve. I want to ebb and flow as I move thoughtfully and simply through life. And though I feel like this possibility is all a choice away, the prospect of truly settling down continues to terrify me.

*

My body relaxes as traffic decreases. I find a steady walking pace and settle into it. The city turns to outskirts and everything quiets. As I cross a bridge on the far eastern edge of town, hundreds of sparrows exit a spinning knot and take turns dive-bombing me and Little Buddy. Some come within inches of my face, veering away at the last possible second. The wind from their wings is a whispered order saying *Go away. Be gone.* "OK, OK! Damn!" I shout. "I'm going! Leave me be!" But they increase their barrage. I pick up my pace to a run, which grows to a full-on sprint as I near the end of the bridge. But even after I'm back on solid ground, a solitary bird occasionally appears out of nowhere for another swoopattack. "I get it!" I shout. "I get it I get it I get it!" I lower my head and press on.

*

Near Bracketville, I get a series of texts from Richard. "Hey Tom, I will be happy to donate you a room on nearby Fort Clark, it will be badass! It's a gated community with mostly old people. The fort has a nice bar where the old people come for drinks...The blonde security lady at the gate (Barb) is without a doubt, badass. If you can get her in a picture, that would be epic!"

When I arrive at Fort Clark, Barb greets me at the guard shack and we take a selfie. I send it to Richard with an accompanying text. "I wasn't sure if I was going to make the 33 miles. But I did the distance in your honor." His response: "Badass."

Day 109

A cold downpour forces me to put on my parka for the first time since Arizona. The rain keeps me in the moment and out of my messy head. It washes away the past few difficult days and serves as a reset. I thank the storm for coming to my rescue.

A fraying American flag waves on a front yard pole. A welcome sign into Hondo reads, "This is God's country, please don't drive through it like hell." On a grassy patch near some train tracks, I park Little Buddy and unload the fixings for lunch. A large truck peels off the main road and stops behind me. I figure it's a police vehicle. A woman gets out, grocery bag in hand, and walks toward me. Exhaust bellows from the muffler. "My husband and I saw you a couple days ago in Uvalde," she says. "But it was getting dark and, you know, there's a prison nearby. So when I saw you again today, I stopped and got some nonperishables." The word *nonperishables* makes me swoon. She hands me the bag. Tells me what's inside. "Water, beef sticks, trail mix, protein bars, and a couple other things." She asks how far I'm planning to go. "To the Atlantic," I say. She shakes her head. "That's too far."

Day 111

The sun is low as I roll into a vehicle rest stop in Castroville. There are no hotels nearby, nor any obvious spots for stealth camping. I call the local police and ask where I can sleep without freaking anyone out. The dispatcher says the deputy on duty will get back with me as soon as possible.

When the sun is down, I lay out my bedroll. All night long, cars park at the curb, their headlights illuminating my illegal spot under the stars. I'm worried they can see me. That they might be afraid of me. I keep a sharp eye on them until they drive off. Then try to relax and squeeze in a few minutes of sleep before the next one arrives. Around 3:00 a.m., a police car enters the lot. But unlike the other vehicles, it doesn't stop before reentering the highway, flipping on its siren and racing away toward trouble.

Day 112

I hold onto LB with one hand as gravity pulls us down a long, gradual decline. I sing "Neon Knights" aloud, an ancient Black Sabbath tune, post-Ozzy, replete with Tony Iommi's definitive heavy guitar and upbeat power stroke. I often play this song as I begin walking each morning. Today, however, I'm the one belting out the vocals, a cappella, doing my best Ronnie James Dio impression.

Later, while I'm putting air in LB's tire at a gas station, a cowboy in a big truck pulls up beside me. My heart races as his window rolls down, exposing the man's tanned and wrinkled face. I make assumptions based on what I see—his loud and lifted rig, faded denim jacket, dirty ten-gallon hat. He's going to give me grief for being a vagabond commie queer hippie liberal. Somewhere in his accented vernacular, between spits of dip into a Big Gulp cup, he'll find a reason to hype Trump or automatic weapons or Jesus Christ or anything else that might pluck a chord of contention between him and an obvious left-winger. My heart races as I brace for the worst. He asks where I'm from. When I tell him what I'm doing, his eyes bulge. "Man, I've always wanted to do that," he says. "Actually, I've always wanted to ride a horse across the US." He then tells a story about a young boy and his grandfather who set out in the saddle from Colorado to the Pacific. The journey had forever been the old man's dream. But the grandfather died before they made it to the ocean. The grandson pressed on, finished the journey as planned, and sprinkled his grandfather's ashes in the crashing waves somewhere on Oregon's desolate coast. "I think it was a movie," he says. "But man, it really got me." He wipes his eyes as he wishes me good luck. Asks if it's OK for him to pray for me.

"Sure," I say. "Thanks." As he drives away, I feel like a jerk for judging him.

*

Approaching San Antonio on foot is onerous. My phone's unreliable navigation sends me headfirst into construction road closures and dead-end detours. I'm forced to start and stop and rethink every route I try. It's good practice for my eventual entry into nearby Austin, but the prospect of future ease is no consolation for present chaos.

I cross multiple lanes of congested highway, dodge vehicles that brake quickly and smash horns when they see me, and try in vain to get the heck off the main road and onto backstreets. Everything about this sort of walking is stressful. When I find a somewhat-safe pullout, I scour Apple Maps and consider my options. The most efficient route bisects the area many people have told me to avoid. A man at a bus stop asks if I need any help. I tell him I'm trying to walk downtown. He shakes his head and recommends I join him on the bus. He'll pay my fare. "It's a way better option than what's waiting for you in this part of town," he warns. I press on.

I wander through ramshackle neighborhoods. Postwar split level houses pressed tightly together. Yard dogs, mostly muscular pit bulls, bark and sling drool in my direction. To avoid them I walk down the middle of the street. Parked cars along cracked curbs make it difficult for me to move out of the way of an oncoming vehicle. Booming bass vibrates its license plate as it nears from behind. I crush LB to the side, make myself small so it can pass. Instead, it stops. The side window rolls down and smoke rises from it. A young Latinx man with face tattoos turns down the speaker. "What's this all about?" he says. I tell him. "I'm trying to stay off the highways," I say. "Taking backstreets toward the northern part of town." He nods. Looks up the road. "Damn, man," he says. "Stay positive, brother. You're gonna make it." He asks how it's been so far. "Up and down, but mostly good," I say. "Lots of nice people, like you, giving me a needed boost when I most need it." He says the least we can do is spread love and take care of each other. He wishes me luck and drives away. Thundering bass ricochets through the neighborhood, then disappears when he hangs a left.

Day 114

I'm still awaiting the day other crossers have told me to expect. The day when everything around me is crumbling and all I want to do is curl up into a ball. The day when all the voices in my head join forces to convince me that stopping makes better sense than continuing. I have plenty of ups and downs. And the last couple weeks of long miles have been draining. And though there are days when everything seems to be falling apart, I can honestly say I have not once entertained the thought of canceling the adventure. And at this point, on the downslope of the trip's duration, I don't imagine such thoughts will ever come.

Every morning I wake up and take time to accept what I've chosen to do. Sit quietly and take deep breaths of appreciation as I repeat my daily intentions. To open my heart. To stay positive. To go easy on myself and others. To say yes to kindness. To remember it's not all about me. I do my damndest do move humbly through the day while doing right. I'm not always successful. But who is?

Day 115

At the Guadalupe Canoe Livery in Spring Branch, singing peafowl in zoo-sized birdcages alarm when I arrive. Peacocks perched on the upper bars watch me and wiggle their tail trains that droop downward like fishing lines. A young girl, maybe eight years old, greets me. She asks if there's a baby in my stroller. "No. Just a bunch of camping gear," I say. Her name is Leah. She asks what I am doing. "You've seen the ocean?" she says. "Is it beautiful?" I show her photos of the Santa Monica coast. She looks close. Says someday she'd like to see it for real. "Don't you have a job?" she says. I tell her I'm an artist. "I'm an artist, too!" she says. "I have a good imagination and I like to draw. I'm also a good dancer." She twirls on one foot, her arms overhead like a ballerina.

It's nearly the livery's posted closing time, so I tell Leah I need to talk to someone about camping. "I spoke with a man on the phone," I say. "He said he'd be here." She seems to know who I'm talking about. "Should we call him?" I ask. "No, that's a bad idea," she says. "He's in a meeting." I call anyway. "Just go ahead and pick a site," the man says. "I'll pass by later and pick up the seven dollars. Cash only."

Leah runs off as I inspect the sites along the river. Trash barrels overflow with refuse, cigarette butts are everywhere. I'm the only camper, and considering the proximity of the sites I hope it stays that way. Leah returns with two others. Levi, about her age, and Levi's grandma, Sissy. Leah bounces as she asks me to tell my story. I do, and afterwards the kids barrage me with questions. "Where's your tent? Do you carry toilet paper? How'd you get these antlers? Why are the wheels so muddy?" Sissy tells them to give me a break. "You're pretty tall. I like your hat. How many tattoos do you have? Where'd you get this one? And this one? And this one?" Sissy apologizes. She tells the kids that Levi's dad has a bunch of tattoos, too. Got his in prison.

Sissy insists I knock on the door of her fifth wheel if I need anything. Levi and Leah hang onto her arms. "So where to next?" Sissy asks. "Austin," I say. "To see my brother and his family." Sissy runs her fingers through Leah's hair and places her hand on Levi's back. Her eyes tear up. "Family is all we've got in this life," she says. "I'll be praying for you and yours. We wish you all the blessings, don't we, guys?" We take a few photos together. I show them to the kids. "Dude!" Levi says. "You can totally see the orange fire on the front of my shirt!"

Day 116

A late model Subaru with sticker-covered windows is parked on the roadside. A road bike on a roof rack. A guy about my age gets out of the car and waves. "Hi, I'm Kevin!" Gives a long handshake. Kevin's a combat veteran on permanent disability. Spends his days as a Subaru ambassador raising awareness for disabled veterans. He gives me a new pair of Subaru-branded sunglasses, which is funny since before I started walking this morning, I asked the road to provide me with a new pair. The ones I found in the gutter a month ago are all scratched up.

Our conversation winds down, and I tell Kevin I'd better get back on the road. "Hey," he says. "One more thing. Don't forget that sometimes less is more." I laugh as I recall my recent extra-long mileage days. And though his words apply to the actual distance I'm covering, the *less* he's referring to transcends this walk. I interpret his less as a purposeful slowness that allows us to see life more clearly. Makes us more able to spare a few minutes with a stranger. To empathize with them. Hear their stories. Because who knows, we may be the only person they talk to today. We may be the only person in their life who actually sees them.

I'm guilty of racing through life trying to achieve status or collect kudos. This drive *to do* is a reflex. Kevin's words, however, are a reminder that life is not defined by what's been done. If anything, *how* I'm doing it is what matters most.

I spend the rest of the day deciding what I'd do if I had all the time in the world. All I come up with is precisely what I'm already doing, walking and meeting people. Opening myself to the world and letting it push me along. Which makes me seriously wonder, *How can I keep doing it?*

*

My brother Mike drives an hour and a half to retrieve me from the intersection of Texas Highways 281 and 290. He, his wife Amy, and their teenage kids, Carsen and Emma, recently relocated to Hutto, a northern suburb of Austin, where the town mascot is a hippo—supposedly an actual hippo escaped from a circus train in 1915 and ran amok before being wrangled back into its pen. I spend a week my extended family as Mike shuttles me back and forth from their home to my previous day's stopping point. I mix in a few off days because my body needs a break. Doesn't take long to grow used to being with loved ones. I need it more than I realize.

Day 118

Two days later, from the apex of Redbud Trail, I take in the view of Austin's skyline. Before I call Mike for a pickup, I veer into downtown for an americano at Houndstooth Coffee on Congress. Park LB on the back patio and tell the baristas I walked all the way from the Pacific Ocean for their killer espresso. They comp my drink and throw in a warmed-up almond croissant. The smell of it on the warm ceramic plate triggers nostalgia.

My great-grandfather, Wendel Kretz, was a hobo in the early 1900s. Hopped trains all around the country following seasonal jobs before landing an internship at a German bakery in St. Louis, Missouri. After mastering the trade, he jumped one final train and took his new skills to San Francisco where he opened his own bakery, the Golden Brown.

The shop was always pristine. Display cases meticulously wiped down to eliminate fingerprints and make more visible the exhibit of decadent edibles with magical names and intoxicating smells. Every item was meticulously packed and presented to customers in a sturdy pink box tied with white twine.

Great Grandpa knew small gestures make a lasting impact. He ran a tight ship and told his staff to never turn away a customer no matter how destitute they seemed. When word got out that the Golden Brown would hand over a pink box in exchange for any coin a buyer could spare, the bells on the front door never stopped ringing. The coins he collected were mostly foreign and useless, but he saved the lot of them in a glass jelly jar. Great Grandpa would pass the annual accumulation of coins to his daughter—my Grandma—to send to me as a Christmas present.

I'd dump the jar on my bed and scrutinize each coin's markings. I'd find the country of origin on my big sister's globe and imagine all the things that had to happen for the coin to end up in my hands. I'd look up the nation's entry in our set of orange encyclopedias. Learn its capital, population, GNP, main export. I'd look at photos of its flag, study the symbolism. I'd move in to better see its people and places, intrigued by new cultures and varied architectural styles. I'd promise to someday travel across vast distances just as the tiny piece of metal had done.

Day 119

For the past few weeks, friends and social medial followers have been asking where they can send me things. Since Mike's was one of my few certain destinations, I passed his address along. Boxes flooded in and Mike stacked the mountain of parcels in the guest room. I spend an off-day opening boxes of new shoes, socks, insoles, sports nutrition, and an abundance of cards with encouraging sentiments and extra cash to fund my momentum.

Carsen and Emma help me carry my loot to the garage where Little Buddy sits in wait. I pack it all into his hold and push him up and down the driveway. Carsen and Emma do, too. "It's so heavy!" Emma says. Carsen is incredulous. And they are right, LB's never been so loaded down. I am, quite literally, overloaded by an outpouring of love. When it's time to move on, I may have to leave some of it behind.

Day 120

I wake in the spare room and find a handwritten note tucked under my bedroom door. It's from Emma. She's asking me to join her for lunch. Ever since she was a little kid, we've had lunch dates at her school whenever I'm in town. Now that she's a teenager, I'm a little apprehensive. At her age I wanted noting to do with adults. Definitely wouldn't have wanted any to come eat lunch with me at school. Mike shrugs off my uncertainty. "You should bring her Chik-fil-A," he says. "She'll love that."

On the drive over, I wonder if Emma feels obligated to ask me to lunch. I worry she's simply being accommodating. At a red light I shoot her a text to make sure she still wants company. Tell her it's totally optional. Seconds later I receive her response. "Yes."

At the front desk I hand over my identification. They print out a sticker for me to wear and ask me to wait for Emma in the adjacent, dimly lit lobby. I sit at a tall table and watch as hordes of students pass through the hallway intersection, slamming doors and shouting. I vividly remember being in seventh grade. My two best friends were both named Tom, I had a major crush on my big sister's friend Alison. The summer after seventh grade is when I got drunk for the first time. Back then I definitely didn't feel as young as these kids look.

Emma enters the lobby with a few friends. She's playing it cool, I assume. But my assumptions are dashed when she spreads her arms and gives me a big hug, thanking me for coming. With a wave she dismisses her posse and they leave on cue. "Got us some Chick-fil-A," I say. She beams.

A large pane of glass divides us and the main office. Emma jokes that we're eating in a fishbowl. We talk with our mouths full, maximizing time between bites of grilled chicken dipped in sauce. We overhear passing students make comments about how good it smells. Emma's wit, intelligence, and curiosity make her the perfect host.

I ask Emma about the school's social groups. "Yeah, there's the popular kids," she says. "Also the theater kids, the sport kids, the smart nerdy kids, and there are some loner kids, too." I ask where she fits in, a question she saw coming. "Now that I'm running cross country, I'm an athlete," he says. "But I'm friends with kids in all the groups." She lowers her voice. "But you know, I'm also sort of nerdy," she says. "So I hang out with those kids, too. Really, I just try to be nice to everyone. Especially to the kids everyone ignores."

Day 121

Walking though cities is a lesson in anonymity. There are more people, but I have significantly less human interaction. I enjoy challenging this norm, so I make purposeful eye contact and say hello to unsuspecting passersby. Folks are surprised, but their reciprocation suggests a certain degree of appreciation. It feels good to acknowledge people, and I want to follow Emma's lead and practice seeing everyone.

On Cameron Road on the north end of town, I meet a man carrying a large McDonald's bag in one hand and a tall soda in the other. From afar he raises the bag like a wave. I return the gesture. We stop where our paths converge. "You a veteran?" he asks. I say I am. He has no teeth, his hair is nesty and unkempt. His fingernails are long and yellow. "Doin' the walk, huh?" He tells me his name is Angel. Says he gets it.

"I've got four combat tours in me," he says. "All in Afghanistan. Last one nearly killed me. Instead, it put me in a wheelchair for seven years. Just started walking again last month. Doctors can't explain it. But look at me now." He holds his arms out wide, looks down at his feet, rocks back on his heels. The smell of french fries wafts from his bag.

Angel lives in a Motel 6. Draws full disability for a spinal injury he sustained when a bomb blew up 10 feet away from him. "Guy to my left wasn't so lucky," he says. "And the two guys behind me died the next day." He's not sure why he got a pass.

Angel asks if my walk is therapy. If there's more to it than just walking. I haven't been asked this question before and don't have a practiced answer. "Well...," I say, "it's not therapy, per se. But I think the time alone is therapeutic." Silence hangs between us. "OK. But then why are you out here?" he asks, stressing the "why." "Because I need more of this," I blurt, motioning my finger back and forth between us. Angel adjusts the bags in his hands. "Shit," he says. "I heard that."

Every day Angel takes a few more steps. Soon he'll be on a bike, maybe even start hitting the gym. "After that I want to jump out of planes again," he says. "I mean, it's what I do after all." I extend my arm to shake his hand, then change to a fist bump figuring it'll be easier with his full hands. He lifts one paper bag and sticks out his pinky. I make the adjustment and hook my smallest finger onto his. "Be safe out there. And hear this," he commands. "Don't go giving two fucks about what other people think about all this." He waves his bags up and down. "You just keep on goddamn walking, you hear me, son?"

Day 123

After coffee with family on my final morning in Hutto, I disassemble Little Buddy and stuff my gear into the trunk of Mike's Ford Mustang. The forecast calls for rain, and Mike says if it gets bad he can be back in a jiffy. I assure him I won't be calling for a rescue. I don't mind a little weather. Still, he assures me, it's an option.

It's a 30-minute ride back to my last stopping point in Thorndale, 25 miles east of Hutto. Emma tags along, and Mike and I spend the time reminiscing about being kids in upstate New York. The messy crabapple trees, raking heavy piles of wet maple leaves, old man Kazimore next door who'd get super pissed any time our Wiffle ball ended up in his backyard.

I tell Mike and Emma a story about my arrival in San Antonio a couple weeks ago. A young white guy wearing a backwards cap and driving a shiny red Saab rolled down his window and shouted, "Go back to Europe!" If I were a quick thinker, which I am not, I might have said, *I'd love to*, or *What a great idea*! But I was confused by his unexpected words and wasn't even sure if they were meant as an insult.

After reassembling LB in the parking lot of a dinky roadside market, I gauge his weight. He's heavy from all the extra snacks, but as long as the road stays paved and horizontal, all will be fine. Mike, Emma, and I say prolonged goodbyes, then they drive off. But then Mike flips a U-turn and passes me with windows rolled down as I take the day's first steps. "Go back to Europe!" he and Emma shout, shaking their fists at me.

*

Gunmetal clouds hide daylight and the tame breeze holds a secret. The air hints of staticky bedsheets fresh from the dryer. I inhale electricity. My breathing is labored. As if I've suddenly reached the mountain top. I'm going to get wet, there's no doubt about that.

I text Mike and thank him for the stay. After I press send, I stare at my phone hoping to see three dots pop up to show he's responding. But nothing happens. My message hangs, marked as delivered. Mike's probably at work. Back to his real life. He'll get to my message later. But that's probably best. Because though I want to make contact with him, doing so will only exacerbate the emptiness filling my guts. I already miss him. And honestly, I don't really feel like walking today. Shoot, I'm not even sure I want to walk any more at all.

If I stopped here I'd be able to spend more time with Mike's family. Put down some roots on the west side of town where there is more open space. Have a garden. A beehive. Avoid the inevitable confusion of going home. I could finally reinvent myself. Maybe I'd introduce myself as TG instead of Tom. Maybe get out of the running industry and start a new career. I've always wanted to get into the coffee business.

Shoot, I've made it halfway across the North American continent. Isn't that enough?

*

The first drops are bullets. An urgent wind builds as the temperature falls. Flashes fill the sky like paparazzi. I roll LB to a grassy shoulder and hit the parking brake. Put my phone in a ziplock and unfurl my rain parka. There's no counting Mississippi to determine the storm's distance. Thunder and strobe are one.

For three hours the rain hammers down. Mike texts multiple times asking when and where he should retrieve me. I send one simple message. "Thx—I'll be fine." And I will, as long as I keep moving. Because right now I'm cold and soaked. Fingers and toes numb. Would be warmer and drier if I were out here walking naked. But the downpour is also cleansing. A baptism. It washes away any doubts I have about charging forward. Forces me to move quickly away from my lifeline. It catalyzes my road legs and gets my goddamned head back in the game.

*

I mock the squalls and scorn the tempest. I dare it to get worse. I push LB, completely waterlogged, into the sucking deluge. Grape-sized raindrops sting where they land. "How's this for a character-builder!" I shout. I wail words of self-encouragement like a madcap incantation: "You got this, Griffen! You totally fucking got this!" I march and squish and march and squish. "You *love* this, Griffen. You totally fucking *love* this!" I scream the eerie opening lyrics from Black Sabbath's "Iron Man."

I ford blacktop creeks toward Rockdale. Tread through shin-deep gutter canals swirling with oily rainbows and buoyant dog turds. I interpret long honks as votes of encouragement and then celebrate in kind. Pump my fist and scream like a human bullhorn until my voice is hoarse. Every passing car is a motorboat that sends a cascading wave two feet overhead. I ride the tube. Wipeout in the whitewash. I'm plowing through the swell. The Texas surf.

After an arduous 15 miles through muck and wet, I call it a day at the first hotel I see. Hang my sopping gear across fixtures and order a large mushroom black olive pizza and mild wings from Domino's. Twelve hours later I'm back on the road. Dry and refreshed. Mike texts to see if I need anything. "I'm good now that I'm dry." He writes back asking how I'm feeling. Takes me a minute to come up with the right word. I type it out and press send. "Reborn."

7

Yesterday I was clever
so I wanted to change the world.
Today I am wise
so I am changing myself.

- Rumi

Day 124

THE ROADSIDE IS AN ENDLESS death trench of mangled wildlife and a heartbreaking number of dogs and cats, too—some with collars still attached. Names like Craig, Milo, Zap, and Rosé stamped on fanciful aluminum tags alongside a phone number. I could call, but I never do. I don't want to be the one to deliver the bad news.

Early on, dead animals were mysterious shapes in the distance that broke up the most barren and loneliest stretches— they were something to look forward to. Eventually I got used to these grotesque piles of twisted limbs, but I never fully acclimated to the rancid stench of decaying flesh. Lately, the road carnage is all armadillos. And though they resemble little armored dinosaurs, their bodies explode into a thousand wet pieces when struck by vehicles.

This morning I stop to watch as a committee of ravenous vultures tears apart the fresh scatterings of a dead 'dillo. In my worst-case scenario, I too am being devoured by these carrion eaters. And hell, if this is how I'm meant to go, I pray I do so in a glorious detonation of limbs: *Dear God, please let me go full armadillo. May I paint the warm blacktop with the splayings of my flesh. May I transform into a twisted and sinewy puzzle. May my splatter mark be Rorschachian. May it call to mind something enchanting. Like smoke from a pipe. A river from space. Pollock's Untitled c. 1950. I ask this in Jesus's name. Amen.*

Beyond Milano, I come upon a couple and their golden lab landscaping the main entry gate to their ranch. John, Liz, and Murphy. Behind them is a mingling of horses and longhorn cattle. "We've had the longhorns since they were calves," Liz says. "Helped us get used to their horns." John and Liz are celebrating Cinco de Mayo and Murphy's birthday. On the menu tonight is barbecue and margaritas. John stoops to pluck some wildflowers. Holds them up to show off the detail. Shades of burgundy and red, bordered by mustard yellow. "These here are definitively Texan," he says. "An Indian blanket and a Mexican hat. Here, take them with you." I place their stems into an end of my PVC. A longhorn runs up to the fence as I walk away. Snorts and shakes its head.

*

A text from John pops up. He and Liz would like me to join them for dinner. I debate the invitation since I'm exhausted after 28 miles. Worry that a late night of socializing will disrupt my routine. But I rarely get dinner invitations from strangers. So I accept and he promptly scoops me up.

We start with their homemade traditional margaritas, then feast on slow-cooked beef ribs, boracho beans, and Spanish rice. Liz insists I keep my plate full. I stick to only one stiff drink since it's enough to give me a strong buzz. I imagine what would happen if I drank two, or worse, three tequila cocktails. I mind my manners. I say "yes ma'am" and "yes sir." Only speak when spoken to. I feel socially inept.

John and Liz are both runners and banter about mileage and workouts and races and PRs. I'm fluent in this language, but I refrain from including details of my own running history for fear of sounding like I'm boasting. John perks up when I tell him I'm from Carrboro. Two of his daughters went to UNC Chapel Hill and one even had an apartment in my hometown. Liz excuses herself to grab dessert. Homemade flan with a crystalized layer of caramel over the top. It's heavenly

By 8:00 p.m. I'm yawning at the table and trying to hide it. "I think we ought to get you back," Liz says. "You've had a long day with more to come." She reaches across the table and taps my hand. Stacks my ramekin on top of hers. "It's been a real pleasure," she says. Thirty minutes later, John drops me at the hotel were I eat a can of Chef Boyardee Mini Ravioli before turning in. It's 9:00 p.m. The same time I always go to bed.

Day 125

I'm guessing it's 90°F, but the humidity makes it hotter. Tar melts on stacks of spent railroad ties. Tracks extend into the past and future and I walk alongside them, mesmerized by the disappearing steel lines. I dig out some change and put a couple coins on the parallel tracks. I hope someday someone finds them, squashed and smooth as paper, and is filled with wonder.

The smell of hot tar carries me back to upstate New York. To when I was a kid and my dad would annually apply blacktop sealant to our long driveway. He'd put on his grubby pants and worn-out blue Nikes. Head off to Chase-Pitkin and return with gallons of protectant and a giant squeegee. He'd pre fill weathered cracks with sticky black gum, wait for it to dry, then gracefully apply the liquid asphalt in clean rows. I'd have to wait for the driveway to completely dry before I could shoot hoops again. Or roller skate again. Or hit the puck around again. Sometimes dad would let me help. He'd say words like "Nice work" and "Good job" and "Keep it up, you're doing just fine." Words he didn't usually say. Which makes me wonder if my dad ever thought *These are the days my son will remember with sweetness.* Because if he did, he'd have been right.

Day 126

The landscape is thick and green. Humidity inescapable. The hushed morning is marked by fog thick enough to delay a safe start. The clearing mist gives way to a dripping jungle. Sometimes I am in Cambodia. Sometimes Laos. Occasionally I mistake a branch for a pit viper, or a tree trunk for a sneaky macaque. There's a symphony of frog chirps and summerbugs. I willingly breathe the heaviness I've chosen. It makes me feel alive.

*

Teeming traffic and narrow shoulders force me to be on guard. I look into the eyes of every passing driver. Tightly grip LB's handlebar to ensure my true course. My head swivels and my ears perk up. I keep pace. I eat a lot of food. I drink a lot of water. I reapply sunscreen and lip balm. This routine is my daily salvation.

And though I have an idea of where I am, I don't really know for sure. I speak the language, but I am unaware of the local nuances. Out here I am vulnerable. More than ever. Which puts me on sensory high alert and causes me to see and hear everything—facial expressions, folks on porches, engines accelerating, spray-painted graffiti messages, names on mailboxes, barking dogs chained to trees.

Day 127

"Dude! You're heading into the buckle of the Bible belt!" Bodie says before we admire each other's tattoos. He honked at me a couple days ago and promised himself he'd stop if he saw me again. Bodie's in the process of moving to Austin where he plans to be a full-time Uber driver. Businesses are often reluctant to hire him because he's got a felony conviction, so he's forced to find more creative ways to cobble together a living. "But I wish I had the fortitude you have," he says. I insist that walking 3,000 miles doesn't prove fortitude. "Frankly, I often wonder what I'm running from," I say. "Or toward," he counters. "But no matter how many times I ask myself what I'm avoiding, the only thing I come up with is me," I say, which makes Bodie laugh.

"On a completely different note," Bodie says widening his arms, "This here is the thick of Trump country. Bright red and right. Be interesting to see how your trip shakes out out from here on."

*

Fifteen + 28 + 35 + 17 + 34 = 129 miles in five days. Averaging nearly a marathon a day in high-90-degree temps. I'm wiped. I've been promising myself I'll stop staying at hotels, but tonight I can't deal with the ever-present strain of finding a stealth camping spot. I want a cool shower and a belly full of bacon and eggs. "Just one night?" asks the hotel clerk. "Well...," I hesitate as I contemplate the cheap rate and multitude of nearby places to eat. "No, you better make it two." I hand over my credit card and driver's license, then dump all my gear into the room. I skip a shower in lieu of dinner number one. Figure I can clean up between meals.

At Denny's I order the biggest breakfast on the menu. Add an extra stack of pancakes. "Anything to drink?" my server, Anita, asks. "Coffee, and a chocolate malt, please," I say. I beat the dinner crowd, so Anita is able to give me extra attention. We get to chatting. She's a single mom and this waitstaff gig is something she does as a side hustle. During the day she's a CPA. "It's not the ideal setup," she says. "But it gives me a chance to make a few extra bucks to put into savings." Her confidence is attractive and I tell her so. "Thanks," she blushes. "Honestly, it's nice to talk with someone about something besides the menu." I assure her the feeling is mutual—and that it's nice to talk with someone about something besides the walk. Which, ironically, segues into her asking about the walk.

Before long the booths around me fill with families. Anita's section is the first to reach capacity. She checks in on me often. Offers to top off my cup. "Yes please," I say. "I hope you don't mind if I hang out for a bit. Looks like you folks are getting busy." She looks around. Says it's a typical night. "But please, stay as long as you want," she says. I ask if all the folks in her section requested her. She shrugs. "Wouldn't surprise me one bit," I say. "I'm definitely requesting you if you're here tomorrow." She frowns. She's off tomorrow. But back the day after. "Will you still be in town?" she asks. "No, I'll be back on the road by then." Which is too bad. Because I'd enjoy chatting more with her.

When Anita brings me the bill, she hands me her business card. I pay and leave a hefty tip. I walk out feeling pretty sure Anita was flirting with me. The fact that she gave me her card is permission to reach out, right? That gesture goes beyond nice—I think—but I also don't want to misread her cue. After nearly a decade with Katie, I have no idea how to navigate this moment. Makes me feel like a teenager.

*

I get cleaned up and eat a second dinner from Little Buddy's hold. Then I spend an hour composing an email to Anita. Then more time analyzing how my words might be received. Because yeah, I would like to talk more with her, but I'd also like more than that. Since I don't have the luxury of time, I don't mince words. I write things to her I probably shouldn't be saying since I have a partner. I tell her how lonely I am. How nice it would be to sit close to her. After a final reread, I press send with a shaky finger. Then I stare at the screen and am both thrilled and terrified by what I've done.

*

Minutes later, instead of feeling excited by the possibility of Anita writing back, I'm overcome by the fact that I let a benign moment get the best of me. I worry I disrespected her by oversharing my desires. My message could be easily read to mean something overtly sexual. Which isn't my intention. But I guess it sort of is, too.

What bothers me most is how my lapse in judgment may be affecting Anita. My words may have made her uncomfortable, or at least confused. I fear my wish for connection is actually a form of objectification. I now want to rewind and take it all back. I consider emailing an apology, but I'm also afraid my state of mind is too jumbled and unfocused to say the right thing.

Day 128

When I wake up I immediately check my phone. There's still no response. With fresh eyes and a clear head, I send Anita another message. I tell her I'm deeply sorry about the one I sent yesterday. I blame the walk, the heat, the miles, for getting to my head. My words feel right, even if they are self-serving. Again, I get crickets in response.

*

I don't return to Denny's even though I know Anita is off. I spend the day with my feet up. I stuff my face with accumulated road snacks and pass the time flipping channels. More than ever, I can't wait to get back on the road. I check my phone every few minutes hoping for some sort of acknowledgment. Minutes creep by. I'm sick with the feeling that I mistreated two people. I disrespected Anita and cheated on Katie.

Day 129

The following morning, I'm up early for a sunrise start. My phone dings to a flurry of bogus spam messages. Mixed within is a response from Anita. I roll LB onto the deep shoulder and read her brief reply. She says my message had, in fact, confused her, which is why she hadn't written back sooner. "I forgive you," she writes. "Good luck and God bless your journey." Her words choke me up. I walk and cry as the morning mist mixes with my tears. I'm ashamed of myself. But I'm also grateful for her absolution. "I fucked up," I say loud enough so Little Buddy can hear. "Wasn't thinking about anything but myself. I better have fucking learned something from this mess." LB's tires crunch over the thin layer of gravel. The sound of rubber treads give way to each minor obstacle. My words echo in my head as I tick off the first dozen miles. When I stop for lunch, I promise myself no more hotels for a while. I tell LB why: "It's too easy to hide there from my real self."

*

As I span two bridges across the Neches River to complete the final miles of the day, I imagine a safe place for my tent on the opposite side. Maybe at the water's edge. I yearn for a restful night with my body pressed against the earth.

A sign ahead is my beacon. Camper's Cove RV Park. I beeline to it shortly after getting off the bridge. An older looking white guy dressed in leather biker gear greets me at the entrance. "Hey there. I'm Frank." I tell him the sign lured me in. Frank says camping, though mentioned in their name, is not their thing. The RV park's occupants are all full-time permanent residents. "Oh," I say. "I'm just looking for a place to stay the night. Can you folks make an exception?" He asks if I plan to do any drugs. I respond with a resounding no. "Hmmm…I have to check you out first," he says. He takes a photo of me posing behind LB. I smile big.

Then he snaps another shot of my ID. Texts both to the park owner who immediately calls him back. I overhear their exchange. "Well, he's white...average height...beard and glasses," Frank says. "He's pushing a cart that has Walk USA on the front. Seems like a nice guy. Legit, I'd say." Frank pauses, listens into the receiver, then hangs up. "Well, he said it's my call. And far as I'm concerned, you're all set." I ask Frank if I should pay now and he waves me off. "Nah, don't worry about that," he says. "Not charging you for the night. We have a peaceful place here, just help us keep it that way." I shake Frank's hand. "I'm Tom, by the way." He laughs. "Yeah, I know. Go on and take that spot over by the boat landing. On that grassy patch out that way."

*

I park LB and plop onto the ground. Three fishing boats sleep on the glassy water. A scattering of small clouds punctuate the sky. Movement to the side catches my eye—curious people peeking through their trailer windows. Soon a few walk by and wave, others welcome me as I set up my tent. A young man, maybe in his twenties, bounds in my direction with two Bud Lights in hand. "Man, I saw you on the bridge earlier today," he says. "I thought you were selling ice cream! I'm Charles. Wanna beer?"

Charles and his wife, Cheyenne, are taking their son for a swim off the dock. "Man, you're so damn lucky you found this place," he says. "This whole area is fuckin' meth city. Our trailer park is about the only place where everyone's clean. Everyone out there—" he points toward the park's entrance, "is desperate as hell. They'd roll you in a heartbeat without thinking twice. Trust me!" Charles tells me he's a recovering addict himself. "But I'm one year sober," he says. "Haven't touched the stuff in forever." We clink our cold cans together.

Charles points to Cheyenne supervising their son on the dock. "My wife's into suicide prevention," he says. "She puts up posters all over town with hotline numbers for folks to call. There were seven suicides in this town last year. Seven, man! That's a lot. People around here ain't got nowhere to go." Charles has had a handful of local jobs. Most recently at a barbecue restaurant where he was being groomed for a management position. "But I blew it," he says. "I let my past take control. I've got anger problems, man. It's real hard for me to catch myself in the moment when I'm losing my shit. But I want to break the cycle, you know." I raise my can again.

Cheyenne's parents join her at the dock. I watch Charles as he watches his wife gather up their son and walk toward us at the child's pace. Charles cracks another beer and hands me one, too. He goes quiet. His smiling face hardens. "My family. My son, man," he says, gesturing toward them. "They are why I try my best. To be the dad mine wasn't. I want to do right by them. Maybe someday go back to school. But you know, I wasn't good in school back then, so I'm not sure things would be any different now." He kills his can and crushes it. "But I can tell you this—I'm a natural leader and pretty much can do anything I put my mind to."

*

For the rest of the evening, people stop by to welcome me to the Cove. I may be invading their space, but they make me feel safe. One of the visitors, a young woman named Alex, tells me that when she first overheard my voice she thought I talked proper. "I think more people should talk like that," she says. "There's a stigma against folks who don't."

Alex is 19 years old, a lesbian, and anti-Trump. "Life is tough here for people like me," she says. Tonight she's cooking a feast for anyone who wants to join. "Consider this your official invitation. All sorts of meats, some sides, and salad too. It's at Lynn's place just across the path. Hope to see you there."

When the sun sets, I join Alex at Lynn's trailer. She fills my plate over and over while telling me how badly she wants to leave Texas. "I imagine anywhere is better than here," she says. "I'm just so tired of worrying. About everything." Lynn shakes his head and laughs, wipes stray sauce from his salt and pepper mustache. When he raises another chicken leg to his mouth, two hound dogs at his feet drool waiting for scraps to drop. "But hell, if she goes," Lynn says, "I lose all this." Alex moves the hot links away from the red coals. Looks at my plate and insists I eat more. She sets a sealed ziplock of leftovers in front of me. "Take this too," she says. "For lunch tomorrow. Something to remember us by."

Lynn excuses himself and the dogs follow. I assume he's just off to use the restroom, but he never returns. The occasional crackle from the grill adds to the whirl of cicadas. We sit quietly under a ceiling of flickering stars. "You're super talented, Alex," I say, pointing to my plate. "I vote you take this show on the road." Alex leans against the cooling grill. Crosses her arms at her chest. "Yeah, maybe," she says. "Maybe someday I will."

Day 130

My checker at Brookshire's Grocery is a short Black woman with a cap on her head and a name tag that says Jill. I put my three honeycrisps and two Valencia oranges on her conveyor. "Morning, honey," she says. She weighs my fruit and taps her register screen. "When I started in this business there were only five kinds of apples," sh says. "Now, oh Lord!" She asks if I'm from the area or visiting family. I tell her I'm from North Carolina then explain what I'm up to. "Wait now," she says. "You're walking?" She stops pressing keys and grabs my hands. Locks her eyes onto mine. "You know, the good Lord's watching over you," she says. "He's walking along every step." I nod. She leans in and says it again, seemingly doubtful I heard her the first time. Then she releases her grip and continues to ring my items. "Boy oh boy," she says. "Everyone has a gift, you know. And it's up to each of us to figure out what that gift is. It makes me so happy you're putting yours to good use."

There's no line behind me, so we take a quick photo. I ask her for a hug. "Looks like He—" she points upward with a single raised brow, "spoke into your ear before mine— because I was just about to ask you the same thing." She comes out from behind her stand and squeezes me hard. "Everything's going to be just fine," she whispers. "Good Lord'll never give you more than you can handle. You can believe that!"

*

I'm still trying to camp every night for at least a week, so I beeline through Tyler, a minor metropolis. Before long I'm out of the town's bustle and I debate over a few so-so roadside camping spots. None are far enough out of sight to meet my stealth camping requirements, so I press on. Not far ahead, a Korean Baptist Church looks promising, so I ignore the private property signs and off-road LB through the lot's dense foliage. I don't stop charging through the prickly brush until I'm out of sight of any traffic and human made structures. It's a perfect spot.

*

I set up camp to the sounds of kids playing basketball at the church. I listen to the tinny ring of a perfectly inflated ball bouncing against blacktop. The clank of a bank shot, a shanked jumper. The metal rim vibrating then going quiet. The squeak of sneakers, of cutting and driving and laughing and layups and finally a wide open J. An abrupt silence marks the game's end and I imagine the players sitting in the shade of the backboard, sipping Gatorade, relacing their sneaks. They consider another game to 21. Winner takes it out. Gotta win by two.

Day 131

The next day, a sign in Winona says, "Sale—Help a Hoarder." As much as I'd love to dig through someone else's junk, I bypass it. A late model truck rolls up and the window rolls down. "Got a minute to chat?" Jason and his son Ben introduce themselves. They're heading out for a day of beekeeping. "Not sure if you believe in divine intervention," Jason says, "but we just stopped for breakfast at Whataburger and they accidentally gave us an extra sandwich. You want it?" I don't hide my excitement.

Jason asks if it's OK for them to pray for me. Since the first time I heard this question, back at the World's Biggest Dinosaurs attraction in Cabazon, California, it's been the second most frequent comment made during roadside exchanges. Folks ask why I'm walking, and after I answer, they ask if they can pray for me. I tell Jason sure, and before I fully understand what's happening, he and Ben are out of the truck, flanking me, with hands on my shoulders. "Oh," I say nervously. "This how we're going to do this?" Their heads bow., and Jason begins with "Dear God," then prays for my safety. Ben ends each of his father's requests with "Amen." Jason asks God to help me grow as a man —which makes me feel a little defensive—but I roll with it. "Dear Lord, may Tom come to find you if he hasn't already." Jason ends with a plea for the salvation of my soul. His eyes press tightly shut, his hand squeezes my shoulder.

*

Six hours later, Jason and Ben find me again on their drive home. They've brought me two bags of supplies and I'm impressed by their choices. Every single item is of practical use. Two water bottles, a large pack of pistachios, a jumbo bag of teriyaki beef jerky, bug spray, sunscreen, and a pack of baby wipes. "And also," Jason says, nodding toward his son, "Ben wants to give you something, too." Ben reaches into his pocket and furnishes a small, red-covered copy of the New Testament. Same as the one given to me at basic training. "Will you accept this?" Ben asks. I note my reluctance, so I assume they notice it, too.

*

I attended Catholic school for 10 of my 12 precollege years. Memories of those days conjure a conflicted sentimentality that resembles how I feel about my time in the military. Mostly I'm relieved for having survived the ordeal without sustaining, or inflicting, much damage. But ripples of my era with authoritarian priests and nuns continue to affect my adult psyche.

Growing up, my religious role models made me feel small. They regularly told me that I wasn't enough. Not strong enough, not smart enough. Not handsome enough, not from a wealthy enough family. They told me I ran with the wrong crowd. That I was immature and had low self-confidence. That I was a dreamer, and did things boys weren't supposed to do—like feather my hair or listen to David Bowie. Over time I grew accustomed to their put-downs. It was attention, after all.

In my teenage years, I embodied their language and used it as a tool to disparage others. I looked for ways to elevate myself while stepping on heads. This self-righteous berating was done to honor a shame-hungry God—a God I'd been taught to fear. I didn't trust this God, but I was scared shitless of him.

In ninth grade, Mr. Finn, a secular man who always wore corduroy sport coats, stood in front of my theology class and told us to "question everything." Until that moment, I had never thought to dispute the idea of a heavy-handed God to whom I owed my soul. I promptly quit being an altar boy, told the Boy Scouts to shove it, and gave my life over to seasonal sports. I boldly shelved Catholicism's pomp, but I didn't quit God altogether. I still prayed. I still did my best to be good. But Mr. Finn's permission was a crucial turning point in my young life as a spiritual being. It allowed me to make my own choice regarding organized religion. I walked away from mine.

Telling Catholicism and its patriarchy to back off was the most empowering thing I'd done to that point. But it left me defensive, and does still. To the point that now, decades later, when someone asks me what I believe in or if I am saved, my heart immediately races and I'm tongue-tied. Which is tricky, because such questions have become commonplace on this walk.

*

When Ben extends the small book in his fragile hands, I gently accept it as Jason looks on. After they drive away, I notice a smell emanating from the holy book. It reeks of something oddly familiar, something from my preteen years. Like it's been dipped in a vat of chemical fruit, leaving a bouquet of stink that reminds me of a crush I had on a babysitter in the '70s. The fragrant Bible emanates a tang of strawberry lip gloss. Which makes me wonder if Ben's gift is merely Jason's brilliant strategy to unload a migraine-inducing stink Bible without having to dumpster it. *How about we give it to the guy we met earlier?* I imagine him suggesting. *After all, he looks like he needs Jesus.* And maybe I do. But I definitely don't need strawberry Jesus.

I stash the Bible in Little Buddy's main hold where it cooks for the remainder of the steamy day. Even when I stop to camp in a wide open field, the booklet's stench is so strong that I simply can't take it anymore. I hurl it a safe distance away and hit the hay. In the morning I collect it, place it into a plastic bag, and toss it in the first trash bin I see.

Day 132

The last actual flat tire I had was back in New Mexico when a needly cactus thorn stabbed directly through LB's tire and tube, sending air screaming out in a cool whistle. The only other time I've needed to dig out my patch kit resulted from a hasty off-road detour across a field of hidden goatheads. Only two flats between California and here ain't so bad.

Since then, my nightly ritual includes tweezing out anything that's gotten stuck in LB's rubber tread. Shards of glass, stray wire, sharp pebbles, plant barbs. A thumbtack once. The nightly surgery has paid off. But after 1,800 miles, the tire knobs have worn smooth, making it more vulnerable than ever. And after a 19-mile morning, Little Buddy's left foot goes limp. I stop at a bait store on the west side of Lake O' the Pines to give it a look. The puncture is a real doozy. The unpatchable sort. It's a pinch-flat in the tube, and it forces me to bust out my last spare. And given the worn state of the tire, I replace it, too, with my last reserve.

I install the fresh setup and pump the shiny tire to 40 psi. Then I sit in the shade and eat a couple ice cream bars. The adjacent fishing resort offers a few meager motel rooms and I'm tempted to stop here for the night. A shower would be nice, and so would a comfy bed. But I'm still feeling my no-hotels-for-a-while promise. So I get back on the road.

*

Ten miles later there's a dirt path through a pine forest leading to electrical lines. I want to explore, but the opening is directly across the highway from a bustling country liquor store and I worry someone will see me. I wait for a break in the action and pretend like I'm messing with my phone. But the place doesn't mellow. When one car leaves, two more show up. I remember something my brother told me about graffiti artists: "The best time to illegally paint is in broad daylight." I apply it to my situation and eventually push Little Buddy onto the path like it's no big deal. I beeline straight through the conifer grove into a hidden meadow where I set up my tent in grass taller than me. The matted turf is a stately mattress. I consider heading to the nearby shop for small flask of Jack Daniels. Would be nice to fall asleep with a buzz. But I'm too tired and can't be bothered to get up. I wonder what Katie is doing right now. Sleeping, probably. But maybe lying in our bed and thinking about me, too. I wonder if we'll ever stop breaking up.

The steady flow of cars is occasionally interrupted by a fit of laughter or a squeal of tires. Hours later I wake with a jump—chilled because I never got myself into the sleeping bag. I am overcome by how much I stink, but I secretly like it. I roll onto my side and breathe myself in. I feel the pressure of the ground against my hip and knee. It's like the bruises have always been there. Like some parts of me are meant to hurt.

I recenter myself on the cushioned pad and absorb the minor discomfort until it settles. I fold my bare arms across my chest and appreciate my warm skin. I make a sound like purring.

It's extra dark. The waning crescent offers no shadows on the tent walls. A breeze whispers through tall grass. The stalks bend and rise, smooth and unbothered, as they drift through the night together.

Day 133

As I walk past a used tire shop in Texarkana, two men shuffle out of the bay and turn their hands into bullhorns. "Hey! Come 'ere! We saw you coupla days ago!" they shout. The older guy introduces himself as Ray, the owner of the place. The other fellow is Bart, Ray's only employee. They ask what I'm doing. "Oh man! Thank you! Thank you so much!" Bart says. "Boy oh boy! I ain't never met no one who's been to Los Angeles."

Ray asks if I have a minute, then motions for me to follow him into the bay. Leads me to an office where stacks of paper fill the desktop. He points to the back wall. It's lined with shelves of vintage glass bottles. "My customers gave me all of these through the years," he says. "Each one means a little something different." He tells me to take a closer look while Bart nods encouragingly. The stacks of shelves are lined with brown glass whiskey jugs, vintage Coca Cola bottles, old perfume jars, blue glass pill vials, and other ornate collectibles. Most pieces, if considered individually, are forgettable bits of rubbish. But as a collection they tell a different, unexpected story. I hold my hands behind my back as I marvel at the way their angles and chips catch the light. One's prism sends a faint rainbow onto the side wall. "Go on, pick one," Ray says with a finger. "Give ya something to remember us by." As I further examine the rows of colored glass, waiting for one to jump out, Ray tells me about another guy who passed through town years ago. "Old boy said he was walkin' all the way 'round the world," Ray says. "And he wasn't no bum, I tell you what. Just a feller out doin' some walkin'."

Ray grew up in southern Alabama. His accent is thick as cold tar. He fills empty spaces in our conversation by repeating, "Yep, yep, yep." The repeated words gradually decrease in volume until settling into silence. "You know, I once met a feller called the goat man," Ray says. "Had a small covered wagon pulled by damn goats. And had a beard that went clear to his feet. He traveled all over the states with them goats just like you are. 'Cept you ain't got no goats!" he laughs. "Yep, yep, yep. You pick you a glass bottle yet?" Ray asks. I choose a green one shaped like a horseshoe that says "Good Luck." A '70s-era Avon eau de cologne container. He chooses a second one for me, a small snail with a golden neck. "Here, take this one, too," he says. "Snail's got everything it needs right there on its back. Jus' like you, son."

Ray gives me directions to the state line then hands me a folded-up shop receipt. "Ray's Tires" is stamped at the top in black ink, and below it, a hand written phone number and address. Ray asks me to call him and Bart when I get to the Atlantic. "We'd sure love to hear from you again," he says. I notice the address is missing a zip code, so I ask for it. "Oh boy," Ray says, scratching his chin. "I can't say as I know." He looks at Bart. His eyes widen, too. "Well, just send it to what I put down there," he says. "We'll get it. Yep, yep, yep. Sure will."

Day 134

Near Queen City, a large silver truck slows and pulls into a nearby driveway. "Hey!" a woman yells out the window. "You're the walk USA guy!" She says she's seen me walking for the past three days. "I just called my husband and told him! God put me in your path enough times for me to get the hint. I'm Michelle!" She hands me $26. Insists I take it. Asks where I'm stopping for the night. My goal is Texarkana where I'll take a day off. "Great!" she says. "I work there. If you need anything in the meantime, I'm happy to help." Michelle also offers to buy me a meal, wire me money, and pay for my hotel stay. We make tentative plans to meet up for dinner. She expects to be off work by 7:00 and I joke that anything past 8:00 is a late night for me.

A couple hours later, I get a text from a number I don't recognize. Angelica says she got my contact info from a photo posted on Texarkana Cheers and Jeers, a community Facebook page. It's public, so I find it easily. After our chance meeting, Michelle posted a few photos of me with Little Buddy, including a closeup of my business card. Her accompanying message says, "Cheers to this gentleman who is on a mission to walk from the Pacific Ocean to the Atlantic Ocean. We saw him near Winsborro, TX Sunday morning and yesterday I saw him in Linden. This morning I saw him in Queen City on his way to Texarkana. If you see him, show him some Love!! Prayers for safe travels Tom Griffen!!" The post has garnered a lot of attention. In two hours, 36 people have left comments. Some are supportive, but others are critical of my motives for this walk, and of my politics and past experiences I've detailed on my blog. I'm on an emotional roller coaster as I read them.

The Cheers and Jeers page leads me to Michelle's personal account. Her cover photo is a close up of a bald eagle's head. Below it is one word written in blood-red letters. All caps. The word, Trump. Michelle's feed is a chain of right-wing memes.

Had I only seen her Facebook page, I'd doubt I'd be interested in spending much time with her.

The comments on Cheers and Jeers offer me a glimpse into how some people see me. And not just as the walking me, but also me as a person. It sucks to be judged. It hurts to witness people getting upset by the details of my life. But frankly, I'm no better than any of these trolling commenters. I mean, I'm guilty of passing similar judgment on Michelle based solely on her Facebook images. I sidestep my assumptions, and do my best to give her, and the plethora of vitriolic voices resulting from her post about me, the benefit of the doubt.

*

At the end of my walking day, I text Michelle and confirm our dinner outing. "I'll take you to some real Texan barbecue," she says. "My husband is working so he won't be able to join us." I warn her my appetite is like a teenager's. She assures me this is a good thing. "I'll come get you and we'll get supper. But I hope you don't mind, afterwards I'll need to pick up my pistol at my twin brother's house."

I figured we'd hit a local hole-in-the-wall barbecue joint. So when we roll up to Texas Roadhouse, a national chain, it throws me. As soon as we are seated, Michelle schools me on the properties of a good cut of meat. We place our order and clink our water glasses together. "Cheers," she says.

In Michelle's 23 years as a nurse, 18 of which have been in the ER, what she most enjoys about her job is the people. "You've got to have a certain attitude to stay that long," she says. "But at root, I just want to take care of people." Michelle asks if I carry any weapons. I tell her I don't want to carry something I'm not prepared to use. She opens her wallet and pulls out a plastic credit card looking thing. "I get ya," she says as she monkeys with the plastic rectangle until it transforms into a double edged knife. "But here, take this. Never know when you might need it. And don't worry, I've got three or four more at home."

*

After dinner, we swing by Michelle's brother Michael's place. She first introduces me to Cody, her nephew, who was just made the percussion leader in his high school band. Then her brother Michael joins us in the hallway and invites us into the living room. As I take a seat on the couch, Cody hands us glasses of ice water. I wonder how long we're staying.

Michael shares details of his ongoing struggle with armadillos. "They're tearing up the lawn," he says. I want to join in the conversation, so I wait for a pause, then I tell everyone about the dozens of mangled armadillos I see every day. "Just last week I saw my first live ones," I say. "They're like little dinosaurs." Michael perks up. "Yup. They're everywhere. And when grubs get hard to find in the forest, they come into neighborhoods." Cody laughs at his dad's comment. Swirls the ice in his glass. Michael gives him a look and Cody perks up. "You see, my dad actually loves armadillos," Cody says. "Like, loves 'em. He wishes he could have one as a pet." Michelle cackles at Cody's admission and Michael doesn't dispute it. I take the comment as a rib, but I can't tell for sure. "Oh my!" Michelle blurts out. "I almost forgot what we came here for!" As she jumps up, Michael reaches alongside the recliner and grabs a black box and hands it to her. "Well, I got my gun, Tom! You ready to go?"

*

Michelle drives me back to my hotel. It's been a great night of stories and togetherness and I thank her many times for all she's done. I don't mention the Facebook page even though I almost allowed it to come between us. Instead I consider the possibility of all people connecting first as humans, rather than as oppositional ideologies, political parties, or religions. Michelle gives me a huge hug and toots the baritone horn twice as she pulls out of the hotel lot.

Later I get a text from her asking what else she can do for me. Do I need more money? How about another hotel night? She insists I let her help me out. I write back telling her that the extra good vibes were enough. "Thanks for taking the risk to stop and stay hello," I say. She thanks me for taking one, too. Which makes me wonder if she knew about my apprehensions all along.

Day 135

After taking the day off, I dine on Mexican cuisine with Pat, another local I met as I approached the border. Pat's a field worker for a fiber optic cable company, but he aspires to be a fiction writer. "In the 1970s I hitchhiked across the US," he says. "I get it. I'm not even going to ask why you're doing this."

After dinner we hit Pecan Point Brewing Company and spend the night talking about religion, spirituality, and the nature of the human condition. Our different perspectives are softened by the high ABVs. "I'm a Christian minister," Pat says. "As conservative as they come. To the right of Rush Limbaugh, even. But even I can see the nation has strayed. There's a lot of misunderstanding out there."

Unlike others who have pushed religion on me, Pat listens. He doesn't try to scare or guilt me. He doesn't try to get me to go to church or be saved. We simply talk. Our conversation dives into heavy topics, but it's framed with a refreshing openness. No doubt the beer is helping keep things loose, but it could just as easily have the opposite effect. For a spell there's no line in the sand between a far-right conservative minister and an agnostic, tree-hugging, hippie liberal. We refill our pints. I've lost track of how many we've had.

"You know," Pat says. "I've been reading your blog. Saw the post about when you dressed up in drag in Mexico City." He's referring to a detail of my recent visit to Mexico's Federal District. To try something new, I signed up for an Airbnb experience where I spent the evening with two men in drag who outfitted me similarly before we went dancing at a couple gay bars. The night ended in the morning's wee hours with a visit to a churro stand. According to my hosts, Skanda and María Magdalena, I was their first straight client.

"Because you did this," Pat says, "because you dressed up as a woman and went to gay bars with homosexuals, plenty of people in my circle would immediately discard the possibility of spending time with you. But here we are. Lord, if they could see me now!" Pat raises his glass. I clink it. "You know, I like the idea of looking over the fence to see what can be learned," Pat says. "To me you are a pioneer who can help translate things for all of us." There's a hint of sadness in his voice. Of longing.

Day 136

On State Line Road, I stop at the post office that sits on the state line. Half in Texas, half in Arkansas. Outside the main entrance, I chat with four Mormon women on their 18-month mission. I ask if folks are receptive to their message, and they assure me they are. "It's easy," one says. "You just strike up a conversation and figure out a way to connect." Another asks if this walk is a pilgrimage, which makes me think of others who've asked the same thing. "Well, it definitely wasn't when I started out," I say. "But I'm beginning to think it just might be."

8

—There's nothing lonelier than the land, he said.
—Why lonely?
—Because it's so damn free.

- Patti Smith
M Train, during a dream conversation with the cowpoke

Day 137

TRAFFIC ON THE ARKANSAS 67 stops dead in both directions. People gawk at me and take photographs as if I can't see them behind their windshields.

A couple men watching the gridlock from their yard shout to me from across the highway. "Hey! Come over and have a cold drink!" It's barely 9:00 a.m. and already topping 90°F. I wave back, then veer easily through the congested cars and park Little Buddy at the bottom of the driveway. "Beer or water?" they ask. I decline the beer with a laugh, but happily accept a water.

The tall guy introduces them both. "I'm Oz and this here is Milt," he says. They're setting up for a high school graduation party later this afternoon. "You should stay," Oz says as he sips his beer without taking his eyes off me. "I would," I say. "But I'm trying to make it to Hope before nightfall." Oz chews his lip. "So...you don't want to come?" he asks. Milt laughs nervously and pats his friend on the back. "Come on, Oz. Let the walking man do his thing." Oz steps closer to me. Cocks his head. "You don't want to come to my barbecue?" I tell him it's not that—it's just that I want to keep moving. "Oh, I see," he says. "You're too good to hang with us, huh?" His posture hardens. He uses his thumb to crack the knuckles of his free hand.

My rebuttal begins with a stammer and Oz cuts me off. "Yeah. I see how it is," he says as he sips his beer. "But hey—let me ask you this—how much money you think I make?" Milt smiles apologetically and I shake my head. Oz repeats his question in a hushed tone. I tell him I'm not going to guess. I thank him for the for the water and excuse myself. "Oh—you see that, Milt?" Oz says. "See that right there? That's exactly what I'm talking about. This man stands here on my property, drinks my water, and then he walks away and disrespects me. It's because I'm Black, huh?" Oz moves in, points his finger at me and I smell his warm, boozy breath. "Let me tell you something, man," he says. "I make more than one hundred thousand dollars per year. I make white money, bruh. You believe me?" I assure him I do. But I also say it's none of my business. "But you still don't *believe* me, do you? You're thinking, *How could a black man make so much goddamn money*?" I feel like my words don't matter, so I say nothing in response. "Come on now, Oz," Milt pleads. "We gotta get ready for this party." Oz glares at his friend, then puts his hand on my shoulder. His eyes press thinner. His lip curls and I brace myself. Three, four, five seconds pass. "Oh man!" Oz says. "I'm just fuckin' with you!" He pushes his finger into my chest. "But I got ya, didn't I?" he says. Her raises his voice to repeat the question.

"But hey, before you go, I just got one more question," Oz says. "You gonna write a book about this walk?" Before I have a chance answer, a woman hollers something from the porch. Oz turns toward her and jerks his arms in the air, spilling a slosh of beer. "Shit, woman! Give me a minute, will ya?" he shouts back. Milt asks if they should get the barbecue going. Oz snaps. "Why don't you shut the fuck up, man! Let me finish up with this white boy first." Oz kills his can and crushes it in his hand. Redirects his attention to me.

"Look here," he says. "How about I write you a check for three thousand dollars right now?" I squish my face. "That's right," he says. "I'll give you three thousand dollars to write a book and put me in it. Would you take the money?" I shake my head. "So wait—hold on then," Oz says. "I'm offering you three grand and you immediately say *no*? See. I knew it. You don't think I don't have the money, huh? Because how could a Black man have three thousand dollars cash?" I step back, thank him again for the water, and he moves his body to block me from leaving.

Oz looks at Milt. "Yo. Tell this man I'm a rich motherfucker and could give him three thousand dollars right now." Milt nods. The woman on the patio hollers something again and Oz points at me. "He's walking across America!" he shouts. She moves her hand dismissively. Oz quiets his voice. "That's my wife," he says. "She's a rich black woman. She's got white people working for her. We're paying for this whole goddamn party, aren't we, Milt?" Milt reaches his fist out for a bump. "You the man, Oz! You the motherfuckin' man!"

As their fists come together, a glittering purple Impala with large polished wheels pulls into the driveway. Its stereo pounds deep bass. Oz and Milt approach the side windows and I slip away toward Little Buddy. I unlock the parking brake, cross the jammed highway, and get back on the roadside. I look back as Oz opens a cooler and hands the new arrivals a couple cold beers. Neither Oz nor Milt pays me any attention. Oz's wife, however, watches me intently from the porch with her hands on her hips. I wave to her, but she doesn't wave back.

*

On the outskirts of Hope, I turn off the highway into a neighborhood, following a GPS shortcut to an interstate hotel. The streets are lined with cars on blocks. Sidewalks jut upward atop untamed roots. A fire-damaged building fills a corner lot. I push LB along a path of tiny ziplocks. Low light hangs in the cumulus sky. I take photos of brokenness and see art.

To some this is home, but to me it is merely a place I want to capture. The allure of an opaque house with a sagging spine. A wheelless truck no longer able to recall the sensation of hot blacktop on its knobby treads. I pass through the old neighborhood and romanticize it. When I notice someone watching me as I take a photo of a car's spider-webbed windshield, it's like I've been caught doing something I shouldn't be doing.

Cars zip past on the main road ahead—an exit off Interstate 30 with hotels and restaurants. I'll stop there for the day. As my pace quickens, I wave to a man leaning on his porch rail. He stands tall when he sees me. Runs down steps and offers me a cool drink. I hesitate as I flash on the men from earlier. But I accept. He returns to the house, then exits with a plastic bottle and a grapefruit. "This one," he says with an accent, rolling the grapefruit in his hand, "might not be so good." We introduce ourselves. "Me llamo Raúl," he says. "I am from Mexico. Soy pobre, but I like to do nice things for people."

Raúl's been in the US for 17 years. Hasn't seen his family since he left. Earlier this year, his father was murdered. "They didn't shoot him, they beat him," Raúl says. "He died slowly. Police found him con una toalla en la boca." Raúl puts his hand on his chest. "Me duele mi corazón. Mis amigos don't know what to do for me. I don't have nobody to give me a hug." His arms hang heavy at his sides. His eyes fill. I set the bruised fruit onto Little Buddy and don't bother asking permission before I wrap my arms around Raúl's body. His shoulders soften and he begins to cry. "Lo siento mucho, Raúl," I say. "I am so, so sorry."

Day 138

Staying fully hydrated in this heat is not easy. It's a constant teeter between drinking too much and too little. If I stop paying close attention, my body begins to shut down. A mid-walk nap is my first clue that things are going south. No matter how well I keep up with water intake, around 10:00 a.m. every morning I nod off on the roadside. But I've developed a solution that seems to be working. First, I find a safe place to stop and drink water until it's sloshing in my belly. A half liter or so. Then I chase it with a small can of Starbucks Cuban Coffee and a Mrs. Freshley Jumbo Honey Bun. I have a stash of both in Little Buddy. The combination of water, caffeine, and sugar reawakens me and sends me into the stratosphere. Keeps me high until lunch.

I follow this routine with a dose of classic heavy metal and for the next few hours I push LB with one hand and play air drums with the other. Sabbath and Ozzy, Scorpions and early Metallica. I sing along to all the songs.

In recent weeks the temps have consistently reached into the high 90s and by mid-afternoon, I'm walknapping again. So I repeat the morning pit stop. Another Cuban coffee and honey bun. I don't sweat the calorie count. Five hundred and ninety per honey bun, 60 per coffee. A mere fraction of my daily intake. My body is a red hot furnace. It incinerates whatever I throw into it.

*

I have a missed call from a number I don't recognize. I mash the receiver between my shoulder and ear and listen to the voicemail. It's Lion. His unmistakable voice is deep and thick. His Jamaican accent. The reception is bad and he talks quickly. I make out the part where he says he's checking in on me. Then a comment about Jah and love. But the rest is incomprehensible. I try to call the number back, but it just rings and rings.

*

Aaron stops his old F150 and hands me a green Gatorade. Sour apple. He's a pipeliner. Home for a stretch of 17 off days. He's spending his furlough helping an old man build a gazebo. "But today I'm just going to sit in my air-conditioned house and drink beer," he says. "I'm jealous," I say. "And hey, I appreciate your kindness." He looks down the road and chews his bottom lip. "You know, Tom. I haven't always been a good person," he says. "But everything changed when I had my first kid. The Lord blessed me," he says. "Seems to me kindness suits you just fine," I say. "It rolls off you naturally." Aaron says he's still working on believing these things himself. "Up ahead there's a gas station in

Prescott," he says. "Go on in and tell Stacie I sent you. She's going to let you have whatever you want for lunch." I do as he instructs and get myself a ham and cheese sandwich, salt and vinegar chips, and a Coke. It's all on Aaron. Stacie says he left her $17 and told her to let me keep the change. I tell her to put the few remaining dollars in the tip jar.

Later, a guy named Chris stops to deliver me a case of water bottles. Same with Nicole. And then Sam and others. The gifts just keep coming. I'm probably more hydrated today than I've been the entire trip. I turn down the last two water offerings since LB's axles are creaking under all the extra weight. After 28 miles, I find a stealth camp site. My bottles are empty, and most of the gifted water is in my belly. Without all the extra kindness, there's no way I'd have made it this far.

Day 139

Today's hit of espresso and honey bun isn't cutting it. The ruthless string of scorching days combined with monster miles is catching up with me. I'm actually having dreams as I momentarily lose consciousness near Caddo Valley. Reminds of me when I was in basic training and I'd take micronaps on the down portion of each push-up during morning physical training. "Up!" the drill sergeant would order, and we'd all lock our elbows in a 4:00 a.m. plank. Then he'd shout, "Down!" and I'd hover an inch from the dewy parade field, where, for a microsecond, I'd disappear from Fort Jackson completely. Amazing how much dream can fit into an instant.

The same thing is happening today. Twice I've released my grip on Little Buddy before jarring awake with a jolt and having to flailgrab the handlebars as drivers flash past shaking fists. Rather than push through it, I stop at a cheap motel hours earlier than usual.

A Black woman named Jennifer checks me in. She gives me a coupon for a free waffle at the adjacent Waffle House. We chat longer than necessary, which, she assures me, is fine since business is slow. We discuss the walk, our jobs, and life so far. I ask what makes her heart sing. She says she works a lot. That she doesn't have much time to do anything else. Her answer leaves an empty space in our flow. I take it as my cue to go get settled in.

*

I'm stoked that Little Buddy fits through the room door. I move furniture around to make space for him under the front window. Then I double check his tire pressure and consider wiping down the accumulated grime from his panels. I decide not to bother.

Little Buddy and I have become trusted partners in this strange wander. He's the only one who's been with me for all the moments that make up this journey. I'm already wondering what I'll do with him when we reach the Atlantic—assuming he makes it that far.

He's taking a serious beating. His axles have a worrisome amount of play and lately have been making a distressing squawk. His solid front wheels are starting to split down the middle. Any time I take a close look, I find more reasons to be concerned. But I suppose the same goes with me. I tell him he'll be fine—that *we'll* be fine—and I hope I'm right.

*

As I'm laying out my gear on the bed for a quick inventory, there's a knock at the door. It's Jennifer from the front desk. She apologizes for interrupting, which I assure her she's not doing. "Any chance I can take your photo for Facebook?" she asks. "I want my friends to follow you!" We snap a couple, then I walk with her back toward the office on my way to the Waffle House where I order the biggest meal on the menu. "Plus, an extra waffle," I say as I lay down Jennifer's coupon.

I detour on my way back to ask Jennifer about the hotel's continental breakfast. She smiles and closes her magazine as the bells on the door ring. "Now I'm the one who's sorry to interrupt!" I say. She laughs, then lays out details for breakfast. Before I leave, I revisit my earlier question. "When I asked about what makes your heart sing, you said it was your jobs and how hard you work," I say. "But I'm curious if that's really all of it?" Jennifer sets down her magazine and stands to join me at the counter. "You know, I've been thinking about it since you asked," she says. "And there is more to me than work. Actually, my three kids are my world." She tells me about them. The oldest who looks just like her, the middle about to turn 10, how she coddles the youngest. "And now that I'm thinking about it, there's also photography," she says. "Someday I'll go back to school, maybe on a scholarship, and learn all I can about photography while being a good example for my children. I'll finally follow my dreams, you know. Then someday be a professional photographer. Maybe in doing that, I'll show them they can follow their dreams, too."

Day 140

On the winding outskirts of Caddo Valley, just as I'm losing breath from an incline, a big truck rolls up alongside me. The driver, an older man with kind eyes and a Santa Claus beard, rolls down his window. An American flag waves on his sleeveless tee. "You got Jesus in your heart?" he asks. Which makes me think, *Oh man, here we go again.*

For the past few weeks, I've been fielding countless versions of this same question. Which makes me wonder if I'm putting off a desperately-needs-saving vibe. Sometimes the tone of inquiry is warm and accepting, other times it carries a weight like judgment. The asker barely hears my response before launching into a diatribe of hellfire and brimstone. I'm immediately oppositional, which probably isn't fair, but it's how I've come to protect myself from my own baggage associated with religion and God.

So when this guy asks his version of the same old question, I tell him, "Yeah, sure man. I've got Jesus in my heart." But my words are a deflection. Between the lines I'm snapping, *What business is it of yours, anyhow?* Without moving his truck from the traffic lane, he puts it in park and takes his hands off the wheel. "You sure?" he asks, and a pause hangs between us. "Yeah man," I say. "I *am* sure." He extends a hand out the window and introduces himself as Brother Lee. I note the homonymic possibility of his name. Brotherly. "Hey. You got time for a story?" he asks. I perk up.

A few years back, Brother Lee and his cousin were chainsawing a forest of felled trees. As Lee worked on a thicker log, a pressurized cut snapped a thick branch directly into his forehead. "One second I was cutting, and then I don't remember a thing," he says. His cousin thought he was dead, but felt a pulse and called 911. An emergency crew airlifted Lee to a hospital.

Lee had seven skull fractures, his neck was broken in multiple places, and his brain was bleeding. He fell into a coma. Doctors told his family to start making arrangements. But Brother Lee held on. A month later he awoke with a gasp saying the same word over and over. *Mercy.* Lee's eyes redden and water as he tells me this. "It was my moment of awakening," he says. "I recall being in a place of deep sadness. But then a sliver of light entered my consciousness and I ran toward it."

Brother Lee had been a preacher before the accident, but he left the church after recovering. "Folks didn't want to believe I received a miracle," he says. "Because, why me and not them? This is the sort of stuff organized religion does to us. We pretend like we're looking after each other when actually we're just in it for ourselves." Brother Lee says the injury taught him how to love differently.

"Finally learning how to love is the reason I am better," he says. "I stopped judging things—myself included. I started accepting love from others. And guess what? It's working." Brother Lee shows me the cavernous scar channeling across his head, eye to nape. A quarter-inch-wide crescent of smooth, translucent skin. He tells me I can touch it if I want. I gently tap it. It's so smooth it barely registers on my fingertip.

"I know you're being watched after, Tom, and that makes me happy," Brother Lee says. "Keep that love in your heart. It's precisely what's going to keep you safe."

Days 141 - 146

As I near and clear Little Rock, Becca and Jeff, the same folks who surprised me at a hotel in New Mexico, pick me up and shuttle me back and forth to their house. I spend a full week with them, including five consecutive off days, the most so far. They absorb me into their routine, including me in their family's activities. I meet their friends, tour the area with Jeff, attend Enzo and Ociee's karate and gymnastics practices, and enjoy a daily espresso with Becca just like we did in the old days. The normalcy of this schedule offers a hint of what's to come when this journey is over. A glimpse into my nonwalking life. And though this reality is still at least two months away, it induces minor heart palpitations. Because right now, I never want to stop.

One night Jeff pulls out an oversized road atlas. We trace my route and strategize the next few days through Arkansas and across the Mississippi River. I stare at the map and shake my head. The days and miles have all zipped by in a flash and I can't believe I've made it this far. How the hell did I get myself to the middle of the country? I *walked* here?

I've covered an amazing distance with what seems like little effort. I've taken one insignificant step after another—then suddenly after 3,000,000 strides, here I am. I wish I could apply this sort of dedication to everything else I want to activate. My life would be prolific—I could write novel after novel, become fluent in Spanish, master the guitar, get markedly better at carving wooden spoons. I could save a bunch of money, formulate solid opinions, shift the fizzling focus of my business, and deepen all the personal relationships I've left to flounder. If I de-emphasize the outcome and simply put in a relentless effort, one day I'll find myself astounded by the details of my life. I'll suddenly find myself as surprised by my progress as I am right now, tracing the bumpy line of my walk from from California to Arkansas.

Day 147

Becca walks with me as I continue east of Little Rock. Besides Katie, she's one of the few people I know who's up for pretty much any physical challenge without much preparation. She is, after all, a Gulf War veteran, an Appalachian Trail thru-hiker, a CrossFit enthusiast, and an amazing mom of two superactive kids.

At sunrise it's already 80°F when we leave her place. I bring Little Buddy more out of habit than necessity. We hit an espresso joint for a couple shots, then pass the capitol building and take a some token photos before we cross over the Arkansas River. On Highway 70, the shoulder quickly narrows and becomes precarious. But Becca navigates the roadside like a pro crosser. She leans to the left as trucks hurl past. She waves at nearly every car, which often leads to a friendly honk. We take a break on the side of a vacant building. Becca's tricky knee is acting up. Years of jumping out of airplanes are to blame. She doesn't want the hitch to stop her, but her increasing limp has me worried that we should reconsider our plan. But Becca insists we keep on charging. "Hooo-rah," I say, because I know it'll make her laugh.

After lunch, Becca's knee forces her to stop and we call Jeff for an early pickup. He scoops her up and later returns for me after I knock out an additional 11 miles. Jeff takes a scenic way home where giant trees canopy a narrow stretch of the old highway. "Feels like a time warp," I say. "Like we'll come out the other end and it'll be a century ago." I wonder out loud if this is how people imagined the roadway would someday look—trees reaching from the edges of front yards and gently coming together with intertwined branches to form a cool, shady tunnel.

*

Back at the house I share my final meal in Little Rock with Becca and her family. The sound of silverware on plates. Sips from water cups. And just like back in Deming, New Mexico, I don't want to leave, but I'm ready to go.

After the kids are in bed, Becca puts water on for tea. As we wait in the kitchen for the pot to boil, she asks what's going to happen between me and Katie. I shake my head. Tell her I'm not sure. "How'd y'all meet, again?" she asks. And I share the story I'm sure I've told her before.

In 2010 I joined a local run group for the Ocho—an annual eight-mile run held on August 8. I was in the throes of ultra training and in top-notch shape. When the gun went off, I zipped out with the frontrunners, hoping to use the day as my speed workout. At approximately mile five, a woman came blasting by. We immediately started talking trash. "No way she'll keep up that pace," we said. But she did. And the woman—Katie—came in second overall.

At the finish line, I struck up a conversation with her. Our chat led to a date and before long we were spending every waking moment together. Within a few weeks, I told Katie I was certain we'd be together for a long, long time. "I hope that doesn't scare you," I said. It didn't. She asked when we were going to move in.

"That was eight years ago," I say to Becca. She nods as she pours the hot water. "Well, maybe y'all will work things out?" she says as she hands me my mug and tells me to let it cool. Then we sit quietly at her dining room table and stare at our cups, charmed by the dance of rising steam.

Day 149

Billowy storm clouds rise west from the Mississippi basin like castles in the sky. After three miles, I realize I've taken a wrong turn and double back. A six-mile mistake. I feel self-conscious retracing my path within clear view of a yellow crop duster that's been flying overhead. I know the pilot must be thinking, *Now where the heck is he going?*

I take an Apple Maps shortcut onto a gravel road. Walk past a silo. Then another silo. I see no cars and no people even though I pass farms and houses and an occasional roadside market. Back on the main road it's the same and I figure the heat is keeping folks inside. Or maybe everyone got called to an emergency town meeting to discuss the strange vagrant man who's pushing a baby stroller and illegally camping while taking handouts from good people? Or maybe I'm the sole survivor of an apocalypse I don't yet know about.

*

I take a farm road into a crop field. There's no sign of workers, no fresh tire tracks. I settle on a spot that doesn't have much cover. Soon as I set up my tent, I'm swarmed by dragonflies, metallic green with black-striped tails. Four wings sprout from their backs. They pay little attention to me and spend the remainder of the evening landing on Little Buddy and the tent. One comes to a stop, then another crashes into it, forcing it to fly off. The cycle repeats like a game. When the sun goes down, the dragonflies are replaced by mosquitoes. Giant ones. The sort I'd been warned about. "Mosquitoes are the state bird in Arkansas," someone said a while back.

Until tonight, the mosquito situation has been normal. An occasional swarm and a bite here and there. But in this field they are truly giants. Bigger than I've ever seen. When I crush them, they explode into red splatter blotches. Large biting flies join in the annoyance, and herd me into my tent sooner than usual. I listen as the blood-thirsty creatures buzz around my setup, desperate for entrance.

It's too hot for a sleeping bag, so I lay on top of my bedroll. I kill time flicking shadows as they appear on the tent's taut walls. "Fly away now or I'm launching you," I warn the winged culprits. The amusement occupies me for a solid hour before I grow bored and close my eyes. All night I wake to the sound of buzzing.

Day 151

I'm up and gone before anyone finds me poaching this patch of private land. The sun's barely risen and it's already wet and humid. It'll be triple digits when I make it to the Arkansas state line. There, Becca's husband Jeff will shuttle me across the pedestrian-unfriendly bridge spanning the Mississippi River. "I've always wanted to see West Helena," he said back in Little Rock. Which is funny, because plenty of others have told me to do whatever I can to avoid it.

*

As I near West Helena, nearly everyone I speak with shares an anecdote to illustrate why the downtrodden town is a bad place to travel afoot. I get private messages on my social media insisting I change course. Concerned folks use words like *crackheads*, *thugs*, and *desperation* to get my attention. It works. "You need a weapon!" a man says to me while we wait together at a stoplight. "You got a gun on you?" He calls me a fool when I tell him no.

*

Once in the town limits, I notice I'm walking faster than usual. Hurrying. Hopping busted curbs to find the shortest route to the bridge. The sky darkens. Thunder is constant. Unwanted fear has a grip on me and I let it take control. I walk past decrepit houses and can't tell if folks are still living in them. Occasionally, a car slows and dark-skinned people look intently at me. I tense up. Feel out of place. Like I don't belong. I wish there was another way to cross the Mississippi. I consider backtracking to find one.

A Black man about my age rolls up on an old mountain bike. Asks what I'm doing. Our exchange is typical: I explain my journey, then he shares a bit about himself. Conversation shifts to the ominous weather. We both look skyward. "You probably want to find some cover before too long," he says. "We're definitely getting a storm later. Be safe out here. I'll be praying for you."

As he rides away, I exhale the fearful fumes from my belly. I shake my head vigorously and remember my daily intention. Project kindness, receive kindness. The energy I give is the energy I get. I park LB beside a dirt lot gas station and close my eyes. I shift my intentional output from fear to love. This choice changes how I see the world around me.

*

My phone rings. It's Jeff. He's minutes away. I text him a pin and he scoops me up. Little Buddy takes his second ride atop Jeff's truck as we bridge the Big Muddy. Jeff drops me on the shoulder just beyond a sign welcoming us to Mississippi. I'm five states down and across the nation's dividing line.

9

To give no trust
is to get no trust.

- Lao Tzu
Tao Te Ching, translated by Ursula K. Le Guin

Day 151

I FIRST NOTICE THE SHOULDER, or more accurately, the absence of one. A solid white line divides the road from a drop-off into thick weeds and I'm forced to push Little Buddy down the middle of the westbound lane. Thankfully there's only a car every few minutes, so I have plenty of time to scoot to the side when it passes. Still, every vehicle is a closer call than usual.

I take a break at Jordan's Kwik Stop in Lula. Patrons take a closer look at LB and want to know about the No Baby sign. A few shake their heads, laughing while telling me I've lost my mind. One man buys me a bag of fried chicken while others offer snacks and money. "You're doing a cool thing that not many folks do," the man says. "And I appreciate that." These first Mississippi locals live up to their state's nickname—The Hospitality State.

*

I make it to the visitor center just as the first rain drops fall. Darryl, the security guard, tells me I'd better get comfortable. "This storm ain't going anywhere," he says. "Best to wait it out. Where you planning to end this walk?" I tell him North Carolina and my words surprise me because I really don't have a definitive finish line plan. "Oh yeah?" he says. "I spent some time there. Joined the Marines in 1966 and went straight to Camp Lejeune. Had a buddy who was a recruiter. Said enlisting would keep me from being a tunnel rat." Darryl went to Vietnam, but spent his tour pulling guard duty at the company headquarters. "They said I was too small for the jungle," he says. "During basic the DIs would separate the fatbodies from small fellers like me. They'd give the smalls half the food from the big guys' plates. Thin them out while fattening us up. I didn't mind that one bit."

In eight weeks of bootcamp, Darryl's weight jumped from 94 to 139. But even after gaining 45 pounds, he still fell in the *smalls* category. Which, he claims, kept him from being a grunt. "Forty percent of my bootcamp platoon was killed in Vietnam," he says. "A handful were left unaccounted for. I lucked out."

After his tour in Southeast Asia, Darryl was stationed in Vieques, a small island off the eastern coast of Puerto Rico, where native inhabitants were displaced to make room for an ammunition depot. As his discharge date neared, the Marines tried to get him to re-up. Offered him $5,000 and an immediate bump in rank. When he declined, the offer grew sweeter. Five grand and a guaranteed spot at Officer's Candidate School. "But I knew better," he says. "I beat the system once, but if I took the bait I'd go straight into the dagum mess. So I said no."

*

Darryl and I sit on top of a table and watch as lightning attacks the distant skies. The Mississippi flag whips behind him as he makes a joke about needing popcorn for the show. Mississippi's state flag is the last to include the Confederate stars and bars, a symbol I associate with white supremacy, racism, and the current presidential administration.

Darryl excuses himself, then returns with a state map and a yellow highlighter. He marks a couple possible eastbound routes toward Sardis. When the storm reaches us, the rain comes down like a hammer. Drops explode like grapes. Together we watch the steel clouds twist into each other. "Sure is pretty, ain't it?" he says. A break in the storm paints the sky a cotton candy glow. Like a deep space nebula. "You're welcome to stay here for the night," Darryl says. "As long as you don't set up a tent, you can stay as long as you want."

When Darryl returns inside, I change out of my walking clothes and get comfortable under the awning on the back side of the building. The horizontal rain and tree-bending wind turn the parking lot into a boiling lake as the storm creeps across the basin. Constant light flashes and thunder pounds with each bolt. I sit next to LB and witness the chaos. I barely missed being out in the thick of this madness. The dagum mess.

*

A man comes around the corner and says hello like he knows me. "Officer Darryl just told me your story," he says. "I brought him this here Snickers bar to tell him thanks for what he does here, but he's diabetic so he told me to give it to you." I accept without hesitation. "Tornado warnings all over," the man says. "Good thing you found this place." He hands me his card. "Name's Taylor. I'm a preacher." He offers me a warm, safe place to stay the following night. I look up his town on Darryl's map. It sits along one of the alternate routes Darryl lined out. One I'm least likely to take. Taylor insists I give a shout if I get in a pinch. He'll come get me wherever I am. "And hey, Sardis isn't the most accommodating town, you know?" he urges. "You might want to rethink it." I look off into the dark sky and right then know for sure where I'll be heading tomorrow.

*

The storm continues as I settle into my nest, curling up to stay warm as the temperature plummets. The wind swirls, spraying me with sheets of rain even though I'm 20 feet under the roof. Every few minutes I douse myself with bug repellant to keep swarms of mosquitoes disinterested. Still, they bite through my clothes until everything itches.

All night long, travelers park in the adjacent lot for pit stops and power naps. Headlights jolt me awake on the regular. Eventually the rain stops and the bugs mellow and I actually get some shut eye. Until a voice stirs me awake and I look up to a tall man leaning directly over me. His silhouette is long against the fluorescent roof lights. He peers down at my bedroll. His wet leather boots are so close to my face I smell the caked mud. I spring up and bark. "What do you want, man?" A tense pause hangs between us. "Where's the bathroom?" he whispers. I let out a huff and rub my face. "Shit, man," I say, then point to the restroom sign lit up behind him.

Day 152

Today must be the hottest day yet. One hundred plus made more extreme by the pressing humidity. It's still morning when I take refuge from the savage sun in a tiny patch of Little Buddy's shade. "Thanks, man. You're a lifesaver," I say. The pounding of my racing heart doesn't slow. I'm definitely dehydrated even though I've been regularly chugging water.

Highway 315 turns hilly. The climbs grow long and sustained. I'm fully exposed. And though I'm drinking a lot of water, I can't keep up with my body's needs. And worst of all, I'm not peeing. All the water I've consumed sloshes in my belly, which makes it clear that my intake isn't the problem. It's my body's lack of salt. If I learned one thing as an ultramarathoner, it's that drinking water must include regular salt intake, too. Electrolytes. Without additional salts, the body's natural sodium stores get diluted, which stops water from bring absorbed into the bloodstream. So no matter how much water you drink, you remain dehydrated.

I desperately need chips or salted nuts or Gatorade or something. But I'm low on provisions and have none of these things in Little Buddy's store. I press on and hope I'm able to replenish before I my body shuts down.

*

With my belly bloated with water, I find myself slipping out of consciousness. Not sleepwalking like so many times before, more like severe lightheadedness and hints of fainting. I see the landscape through a straw as my thoughts press through the same narrow space.

There's a large sign in the distance. Its shade is enough to keep me trudging forward. I march on, focusing on my breathing. I take a step and breathe in. Take another step and breathe out. Repeat. One step, breathe in. Another step, breathe out. I relax my chest and shoulders. Step, breathe in. Step, breathe out. I accept my pace. My snail's slowness. Step, breathe. Step, breathe. I imagine I'm on the final stretch toward the summit of Everest. I'm in the death zone. Where oxygen is insufficient to sustain human life. The only reason I don't pass out is because I choose not to. I step, breathe in. Step, breathe out.

*

I make it to the sign. It's a volunteer firehouse. I park LB in a sliver of shade and lay down on the blacktop. The pavement is gloriously cool. I know my symptoms: clammy skin, no sweat, near confusion. The first stages of heat stroke. I maintain my intentional deep breathing and busy my mind with memories of a podcast about the benefits of ice baths. With my cheek on the rough ground, I imagine submerging my body in icy cold water. I imagine the cool Atlantic. I imagine finishing my walk and feeling the refreshing water overtake me as salt water drips from my beard. I taste it on my tongue. My lips. I feel the effects of the freezing water on my toes, my balls, my chest, my nose. I visualize this exhilaration while my heart pounds through my ears.

At some point I lose consciousness. No idea for how long. But when I come to, the shade has shifted and I'm soaking wet. The slight breeze feels nice on my damp clothing. I can finally

227

think straight. LB also sits in a solar laser beam and I wonder if my cans of Hormel chili are compromised. Doesn't heat cause botulism? I wonder if my wedge of cheese is now liquid. I debate camping here. Then I stand up and do a quick physical inventory. "OK. I think I'm good. But that shit was close," I say. I refill my belly with water and focus on making it to Sardis before I pass out again. I still desperately need salts. I return to the side of the highway, stumbling while LB rolls true, holding me upright.

*

The shirtless and hatless cyclist is a mirage. A mirage that talks. Says his name is Chris. He's riding from Florida to the Grand Canyon. Sweat cascades off his hairy shoulders and down his greasy chest. "I can't walk more than a half mile without my knee filling up with fluid.," he says as he gives me a once-over. "But I can pedal this thing all goddamned day." He tells me there are more hills ahead. Compares them to mountains back east. "Rolling ones, you know, like the Appa...the Ada...Acha...Oh shit man, you know what I fucking mean." He presses his arms against the handlebars, shakes his head and tells me I need to be extra careful in Sardis. I ask why. "Dude!" he says. "It's all Black people!" I shrug. Tell him so what. "Yeah, well..." he stammers. "I'm just saying, you know? Some places you just gotta be extra careful." I shake my head and walk away.

*

I enter the Sardis town limits. The long stretch of exposed road gives way to canopied and shady sections past single-wide trailer homes and long dirt driveways. I pass a bunch of Black children playing ball in a yard. They stop to watch me pass. I wave. "What's your name?" one shouts. "You really got no baby in there?" asks another. A toddler in a diaper points at me. Looks at the other kids. "No baby!" I holler back, and they go back to playing.

Minutes later, a man flies past me on an ATV quad, looks over his shoulder and does a skidding U-turn across the lanes before pulling up alongside me. His name is Darren. "My cousins back there said some guy was walking on the side of the road. I figured you must be somebody famous." I assure him I am not. "Well, no matter what, I definitely want to remember this moment." Darren pulls out his phone and asks for a selfie. We take one with my camera, too.

Darren says this kind of heat is normal, the beginning of what's to come. He asks if I need money. Or water. Or food. "Because I can go get you some," he says. I assure him I'll restock a couple miles ahead in Sardis. We talk sports. He wants to know who my favorite football team is. I tell him I'm not much of a fan, but as a kid I liked the Cowboys. His jaw drops. "Oh hell no!" he says. "Tennessee Titans right here!" he pounds his chest. "I'm going to need to rethink my first impression of you!"

Darren asks if I think LeBron is going to get another ring. "Nope," I say. "Dub City this year!" Darren laughs and shakes his head. "Man! You're crazy!" he says. "And not just because you're out here doing this!"

*

After 36 miles I reach Sardis. My hotel sits perfectly close to a barbecue truck and I manage to shuffle to it with great effort. The wait is ridiculously long, nearly an hour, but the crowd of waiting customers validates my decision for this over a bag of Chinese take-out. Still, I'm famished, and pining for my double order of beef ribs and fried chicken with sides of mashed potatoes and coleslaw. When I do finally get my feast back to the hotel room, I eat with abandon and taste nothing. Afterwards I feel sick. I consider making myself vomit but decide against it. I put my trust in the high calorie and salt medicine. That this saucy, gluttonous feast will replenish my sodium reserves for another superhot day tomorrow. I know that eventually I'll acclimate to this heat. Or, at least I hope I will.

Before turning in, I walk across the street to a busy mini mart. I'm the only white guy in the place. I purchase a few bags of chili cheese Fritos, some generic pretzels, four bottles of Gatorade, a few Snickers bars, and two ice cream sandwiches because I'm already hungry again. The checker looks me square in my bloodshot eyes and wishes me a blessed evening. I wish him the same. He smiles and says, "Next!"

Day 153

I reach downtown Oxford after a big week in extreme conditions. I take a couple off days during which I rest up, do actual laundry, and eat nonstop. A local pizza place within walking distance of my hotel is decorated with imagery of a red-hatted, cross-legged Confederate soldier leaning on a cane. This decor pays homage to Colonel Reb, a Civil War caricature who, until 2010, was Ole Miss's beloved mascot. The pizzeria advocates for his reinstatement by posting links and placing literature for the foundation fighting for his return.

Day 156

As I leave town, I take a shortcut through old Oxford neighborhoods. I pass elegant mansions with enormous yards as I navigate my way back to Highway 30. Shiny Teslas and other high-end vehicles drive past me, rubbernecking. I'm out of place, and I figure it's only a matter of time before someone calls 911.

My pace overtakes two white haired women wearing matching blue windbreakers. They could be sisters. I say good morning. "Is there a child in there?" one asks about Little Buddy. I say no, and tell them what I am doing. "Well then…bless your heart," one says. The other echoes her sentiment. Having lived in North Carolina for while now, I know darn well that *Bless your heart* sometimes means, *Poor thing can't help but be dumb*. Words I can't rightfully dispute.

*

Away from the antebellum neighborhood and finally on a far reach of town, a police cruiser stops alongside me. Officer Hollowell introduces himself, cuts his engine, and gets out. His thumbs hook in his pockets as he asks, "Is there anything our department can do for you?" I shake my head and tell him I'm all set. His subsequent interest seems to be more his own than police business. "So what's the scariest thing you've experienced out there?" he asks. Though this common question may come from a place of genuine human curiosity, I often wonder if folks assume this sort of journey goes hand-in-hand with peril. Even I find it hard to imagine walking a couple thousand miles without a few sketchy anecdotes to show for it. But fact is, I have none. Not yet, anyhow. Which always makes me preface my response with, "I'm sorry."

I answer Officer Hollowell's question after taking liberty to reword it a bit. "I've been lucky so far," I say. "Haven't dealt with anything too hairy. But the most unexpected detail of this journey has been the people. Every day a handful of superkind folks come out of the woodwork to do nice things." I can't see Hollowell's eyes behind his dark glasses, but I can tell he's dissatisfied. Or, at the very least, in disbelief.

"OK then," he says. "What about any weird or strange things you've found along the way? You got any stories about *that*?" I mentally scroll through the inventory of items I've found. All the coins, arrowheads, cell phones, poker chips, cowboy boots, doll parts, spoons, dead things, and so much more. "Well," I say, "this may be mildly inappropriate but...," His raised eyebrows give me permission to continue and he leans in. "On a regular basis I find...well...adult items." Hollowell stops chewing his gum. "Like, dildos," I say. "In fact, four so far." Hollowell says nothing and I continue. "It's like I'm following a trail of rubber penises across America." Officer Hollowell bursts out laughing then composes himself. "Here," I say. "I'll show you." I pull out my phone and scroll to an image of the last one I encountered in Coffee City, Texas. "This one was right there on the shoulder like someone had chucked it out their car window." I turn my phone to face him. He lowers his sunglasses. "Well I'll be," he says. "I definitely didn't expect that to be your answer."

*

East of Oxford there are more confederate flags than I've seen this entire trip. One house on the opposite side of the road has five. Two on flagpoles, two draped over porch rails, and one planted on a tall branch in the back of a rusting truck.

In the center of the yard is a raised flower garden. Bright purple petals on tall stems sway in the warm breeze. A few nearby pots with clusters of spring colors and tall stalks. A man in coveralls works under the hood of a late model Ford pickup. I focus my attention on him, ready to offer a greeting when he sees me. But he pays me no mind. I pass without acknowledgment.

*

It's pushing 100°F again. And though I'm fresh off a rest day, I remain unrecovered. My legs ache. My low back hurts to touch. The yellow corns that recently developed between my toes stab like needles. The chafing in my butt crack seeps blood. I am exhausted. And I'm pretty sure I won't be 100% again until this journey is complete.

My thoughts echo my physical state. All is mussed up and unclear, like my mind's eye has a cataract. My brain is a bowl of thick soup. With effort I drag wet air into and out of my lungs. My muggy shorts sag like a full diaper.

The road's backdrop is creeping kudzu. Invasive vines overtake entire trees and look like massive mittens. For a moment I am disoriented, lost in thought with memories of other lush, labyrinthine places. This could be Ireland, Laos, China, North Carolina. This could be anywhere. A flood of faraway worlds rushes into my consciousness. I'm dreamwalking. Suddenly on a jam-packed bus in Southeast Asia. Sitting three to a seat for the entire day's ride, tightly pressed shoulder-to-shoulder and sandwiched between two toothless old women. I'm trapped by the extra riders crammed in folding chairs down the center aisle while a river of unknown liquid sloshes over my sandals. A mounted television churns one solitary music video on loop. Its chorus, "Happy ya ya ya, happy ye ye ye," is meant to lift spirits but serves only to brainwash passengers who have nowhere else to put their attention. I'm startled by the toppling of the live pigs in the hold below. Muffled squeals every time the bus makes a turn. On every mountain curve I imagine the driver missing a cue and losing control—all of us hurling over the cliff, plummeting down the rocky chasm like a body-filled bullet. I lean toward Kent, my travel buddy, squashed one row ahead. He's scowling. I tap his shoulder. "Don't worry," I say. "It's only a six-hour ride." He shows me his teeth.

The straining engine of a passing car snaps me out of my reverie. I am suddenly back in Mississippi.

*

The insufferable heat mixed with my accruing exhaustion makes this stretch a trying one. All I want right now is to get my miles in so I can sleep again. But the highway's nonexistent shoulders and surprised drivers make it impossible to find a groove. When I'm not fully alert, not fully engaged in my surroundings, I accidentally play chicken with vehicles. I think back to Chester, the cyclist I met in Duncan, Arizona. His comment about me being flattened into a grease spot. At any second, this could become my reality. Me and LB, splattered amongst roadside vines and racist flags, never to be seen again.

Being struck by a vehicle is a valid fear, one I carry with me at all times. I step over a pile of mangled animal flesh and imagine how my body would look if I were struck at 70 mph. The word *liquify* pops into my head and I spell it out loud to the dense jungle until the letters sound like gibberish. "El, i, cue, u, i, ef, wye!" I shout. "Liquify. Liquify. LICK—WUH—FYEEEEE!" I wonder if I'll feel pain as my internal organs and bones turn to jelly. Maybe getting blasted by a high-speed truck is like jumping out of a skyscraper window? Your heart stops before impact. Before any pain is registered. But who could ever know this? Maybe we tell ourselves such stories to make dying easier?

But more than being afraid of pain, I'm afraid of being forgotten. Which is funny, because when I try to think of who I'd want to remember me, I think of the children I don't have. The older I get without kids of my own, the more I've discarded the personal artifacts I figured I'd someday pass down. Yearbooks, my varsity jacket, military memorabilia, love letters, trophies, commendations, photo albums. You name it. It's trendy to lighten the load, isn't it? To make everything except me disappear? "L-I-Q-U-I-F-Y," I sing. "L-I-Q-U-I-F-Y! Give me a LICK! Give me a WUH! Give me a FYE! LIQUIFY! FUCK YEAH!"

*

The echo of my madness rings in my ears as a flatbed truck stops on the opposite side of the road. A man gets out. Saunters across the street like a cowboy in a standoff. I try to read his body language to decipher his intentions. But I can't make it out. When he doesn't mirror my extra-earnest greeting, my body shifts into fight or flee. His voice is slow and deep. Calculated. His sullen eyes angled like his down-turned mouth. "Was out delivering a load of building materials," he snorts. "Wondering what the hell you're doing out here." The way he says *out here* makes me feel like an intruder. I tell him what I tell everyone and he glares at me. He slowly reaches into his back pocket and removes a tattered leather wallet. "I'd like to give you something," he says. He pulls out a crisp hundred dollar bill and hands it to me. "I figure you got a reason for doing this. And son, I hope this helps." I'm dumbfounded. He nods when I tell him thanks. "Can I at least give you a hug?" I ask, and immediately wish I hadn't. Because he doesn't budge. I figure he's regretting the gift. But he shifts his weight and throws his arms in the air. "Ha. Yeah, sure. Come on with it." He widens his arms and I squeeze him. He squeezes back. "Be careful out here," he says. "These truckers aren't paying no attention. It gets narrower ahead. So use that side shoulder even though it ain't much of one. Look out for yourself, you hear?"

I notice a blurry tattoo on his arm and ask about it. "I did it myself when I was fourteen," he says. "Sewing needles and ink. Meant to be a heart with the word *love* right here in the center." His giant fingers pass over the bleeding letters inked into his arm. "I didn't even know what love was back then. Not sure I do now, even." I ask if I can photograph it. He holds it out. "Anyone ever taken a picture of it before?" I ask. "Once," he says. "Back when the law thought it might be necessary to note my identifying features." He winks, returns to his truck, and drives away.

Day 157

Dusty, my good friend in Sacramento, links me up with his aunt and uncle, Ann and Scott, who live near my route through northern Mississippi. Back when I was broken down in Blythe, California, Dusty connected me with his dad, Dan, who took me out for a big breakfast and lifted my spirits. Now Scott, Dan's brother, retrieves me from the roadside, loads Little Buddy into the bed of his truck, and puts me up in a spare bedroom. I fill my belly with Ann's spaghetti and too much garlic bread. The house, though smoker-friendly and crowded with stacked boxes, is a welcome change from stale hotels. I don't even mind when I have to flick a couple silverfish and a baby cockroach from my bedsheets. The mattress is blissfully soft and I'm too tired to worry about bugs that don't bite.

Day 158

After hearing my horror stories about fast trucks and narrow shoulders, Scott recommends I walk the Natchez Trace into Alabama. As a national parkway, it doesn't allow commercial vehicles and is likely to have fewer motorists than a proper highway. The first sign I see on the Trace is promising—it asks drivers to make way for cyclists. Finally I'll have some breathing room.

After a couple hours, I across the Alabama state line and enter the seventh state of the walk. Blue sky reflects in my sunglasses as I make a video for my social media. I post it with the headline, "Mississippi…check!" and watch as comments trickle in. A cross-country cyclist I met in Arkansas writes, "Maaaan ive been in texas for what feels like forever and here you are passin through states like its nuthin! Glad your gettin thru safely brutha." Texas seems like forever ago. Suddenly I'm flying.

*

Minutes into Alabama, I have to run, nearly dive, to get me and Little Buddy clear of a minivan that's gunning for us. After it passes, it comes to a skidding stop, then slowly reverses, creeping back to where I'm standing in the tall grass, crushing Little Buddy's bar in my fists. I figure the driver is going to apologize. So I engage LB's parking brake and lightheartedly approach the open passenger window. "Man oh man!" I say with a nervous laugh. "My life just flashed before my eyes!" I expect the driver, a man with a dirty ball cap and aviator glasses, to follow suit. To tell me he feels bad for not paying attention to the road. I'm ready to accept his apology. Because shit happens. But the man mutters words I can't make out. So I lean in closer to the window as he glares out the windshield with his hands flat on his lap. Short bursts of incoherent mumblings drop from his wet lips. My gut tells me to back off, but I don't. I decipher one marbled question, "Thefuckyoudoinhere?" as his right hand reaches under a pile of fast foot wrappers on the passenger seat. I expect a gun. But it's a pack of smokes. He finally turns his face to meet mine. "Yagotalighter?" he growls as he puts a cigarette between his yellowing teeth. When I say no, he throws a handful of food litter in my direction and barks something incomprehensible. I back up with my hands in front of me, wish the man good day, then return to LB. The minivan just sits there. Isn't until I've walked a good quarter mile that his tires chirp and kick up a poof of dust. Space grows between us, but something tells me I haven't seen the last of him.

*

For the next hour, every car that approaches from behind is an enemy. I pull LB onto the minuscule shoulder, far enough away to thwart any attempt to swipe us. Drivers must think I'm some kind of nut job as I hurl myself into the shrubbery as they pass. But I know, *I just know,* this guy's coming back.

When I see a van recklessly nearing, and hear the distant scream of a four-banger pushed to the limit, I know it's him. But this time I'm ready, far enough from his trajectory to be out of immediate danger. As he blazes past, he leans out the driver's side and points at me, laughing like a maniac. Then bright red lights as he hits the brakes and flips a U for a third pass. The van bounces side to side as he evens the wheel. I am in his sights. I race further into the roadside gully and hope it is too angled for his car to take without rolling. He must notice this too, because the van keeps a safe distance from where I stand in wait. I look for places to take cover if need be. This time he slows to pass, reaches across the passenger seat with his hand in the shape of a gun, and pulls the trigger as he streaks by. His loud cackling voice going quiet as the van races away.

Before he's out of sight I'm dialing 911. I tell the operator I'm afraid for my life. She asks me to describe the car. "Did you catch the make or model? The color?" But it all happened so fast. I tell her I'm terrible with cars anyhow. She understands. "What about the driver? Can you describe him?" I say he was white. Maybe middle-aged. Had facial hair. Maybe wrinkles. Dark sunglasses. And as I'm talking into the phone, I realize I just described most of the men I've seen in the area. Shoot, I just described myself. She asks about his shirt, the car's tags, and any other identifying features I might remember. But I've got nothing. I keep looking behind me down the Trace, worried he'll return. "I'm getting off the road," I tell the dispatcher. She assures me they'll try and get someone out here as soon as possible. "But the Trace is managed by the National Park Service and not local authorities," she says. "So our officer is heading your way from our headquarters in Nashville, about three hours from your location."

*

I stop for a breather in a rest area and take an emotional inventory. My hands shake, my heart pumps hard, still full of adrenaline. I'm angry and scared, but mostly scared. I compose a text to Katie. "MF just tried to run me off the road," I write with shaky fingers. "Some kind of welcome to sweet home Alabama."

A beater truck rolls up and I'm on immediate guard. The driver, a large, bearded white guy wearing a green polo and a scarf around his neck, takes off his sunglasses. "Man, I thought that cart was a wheelchair! I'm Nathan. You alright?" I tell him about the near miss. "Fucking asshole," he says. "Sorry about that. Mind if I get out? Would be nice to stretch my legs a bit."

Nathan is a retired and disabled Army vet. Did multiple tours in the desert. He asks if I am a veteran. "Yep. Army, too," I say. "But I didn't deploy." I often feel bad around veterans who went to combat while I sat in an office pushing papers. I want to apologize for getting lucky. "Be happy you didn't go, brother," Nathan says. "Hey, you wanna get high?" I hate to tell him no, because getting stoned with him might be exactly what I need to stop my body from trembling. But I worry the cops may actually respond to my emergency call. Bad enough that I'm the guy on the roadside with a baby jogger, I don't want to be the *high* one, too. "Gonna have to pass, man," I say. He shrugs, then lights a joint and opens the side door. A large German shepherd is sleeping on the floor. It casually lifts its head. "This guy here's my service dog," Nathan says. "He's my best buddy. Keeps me from being depressed. He's nice, but he's not the petting type. Likes his alone time. Which makes us perfect together."

On the back seat of his van is a case of MREs. Nathan knows what I'm thinking. "They ain't like they used to be," he says. "No more hockey puck pork patties and all that shit." Nathan insists I take a couple for dinner tonight. Hands me a Menu 12, Penne with Vegetable Sausage, and a Menu 21, Asian Style Beef Strips With Vegetables. The slogan on the packaging says, "Warfighter Recommended, Warfighter Tested, Warfighter Approved." He also gives me a couple bottles of Gatorade. "Now go find yourself a place to hole up. Somewhere off the road. Fill your belly and get some rest. I'm not down with what just happened to you. I can't handle violence anymore. It causes too many flashbacks."

I take Nathan's advice and muscle LB off the highway, drag us though a stretch of forest, then pull onto an unpaved service road. I march for a mile before finding a spacious pullout at the top of an incline in view of the surrounding landscape. I set up camp. As the sun sets, I watch billowing clouds ripple in slow motion. There's not a hint of noise from the road. And no mosquitoes. I check my phone and am relieved to have no service.

*

I eat both packs of MREs. My favorite back in my day was Chicken a la King. A gooey mass of saturated chicken in beige gravy. I'd warm it under my armpit or between my legs before tearing off the tab to reveal a meal resembling dog food. Or vomit. Or dog vomit. It came with a tiny glass of Tabasco that I never used yet collected to give as gifts to civilian friends.

Five hours later I receive a call from an officer in the National Park police. "Calling to see if you're OK," a man says. "Where are you?" I tell the officer I've already set up camp illegally on the Trace and am hunkering down. "That dude is long gone," I say. "But thanks for reaching out anyhow."

Day 159

In the morning I'm still traumatized by yesterday's events. I walk uncomfortably on the slanted grass adjacent to the highway, against traffic, and eyeball every passing vehicle. I fantasize about being on a busy thoroughfare again. I imagine the loud and windy rush of busy traffic. Maybe the shoulder on the highway ahead will be wide and paved like it was in Texas. My dreaming passes the time.

The sky darkens and I make my poncho handy. Finally get off the Trace and join Highway 72. There's a proper shoulder, just as I hoped. I push LB with one hand and sing Bon Jovi's "Blaze of Glory" as rain starts to dump.

Trucks blast past like rockets. I press into the walls of wet air, put my chin out as each wave thrusts back my beard. The morning heat cooks steam from the puddled highway. A woman stops to give me water. Then two more people pull over to give me a bag of green apples. I find a pile of Barbie doll parts, the ceramic head of an angel, and an antenna flag with an image of Bear Bryant's houndstooth fedora. In Sheffield I pass a mural of one of Robert Crumb's cartoon characters with the caption, "Just Passin' Thru." I take a photo thinking it would be an appropriate design for another tattoo.

*

Thunder rattles windows. Cars shine afternoon high beams and slow their roll through temporary lakes. I take refuge and put my phone in a ziplock bag. I hop from overhang to overhang between cloudbursts, heading toward a bridge spanning the Tennessee River. I return to the road when the sky turns blue and pass 3614 Jackson Highway, the famous Muscle Shoals recording studio where pivotal albums were cut by the likes of the Rolling Stones, the Staple Singers, Bob Seger, Lynyrd Skynyrd, and others. It's a blink-and-miss-it sort of place. An unlikely brick box that changed the world with its definitive southern sound.

My plan is to cross the river ahead using the pedestrian path. A Sheffield police officer stops me as I'm strategizing my approach. The rain has turned to a sprinkle. I tell him I'm headed to the pedestrian crossing ahead. "No can do," he says. "That bridge doesn't go all the way across." He offers to get me to the other side. And since the drive-across bridge doesn't allow pedestrians, I have no alternative. But Little Buddy is too big for the cruiser's trunk so I begin the disassembling process. Just then a landscaping truck pulls up. "The Lawn Man" is printed on the truck's side. "Hey Tate!" the driver says to the cop. "Need a hand?" We load LB onto the truck's mower trailer. I engage LB's emergency brake and tell the Lawn Man that the brake lock is worn out. The cart may end up rolling around on the flatbed. "Nah. It'll be fine," the guy says. "But Tate, you'll have to give this guy a ride. My cab's full of junk." Tate nods, then tells me his front seat is too cluttered for a passenger and I'll have to ride in the back. Officer Tate opens the door for me, and in I go. The hard plastic seat is cold and uncomfortable. I don't want to touch anything. I wonder about the people who've been cooped up back here and try not to think about what's been hosed out of this temporary hold.

As we cross the bridge, I keep my eyes peeled on LB as he shimmies this way and that, bumping against tractors and weed whackers as the trailer jumps over the bridge's uneven seams. I fully expect him to launch from the rig and pull a header, exploding into a thousand pieces.

On the opposite side, the Lawn Man gives me a sticker for LB's side panel, and Tate wants a photo for the department's Facebook page. That done, the men start talking about somebody's barbecue and I no longer exist. I walk away, amazed by how efficiently things worked out. From no plan to success in a matter of minutes. Privilege comes in all forms.

Day 160

East of Center Star, a pickup pulls off the highway and comes to a gentle stop. The soft tap of the horn. It's two Black women. "We are sisters," one says. "This is Amena, like 'amen' with an A, and I'm Sadiqa, but most folks around here just call me Q." As we're talking, a black and yellow butterfly lands on my shoulder and fans its wings. "Oooh, that's beautiful!" Amena says. "Looks like it wants to come along." I tell her butterflies land on me all the time. Amena's eyes widen. "You realize that means something, don't you?" she says. "Oh yeah?" I say. "What's it mean?" Amena looks st Q. "Not sure," she says. "But it definitely means something."

"We're retired," Q says. "Now we're gardeners. We moved here from Chicago to be with our mother. She's ninety-seven. Want to see a video of her dancing?" Q scrolls through her phone. Finds the video and hits play. Their mom has some sweet moves.

Their family has lived in this area for multiple generations. Their grandfather was one of the first Black landowners in Center Star. He bought up parcels and eventually held more than 400 acres of land. "He employed the whole town," Q says. "Our family was like the Black Kennedys!"

Amena and Q give me some lunch money, take photos, and drive off, honking and waving in the rearview. A few hours later, they return. Seeing them again makes us laugh like old friends. "Talking this morning made our day," Amena says. "We couldn't stop thinking about you." I assure them the feeling is mutual. "What you are do doing here is so important," Q says, brushing the corners of her eye with the back of her finger. "I'm really curious how many people stop to talk with you?" I tell them probably five or six folks per day, on the average. "But I'm always amazed folks take time to talk with a complete stranger," I say. "Makes me wonder if I'd do the same." Q assures me it's all about energy. "You're vulnerable out here," she says. "But you're not putting off a fearful vibe. Fear pushes people away." Her sister nods. "Yep," she says. "It's true. Kindness is magnetic. And with all that's going on in the world, we need do more of it."

*

A five-minute conversation with a half-dozen people per day is not the same as having a deep connection with one person. The novelty of the moment is certainly a factor. But it also requires trust, openness, and vulnerability.

I crave these real connections. They exist in my nonwalking life, but they are few. I can count on one hand the number of people with whom I am my fullest and truest self. For everyone else I shapeshift. Social transformation has been a theme of my life, and finally, at age 46, I've reached a threshold. I'm tired of being a version of myself. I want to be publicly whole.

The roadside has become a place for me to experiment with this new way of moving through the world. This wasn't part of the plan, but it's how things are shaking out. And with nonstop validation, day after day, I'm finally starting to believe that all my past efforts to turn heads have been unnecessary. The highs of life come from truly seeing someone, and from being seen. The walk may be what's finally teaching me this, but it isn't a necessary factor for me to put the lesson into practice.

Day 161

Back on the road I consider where to stop tonight. I could make it all the way to Huntsville, but I don't want to. Huntsville means a hotel and I'm sick of hotels. I want to camp. During a late afternoon rest break and under a sky of mountainous clouds, I follow a winding dirt road to a forested nook bordering a farm field, away from the sound of traffic. I wander the area and study the ground trying to find a good spot. I'm distracted by old perfume bottles and arrowhead chips. Seems I stumbled upon a Native American tool procurement area or trash midden. Maybe both. I quickly set up camp, then take advantage of the low light and spend the evening treasure hunting until my neck hurts from staring down. The cumulus skies are an orange and pink heaven. The storm changes course.

*

At the trip's outset I figured I'd end in Maine. But since my injury delay messed with the timeline, my plan A shifted. Back in Texas, I settled on the idea of ending in North Carolina, but that idea never fired me up. Tonight, as I sit outside my tent and consider my next few days of walking, I learn about Lee Highway, one of America's original national auto trails. A satellite view on my phone shows more shoulder than I've had in a while. I can pick it up in Tennessee and follow it straight across Virginia. And shoot, if I'm going to go that far north, I may as well head for a finish spot as iconic as my starting line. LA to New York—that's got a nice ring to it.

I lock in. Stop researching and write a post on social media. "Starting tomorrow I'm heading north," I say. "Taking Lee Highway from Huntsville en route to New York City." Finally, an ending that feels right.

Day 162

I break camp before sunrise to avoid the chance of an awkward encounter with a farm worker. Frogs are still chatting, the dark air already hinting to the day's scorch. A slight breeze gives voice to the trees. More rain is in the forecast but I aim to beat it.

The pinnacle of a ridge affords a view of the city to come. In the distance I see mountains, the first bit of jutting geography since New Mexico. Soon I'll be in the thick of it, and that thought alone makes it easier to swallow the subsequent pile of strip malls and thick traffic made exponentially dangerous by an unsurprisingly minuscule shoulder.

At an extra-wide intersection without a crosswalk, I wait for the light to turn green. Then I run across it, hoping LB's wobbly front wheels don't lock up like they sometimes do when increasing speed. Halfway across, a guy in a truck gives me an encouraging beep and thumbs up. I'm happy to be noticed.

Minutes later, the same honking guy has turned back and pulls off the road next to me. The driver is a young Latinx man wearing a Pink Floyd shirt. His name is Zayas. He hands me a bag. Three plums and a peach. "I live right over there and these are fresh from the orchard," he says. "I'm happy to run home and get you more. Or money? You need some money?" I tell Zayas I'm good. The fruit is just right. "I'm a cyclist," he says. "I've got a buddy who rode his bike across the country. But I can't imagine walking it. That's nuts. But I also know a guy who runs ultras, so I have a sense of what you're up against." I tell Zayas most of the time I feel like I'm witnessing someone else's journey. Looking at a map freaks me out. Zayas says it's important that our own life occasionally surprises us. He pulls out his phone and asks if I'd mind doing a Facebook Live video. I agree to it, self-consciously wave at his camera while he introduces me to his social media followers. Hours later in the hotel, I'm still receiving encouraging messages from Zayas's social media community. The rallying support may be virtual, but it matters.

Day 164

I leave Huntsville on Highway 72 heading toward the Tennessee border. Just beyond the congestion of town, a car stops ahead in the center median. Just sits there. When I get close, a guy steps out holding two waters. "Hi Tom!" he hollers. "I watched you on *What Dink Says!*" He's referring to the live video show I did yesterday with the owner of the Fleet Feet store in Huntsville. I stopped in the shop to say hello to Dink and his wife Suzanne, colleagues from my days in the run industry.

The man hands me the waters and says he took note of the exit plan I mentioned on the show. His name is James. "Actually, people call me Big Game James," he says. "Probably because I work multiple jobs and make a lot of money." James is a waiter at a diner, an occasional chef, and a handyman. "I'm on my way to the Unclaimed Baggage Center," he says. "Place where you buy stuff people never claimed at airports around the world. Maybe find some things to resell. I'm always hustling."

James is getting ready for a 10-mile footrace. His longest ever. "I worked my way up through shorter distances and now I'm up to this," he says. "Probably will do a half after that. Who knows, maybe someday I'll run the Huntsville Marathon, too." Before I leave, James sneaks in an awkward hug that I don't see coming. "I'm happy I found you," he says during our embrace. "Wish me luck at the baggage store!"

*

In Scottsboro, I walk beneath an osprey nest atop a telephone pole. Nestlings chirp as a parent returns with a fish in its talon, then flies away to repeat the process.

The road splits at Mud Creek, a branch of Lake Guntersville, and Little Buddy and I dodge a massacre of turtles. These massive animals seem to have been pressurized before impact. Pieces and parts of their shells and limbs scatter the highway. Bright red blobs of brawny mush. There is no stink of death. Not yet, anyhow. Maybe they were all alive an hour ago. I wonder if dead animals have ghosts. If so, will these turtles forever haunt this section of the highway?

*

I set a stealth camp at a construction dump and take a half hour to compose a detailed text to Katie. I share details of the past few days, the people and places. I write and rewrite what's on my mind, posing lofty questions for which I seek answers. After I hit send, my latent frustration with our situation reignites. I desperately want her to share my excitement and curiosity. I want her to validate all I've done. And yet I'm never satisfied by her words. And though I project my dissatisfaction onto her, I know she's not the problem. It's me. I should be able to validate myself. I should be able to say, *You're doing great, Tom! You're killing it!* But my awareness of this fact doesn't change things. If anything, it just makes me even more frustrated.

*

Lying in my tent surrounded by piles of concrete blocks, spent blacktop, loads of gravel, and tar-caked plastic buckets, I toss my phone toward my feet and scream until tears wet my face. Until my face boils red and my abs grow sore. I howl empty echoes. I long for somewhere else. I miss my past. I miss the less examined version of myself. I want to stop thinking.

Through clouded eyes I swipe through hundreds of photos in an attempt to feel something. But all I muster is emptiness. All this fleeting contact with other humans has made me desperate for something substantial. I take note of my need to truly love myself but promptly disregard it. Because, how do I do this? And especially now? I scream some more and beg animals to scream back. A coyote or an owl or whatever. I need something to prove that I am not alone. But there's nothing. Just me and this brutal quiet.

Day 165

I wake to singing birds and a dull glow illuminating the tent. I feel different. Lighter. Like something has left me. Like maybe I let something go.

I unzip a stretch of the flap door to allow in some fresh air. I peek my head outside. The morning fog is thick cotton. I break camp and get back on the road following the Trail of Tears Corridor. For the past seven days and 152 miles, Neil Young's song "Alabama" has been stuck in my head: "A wheel in the ditch and and a wheel on the track." I replace it with Arrested Development's "Tennessee" as I cross another border. I enter this new state with budding energy. My due east path has started to shoot north. Every step bringing me closer to something I'm calling the end. But for now, "Tennessee, Tennessee," making it impossible not to dance a little bit.

10

You can't hear birdsong
through the hum of an air conditioner.

- Scott Larson
Notes From the Colorado Trail

Day 165

AFTER WALKING 32 MILES, I reach a hotel in Kimball, Tennessee. There aren't many options for dinner, so I choose Shoney's. Never been there, but figure it's probably like Denny's. Average is average.

The restaurant is big. Like they're used to large crowds. With the exception of one occupied table, however, it's empty. I take a seat and order the salad bar. I pile lettuce and spinach on my plate. Sliced red peppers, limp beets, leathery criminis. A few scoops of black olives and bacon bits. As I head to the dressing section, a hint of movement on my plate catches my attention. I pull the salad in for a closer look. As if on cue, a medium-sized cockroach crawls out from a wrinkled crevasse of wilting romaine. "You gotta be fucking kidding me," I say as I tilt the dish to a different angle, hoping I'm imagining things. I'm not. I walk over to my server who's chatting with a coworker. She seems surprised by the role reversal. "Pardon me," I say. "Just thought I'd show you this." I point to the bug. She and her colleague cover their mouths with their hands. "And if there's one, there's more," I say. "I'm sorry, but I can't eat here." I set the plate down and walk out the door.

*

There's one other dining option across the street. A Waffle House. I'm warmly greeted upon entry and tell Amber, my server, the roach salad story. As she shows me to my seat, I warn her about my appetite and explain why it's bottomless. She tells her coworkers about me and they gather around as I share anecdotes about my journey. I tell them about Art and Lion and others whose paths I've crossed. Jennifer, the manager, asks if she can buy my dinner. "I just got a $33 tip and I'd like to pay it forward," she says. I accept, but then apologize for having ordered so much food—an All Star Special with eggs over easy, crunchy bacon, an extra side of hash browns, and a signature waffle with a la carte sausage links. Jennifer waves it off as Amber hands her my ticket. "Please eat up," she says. "I'm not even worried about that. All of us are grateful for that roach."

Day 166

By midday I'm nearly maxed out. My body is used to the heat, but the Appalachian foothills add a new challenge. I climb nonstop as Highway 41 grows lush and hilly toward Chattanooga. My water stash drains quicker than usual and I take breaks in the infrequent patches of shade. When I enter the twisting and blind curving road up Lookout Mountain, the shoulder narrows to nothing and it's quickly obvious a different approach would have been safer. This byway is evidently a popular commuter route and I've hit it smack dab in the middle of rush hour. Drivers hurriedly navigate hairpins as they race to get home. None are ready for a human pushing a double-wide baby jogger. Cars lay on their horns in anger and fear as they miss me by inches. But there's nothing I can do. I've committed to it. I just need to keep grinding so I might hurry up and put this godforsaken mountain road behind me. I try to make myself conspicuous and predictable, but cars are herky jerky as they pass.

When a police cruiser slows with lights flashing, I'm overcome with relief. The smiling cop rolls down the passenger side window. "Hey. Want a ride?" he says. "Or would you prefer to continue risking your life?" He then instructs me to walk another 50 meters east then move into the pullout. There I disassemble LB and load him into the cruiser's back hatch. I tell the cop I never take rides unless safety deems it necessary. "I'd say this is one of those times," he snickers.

Minutes later we're off the mountain. He parks downtown near the Tennessee River and cuts the engine. He opens the center console and hands me one of his old shoulder patches. City of Chattanooga Police, 1852. An image of a cannon, the river, and the city skyline. "We don't usually give these to civilians, but you're doing something special here." I show him a photo of Officer Bencomo from back in Sanderson, Texas, who also gave me a patch. "The Cactus Capital of Texas," he reads. We shake hands and he finally introduces himself. "I'm Taylor," he says, pointing to his name badge. Says that someday he hopes to do the Appalachian Trail or the PCT. "Life's too short," I say. "Don't wait a quarter century to make it happen."

Day 167

As I'm getting ready to hit the road again, I realize I left my floppy hat in the back of Officer Taylor's cruiser. I don't have his direct contact information, so I get on the Chattanooga Police Department's Facebook page and mention the missing hat. Meredith, a long-ago running buddy who lives in Texas, sees my comment and asks her friend, Fred, an ex-Chattanooga police chief now living in Colorado, if he can help. Fred tags Elisa, the Chattanooga PD's communication coordinator, who says she'll get in touch with Officer Taylor. Meanwhile, I'm trucking hatless along the roadside, getting further from Chattanooga as the degrees of separation between people grow smaller. In this heat, my LA ball cap is good for nothing.

*

While I'm taking a break just off the shoulder, a car pulls from the road and flashes its hazards. The driver, Eric, approaches. "Oh man, I totally get what you're doing," he says. "What do you need? How can I be of assistance?" I tell Eric about the hat fiasco. "Oh, you definitely need a hat today. I'm going to get you a new one." Eric hits a Walmart, buys six options, finds me again and tells me to choose. My relief is immediate. I send Elisa a message asking her to forget about the hat. She texts back, "It's too late. Taylor's out looking for you. Where are you?" I do my best to provide my exact location.

A couple hours later I perk up to the chirps of a police siren. It's Officer Taylor. He parks in an empty lot and I run across the highway to join him. He gets out of the vehicle with my hat in hand. Says he's been looking for me for a while. I ask if Elisa told him about my replacement hat and he says no. I apologize for wasting his time. "No big deal," he says. "I was watching the Lego movie with my kids when I got the call. Trust me, it was a welcome interruption. Plus I figured this hat might have some sentimental value." He hands it over. "It's my *go to hell hat*," I say. I tell Taylor about Kenny, the man I met in Arizona who's spending his retirement riding his bike around the southwest. Kenny called my hat a go to hell hat and said that's how I should respond when people laugh at it. Taylor cracks up. "That's how I feel about my hat, too," he says. Taylor reaches into the cruiser and pulls out a worn Tilley. Puts it on. "I'd be lost without this thing," he says. We take a photo. "Gonna post this on the department's social media," he says. "People need to hear good news once in a while, too."

*

I had hoped the short 22 miles into Cleveland, Tennessee might leave me refreshed, but it's the opposite. I stop at the first hotel I see and book a room. My home for two nights reeks of smoke and has door damage suggesting a break in. The adjacent rooms both have busted out windows. It's not the worst place I've stayed on this trip, but it's close.

I have friends here, too. Brittany and David, owners of Terra Running and Bear Brew Coffee. They shuttle me around town as I restock gear and food, take me to Cracker Barrel for my first time ever, and keep me caffeinated. Brittany calls me on my second day in town and says they don't like the hotel I'm staying at, so they booked me a night at a swanky place up the road. "It's walking distance from where you are and ready whenever you are," she says. I try to resist, but she cuts me off and tells me it's nonnegotiable.

Day 169

Tall morning clouds rise above the blue. Rain is expected, but not until later. After a night in luxurious digs, I feel clean and rested for the first time in a while. I hope to beat the weather to my stopping point which, hopefully, will be some kind of campground.

As I depart through the hotel lobby, employees at the front desk bid me farewell. "Have a nice day, Mr. Griffen." The *mister* part seems too formal, but I roll with it.

At the first crosswalk beyond the parking lot, a skinny white man with stringy hair and missing front teeth runs toward me as I wait for the light to change. In his hands are colorful cans of some kind of energy drink I don't recognize. "Hey!" he shouts, "Give me five dollars for these drinks!" I tell him no thanks and wish him good luck selling them. "Oh yeah?" he shouts. "Fuck you too!"

*

In Sweetwater, I take a break in the parking lot of the East Tennessee Livestock Center. It's still an hour before an auction begins and yet the place is already bustling with big trucks hauling trailers filled with live inventory. Everything kicks up dust. I didn't grow up near farm animals so I don't know how to interpret their sounds or behaviors, but still I can sense desperation in their calls. I feel it in my body too. The reality of their fate is obvious.

*

In downtown Loudon I meet Steve. He's a retired teacher, coach, and high school principal. In a span of a couple years, he retired, got divorced, was diagnosed with colon cancer, beat it, and thru-hiked the AT. "Me and my buddies get together for burgers every Wednesday," he says. "Want to join us tonight?"

Later, Steve picks me up from my roadside motel and we head into Knoxville. Steve cries as he tells me about the kind people he met on the AT. I tell him about Art and Lion. He nods like he knows them. "It's amazing how sometimes it takes a thing like this to realize what matters the most," he says. "You're meeting all the right people, Tom. Everyone out there is a teacher in some way."

Steve pays for my dinner and offers to buy me a second one to go. "I know how it is," he says. "I know that hunger. You sure you don't want something else?" I tell him I'm good. "You really sure?" he insists. "How about some pie? Apple or cherry? Or cheesecake, maybe?"

Day 171

I decide to get Little Buddy's wheels checked out. Lately I've grown increasingly concerned about how loose his axles seem. But maybe they've always been like this. I don't know much about wheel mechanics, but I'd hate to ignore it and be forced to ditch him somewhere between here and the finish. I stop at Echelon Bikes in Farragut where Justin disassembles his wheels. He assures me I'll be fine. "You might get more play," Justin says. "But nothing's gonna bust." His words are music to my ears.

With renewed drive I push LB on the sidewalk. The traffic is too loud to listen to music, so I walk to what's rocking in my head. My steps are in tempo with Rush's "Tom Sawyer" and I sing a broken assemblage of erroneous lyrics. "Monday warrior mean mean stride, today's Tom Sawyer mean mean guy." I roll along to the steady beat, quickly working up a sweat while paying homage to Neal Peart by pounding expertly on the air drums with my one free hand. "Catch the wind! Catch the wind! Catch the spirit! Catch the wind!"

*

Instead of raging temps, I'm suddenly dealing with a minor flood. I opt for a detour toward downtown to find refuge, but it only brings more cars and no shoulder whatsoever. I'm literally walking in the lane against heavy traffic in a dirty gush of rushing water deeper than my shoes. My eyeglasses are useless and without them everything is blurry. There are no more songs in my head. Just the fury of accelerating engines and the splash of road river spray. My earlier elation is now frustration and I'm reminded how much I despise walking into cities. I pull over and mope in an empty service bay. Catch a chill that briefly snaps me out of my funk. I need a plan. My phone says there are hotels a couple miles ahead. I bite the bullet and beeline toward one of them. I don't even care that it's going to cost me a fortune.

*

The lobby doors slide open and a blast of cold air makes my skin hurt. My shoes squish as I walk to the front desk where two employees, Lisa and Kevin, enthusiastically check me in. Lisa leans over the counter. "Hey! I've got calves just like yours," she says. "From growing up walking these Knoxville hills." Kevin wants to interview me for his podcast, *The Mouse Knows Best*. "But it's all about Disney things," he says. "So it probably won't work out so well."

I get settled into my room and return to the lobby for a roll of quarters and soap for the laundry machine. Lisa covers me.

"Don't worry about it, I got you," she says as she hands over the items, all on the house.

*

As I lean up against the vibrating machine and wait for my laundry to finish drying, I get a text from Katie. "Got a minute to chat?" She's curious if I have a ballpark timeframe of when I plan to finish in New York. "I want to buy my tickets," she says. "And the longer I wait the more expensive they'll be. Plus, we should give my brother a heads-up. You are planning to pass through Manhattan, aren't you?" Dang. I can't believe it's time to start planning the logistics for the end.

As my clothes tumble in the cool-down portion of the dry, Katie and I hammer out the trail math. It's June 21, and I've got 800 or so miles left. I've been doing about 175 miles per week, sometimes more. I need a day off every six days or so. If I keep charging ahead at this pace, barring any injury or incident I should reach the Atlantic in four and a half weeks. She buys a ticket to arrive at La Guardia on July 24. I may arrive there later, but sooner doesn't seem likely. Her ticket is one-way because we'll rent a car in Manhattan and drive back to Carrboro together. These plans are exciting, but they also freak me out. How can home be just over a month away? I feel like I just started.

But I need to keep my focus on what's before me. Because a lot can happen in a month. We hang up and I lug my laundry back to the room where I plan the next few days. I inspect LB's tires for scree. Make sure I have enough food. Write a post on social media. And keep the TV on, but muted.

Day 172

Around midday, Stella, an old white lady with auburn hair and rose lipstick pulls over. Her pink blouse matches the steering wheel and seat covers. A dangle of keychains swings from the ignition. We talk though her passenger's side window. I'm struck by the musicality of her twang and anything I say sounds terribly boring in response. "Two months ago a man passed through Blaine on a horse, ridin' all the way 'cross the country," she says. "People took him in and made sure he was taken care of 'long the way. I'm tellin' you this because I don't want you to be afraid of the people here. If they wanna help, go on ahead and let 'em." I assure her it's something I'm actively working on. "Well then good for you, honey," she says. "Good for you."

Stella hands me a box of peanut candy bars. "They're my favorite but I sure don't need 'em all," she says. "Look here," she says. "Just ahead is a restaurant called the Little Dipper. Find Mary there and tell 'er I sent you." The way she says Mary sounds like Murray. "Mary'll let you camp behind the building. Probably even give you a free ice cream cone."

*

I reach the Little Dipper and follow Stella's advice. But Mary isn't here, so I run my story past one of the wait staff who makes a quick call. To Mary, I assume. She pulls the phone from her ear. "You're not gonna rob us or nothing, are ya?" she asks. A few patrons stop chewing and watch for my answer. "No ma'am," I say. She gets the green light and hangs up. "Go on ahead and pick any spot you want behind the building," she says. "But be careful out there. We have bears."

Another staffer then hands me a menu, hinting at what I already planned to do. I sit down and order two fried chicken sandwiches, a side of potato salad, and some coleslaw. Afterwards I ask for a dessert menu. And though the camping is free, just like Stella said it would be, the ice cream is not.

*

I situate Little Buddy and my tent under a canopy of tall trees. It rains steadily while I pound metal stakes into the ground with a hammering rock I've been carrying since Arizona. I stay mostly dry. The sky clears when the sun goes down, and for the first time in a while, I have a view of stars. To decrease the chance of a bear encounter, I make sure all my food is ziplocked and buried deep in LB's hold. Before calling it a night, I wish him good luck. "You're on your own, homie," I say. I sleep deeply on the mattress of thick grass.

Day 173

The Little Dipper is open as I prepare to leave. The staff welcome me back and ask about my night. "Any bears?" they say. I shake my head like I wish I had a story to tell. I order a pre walk cup of coffee and figure I'll take it to go. But someone suggests a wedge of warm, cherry cobbler, too, and there's no way I'm saying no to that. Workers prepare the place for the morning rush as I savor every bite and sip. When I'm ready to go, they bring me a couple bottles of water and tell me breakfast is on the house. "And hey, if you're ever in the area again, please come on by."

*

Up the road a bit, a local reporter asks if I have a few minutes for a quick interview. I'm always down to answer questions about this trip, and she hits me with the standard ones: Where and when did I start? Where will I end? Why am I walking this far? Where do I sleep? How much do I walk per day? Before wrapping, she asks if I have anything else I'd like to add. I say Yes, then add something about this walk being a way for me to stoke the hottest fires in my belly. I include something else about life being too short and doing things before it's too doggone late.

Later, when I'm alone again, I listen to the echo of my answers and kick myself. I wish I had said something about all the amazing people I've met so far. I wish I said that kindness has become the unexpected theme of this journey. I mean seriously, how the hell could I have forgotten to mention that? I wish I had said it's the people I meet who propel me forward. I wish I told her that by experiencing this national outpouring of generosity, I'm learning more about myself than I could have ever imagined. But I choked. I left out all the most important things and talked only about me and my goal and some dumb shit about capitalizing on opportunity. What a self-centered response! How white can I be! Even after all the powerful lessons in humility offered me by the people I've met along the way, I'm still only thinking about myself. Apparently I've learned nothing. I'm almost done with this thing and still it's all about me. Damn.

Day 176

Shoulders widen as I cross another state line into Bristol, Virginia, nicknamed "The Birthplace of Country Music." I pose Little Buddy on Lee Highway next to a guitar as big as a house. A nearby church marquee says "In the Tapestry of Life We Are All Connected." Another one, "Doing Right is Never Wrong."

Like all older American roadways, Lee Highway, also known as Route 11, retains remnants of its past. Kitschy diners, motor inns, drive-in movie theaters, roadside attractions. Lots of gaudy neon signs. All very reminiscent of the stretch of Route 66 I walked back in California. I've never before been to this part of Virginia, yet these relics make my heart pang. I wonder if I'm seeing these iconic attractions for the last time. It's only a matter of time before they'll be leveled in favor of soulless strip malls. Places filled with people, yet devoid of life. The sorts of places we've all grown used to.

*

Less than an hour after my arrival into Virginia, the wide and welcoming shoulder disappears completely. A familiar panic resurfaces as I walk in the westbound lane, headlong into unsuspecting motorists. Out of breath and edgy, I park in a pullout to look on Apple Maps for an alternate path. It's hard to tell for sure on the satellite view, but my situation looks temporary. Not far ahead, an adjacent road detours away from, then back toward Highway 11 right about where the shoulders return. The detour is under construction, but I take it anyway and am initially overjoyed by its paper-smooth concrete sidewalks. My delight, however, is short-lived as the walk quickly changes to a gravelly lane. Still, this spur is easier going than the highway, and arguably safer, too. But when the gravel gives way to a top layer of thick, red mud, I regret the diversion. Every hundred feet or so I have to scrape pounds of caked clay from the soles of my shoes and Little Buddy's wheels. Distancewise, this sidestep is only two miles and should take a half hour or so. But with bricks attached to my and LB's feet, it takes us three times that.

Where the new road rejoins the highway, there's a self-serve carwash aptly named Griffin's Lee Highway Supercenter. I park LB above the water drain and powerwash a half ton of muck from his wheels and underbelly. Then I turn the nozzle on myself and spray off my shoes and pants. The pressurized water on my legs feels like a massage.

*

Back on Lee Highway, the minuscule shoulders look the same as they did before I deviated, but now they are a relief. Happiness is so damn relative, and yet I always seem to be seeking it elsewhere. I want to be able to look at my situation, like this nearly nonexistent shoulder, and think, *Yeah, this blows. But odds are it'll get better. And even if it doesn't, at least I know what I'm working with.*

I can choose to be happy with my now. But that's just it, I have to live mindfully enough to make that choice.

Day 177

I am soothed by Chilhowie's sidewalk. It's broken and irregular, but it gets me out of the traffic lane. I push LB with one hand and relax into my pace.

Ahead, two men amble toward me. A younger guy on foot and an older man scooting along on a BMX bike that's way too small for him. There's no way we all are going to fit on the busted sidewalk together, so I maneuver into the gutter. As I do, the younger fellow scoots off to the side, waving for me to pass first. "Come on past," he hollers. I wave back and continue, pick up my pace a bit. When I reach them, I notice a brick in the young guy's hand. He catches me looking. "You wanna see this brick?" he says. I stop walking. Not sure how to interpret the question. "This right here," he says, "might be the most valuable brick you'll ever see." They introduce themselves as Vincent and Calvin.

Vincent just found the brick in a pile of rubble near a newly razed building in an older part of town. "When I was a kid, I heard about these Chilhowie bricks," he says. "They're rare." He holds the brick at eye level. Inspects it with a squint. Says they stamped the town name with a missing final E. "Last I heard only thirty-two of these were made before they realized the error," he says. "Which means this is nearly a one-of-a-kind." Vincent claims the rare bricks are worth $15,000 each. "To a brick collector," chimes Calvin, which makes them both laugh like it's some kind of inside joke. "I like looking for stuff," Vincent says. "And I always find things, too. Old jars, arrowheads, and once I even found one of the first vodka bottles ever made in America." He says the best place to find collectibles in town is behind the Health and Human Services building, where he lives. "Treasures are hidden in nature," he says. "Lots of people are afraid to go in the forest, but not me." I ask Vincent what he's going to do with the brick. "Shoot! We're on our way right now to the museum! We're gonna sell it! I heard they'll pay top dollar for one of these!

It's local history, you know!" He holds up the red block again and gazes at it. He's already spending the windfall. "Man oh man!" he says. "I've been looking for this beauty my whole life." I wish the men good luck and Vincent shakes his head. "All the luck I need is right here in my two hands!"

*

As Vincent and Calvin continue on toward the museum, I do some quick internet research. The archaeologist-slash-junk-hunter in me is itching to know the truth about that brick. I check eBay and find nothing, then Google a few keywords and come across a handful of websites dedicated to the topic of brick collecting. Turns out it's a thing. And though the Chilhowie brick is an item listed on the sites, Vincent's brick, unfortunately, is no more valuable than any other single brick. The missing letter on his block resulted from a break. The final E is quite likely on a smaller chunk in the same debris pile. The actual collectible is a true error in fabrication and misspells the town's name by leaving out the second H, not the final E. But according to the internet, even that one isn't very rare, and definitely not worth $15,000.

I catch myself playing out the exchange between Vincent and whoever gives him an ear at the museum. I hope this person responds tenderly, knowing Vincent's dreams will be crushed by the truth. I imagine Vincent absorbing the blow then exiting the museum, deflated. The brick that he so revered minutes earlier now heavier in his hands. A tangible object of frustration and disdain. I imagine Vincent hurling the worthless hunk of red clay into the museum's parking lot, shattering it further. He and Calvin will shrug it off, then go about their day as they always do.

Still, I hope the moment won't discourage Vincent from looking for more treasures. In fact, I hope it does the opposite. I hope that worthless Chilhowie brick turns out to be priceless for other unexpected reasons. I hope it's the thing that leads to another thing that leads to an even more important thing that changes everything.

Day 178

Near Rural Retreat I stop to gawk at a herd of shorn alpacas. I stand near their pen and coo hoping they'll approach. But they're only concerned with Little Buddy. They stand still with ears back and emit a high pitched hum, ready to bolt if he makes a sudden move.

Later, I pull off the highway onto an elevated, unpaved lot. I roll LB to the leveled-out section at the top and inspect the roadside apiary I find there. It seems out of place. Wooden beehive boxes, labeled by swatches of bright colors, sit atop cinder blocks stacked two high. The collection looks like a gathering of file cabinets. I'm intrigued by how they contrast against the thick green forest backdrop. I want to take a few photos. So I release my hold on LB and don't bother depressing his emergency brake like I always do. I'll only be a second.

I hesitantly investigate the rainbow rows, jumping every few seconds to jerk out of the way of a curious bee. I'm terrified of stinging insects and walking amongst them makes me feel brave. The wasp tattoo on the top of my left hand is meant to remind me to keep my fears at the forefront. The fact that the image looks like a flea is simply the ironic outcome of my failed attempt to be profound.

I slowly weave between the cabinets and tune in to the gentle buzz. I think about my friend Matt, a visual artist and founder of The Good of the Hive, an organization meant to draw awareness to bees and the importance of community. He travels the world giving lectures and painting bee murals. His goal is to paint a total of 50,000 bees in all, a multiyear project. I inspect various angles of this bee community as I compose a photo to send to him. I consider the midday sun as it reflects on the colorful boxes. I squat down for a zoomed-in portrait of a resting worker. I think Matt would especially like this one. As I do, I hear the crunching of gravel and hop up, assuming it's the owner of the hives wondering what I'm doing on the property. But the noise is coming from Little Buddy, already moving at the pull of gravity. He's gathering speed as he heads down the parking lot decline. Nothing but space between him and Lee Highway.

*

I explode from the hives and give chase. For the first time in years, I sprint. Big arm swings and wide leg turnovers. I shoot after him toward the two lanes of highway traffic. LB accelerates, extending the gap between us as he bisects the empty road. I'm two, maybe three steps behind when I reach the blacktop. I don't bother looking both ways before I lunge at his handlebar. But in my effort, I only grasp air as he finds a new gear and motors to the far end of the westbound lane. Momentum hurls him onto the opposite shoulder then down the reach of a slope on the south side. As I continue my charge into the grassy downhill, a resounding pop in my left quadricep interrupts my clean gait. I grab the front of my leg and limprun down the hill between LB's fresh wheel tracks. He's finally free, fully exploiting a chance to be off-leash. I watch in amazement as his tempo surges and our rift grows insurmountable. I fully expect him to fishtail and topple, spewing his guts. But he glides down the dewy ramp, his path straight and true, and reaches maximum velocity just before coming to an anticlimactic stop surrounded by yellow wildflowers on the edge of a farmer's field.

I catch up, broken from my failed rescue attempt. With each step, a driving pain stabs across the top of my thigh. "What the fuck you do that for!" I scream. After giving him a thorough once-over, I softly kick his frame before dragging him up the hill and back to the hardtop. My upper leg collapses every time it flexes. Plus, it looks wrong, like the muscles within have all come loose. The skin around the injured spot is already hot and red.

Pain is so intense I expect something to jab out of it. It itches like a beesting.

*

At the top of the incline I wait for a string of cars to pass before I carefully recross the road to the apiary side. I press LB's foot brake, look up toward where the hives sit, then back down to the field below. Five minutes ago all was fine. And now, another goddamn injury. But I'm also hyperaware that the whole scenario could have played out significantly worse. Had the timing been different, I could have easily become that grease mark. Day 178 marking not only the end of my walk, but the end of my life. I'm immediately overcome by gratitude and hope things aren't worse tomorrow. But I already know they will be. The real question is *How much worse?*

*

Swelling increases as the day lengthens, but my steady stride isn't hindered by the mounting pain. Somehow I still manage big miles, pulled eastward by the prospect of a motel ice bath, but also by the adjacent Denny's. The thought of its illuminated red and yellow sign draws me toward it like a magnet. Thoughts of a sticky booth where I'll sip flavored coffee with extra cream and devour a Lumberjack Slam sided by an extra order of two blueberry flapjacks dripping with warm butter and maple syrup. Today I endure more than 70,000 painful steps to satisfy my insatiable hunger. Food moves me. Quite literally.

*

I spend the evening icing my quad. Watch another marathon of *Pawn Stars* where somebody is selling a signed Abraham Lincoln parlor card for $100,000. I think of the Civil War battlefields ahead. I'm not a blue and gray enthusiast, but my grandfather was. And if he was still alive, he'd be thrilled to know I'm moving at the pace of the regiments. He'd be proud of this journey and tell me so. Even though he passed on years ago, knowing this is true causes tears to drip onto my icepack as I sit slouched in my underwear atop the coarse comforter.

*

I think about the various landscapes I've seen along the way. Big cities and empty deserts. Swamplands and mountains and forests. Every day's been a mix of past and present thoughts, new memories, and so much unknown. After her own walk across America, my crosser friend Lindsay wrote about her favorite tree from the journey. I wonder if I will end my walk with any favorite things. So far I don't have any. And since I'll reach the ocean in a few weeks, I doubt any will manifest in the meantime.

"What's been your favorite...?" is another common question people ask. Favorite state, meal, homestay, whatever. I want to have a favorite tree like Lindsay—or at least a favorite *something*. I want to feel extra-connected to a thing that will forever remind me of this undertaking. For the past few weeks, I've been looking more closely at everything. Trees, roadkill, fence posts, barns. But all this close looking hasn't led to any kind of ranking system. All it does is remind me that nothing is better or worse than anything else. When I look close and long at anything, I can't help but fall in love over and over. My favorite tree, turns out, is the one I am looking out right now. Because really, it's the only one that I'm certain exists.

Day 179

I thought I would wake up and knock out a short 21 miles on the shoulderless frontage road into Dublin where I'm planning to meet my good friend, JP. Plan is to take tomorrow off and spend it with him. But the morning fog is thick as chowder. And though

I can hear tractor trailers coming in and out of the nearby truck stop, I can't see them. Not even a glimmer of their lights. If Little Buddy and I try to walk in this soup, we'll be invisible. The low clouds delay my departure until any chance of meeting JP as planned is impossible.

*

I press into my swollen thigh. The skin hurts to touch. A red bruise darkens around the area of acute pain. It looks ugly. Still, I'm pretty sure it's minor. Otherwise I wouldn't have been able to walk as much as I did yesterday. But it will only benefit from rest, so I decide to make today a down day. Which gives me two zero-mileage days in a row. I thank the heavy fog for making my decision easy.

I call JP. He offers to pick me up. Tells me he's in his new sports car which doesn't have room for LB. So I book another night at the hotel so LB has a place to stay. As JP rolls up, I close the drapes and switch the TV on low. "No parties, OK?" I say. Then I close the door behind me.

*

JP and I have known each other for more than a decade, but our relationship as friends is newish. He was the CEO of a company I worked for. After I left, we'd get together to sip bourbon or sit around a campfire. JP follows my social media, and when he heard I was following Lee Highway, he reached out. Drove three hours to meet me here.

We go to his family's getaway in Indian Valley. For years I've heard him talk about this place. The Farm. A vast and quiet span of long-standing family land where his grandma and her 11 siblings grew up. These days it's a modest home with country decor and a scattering of Virginia Tech Hokie memorabilia. There are locks on the property gates and unpredictable internet connectivity. The Farm is JP's refuge. A release valve where the

269

tumults of life are easily forgotten. Where the creaking of porch rockers is drowned out by cicadas, crickets, and melting ice cubes in a tumbler. And later tonight, with a bottle between us, the night shadows will grow long under a lemon moon.

*

JP takes me to Floyd where we meet up with Winfred, his high school track coach and one of his oldest friends. Winfred's still coaching, and considering the town of Floyd's meager population of 400, his ability to consistently produce competitive teams is impressive. Spending time with Winfred is like hanging out with a celebrity. People don't just know him, they love him. The three of us can't go anywhere without locals wanting a hug or a photo with him. It's nice to relinquish the center of attention.

*

Each homestay of this walk has been serendipitously timed, which further validates my belief that everything happens when it needs to happen. This stay with JP, however, seems extra special. He is the closest connection I've had to home in months. And though I'm in denial about how little time I have remaining before I hit the Atlantic, time with JP ignites my desire, albeit a tempered one, to put a cork in this walk across America. The prospect of soon reconnecting with my people back home—of reconnecting with Katie—now feels more appealing than ever.

Day 181

I'm anxious to make up the miles I missed. I find a shortcut along Lead Mine Road and assume that since it's off the main highway it'll have less traffic. But I waver. Intuition tells me to stick with the plan and stay on Lee Highway. Still, I hem and haw, waffle back and forth while staring at the map. Finally tired of being indecisive, I commit to the detour and get on with it.

My sore leg is swollen but it doesn't impede my stride. I begin the weekend with a demanding climb, reach the apex, drop down, then repeat it on the next lip. This rollercoaster scenario replays as the day heats up. Soon I'm ascending blacktop grades fully exposed to the summer oven. It's got to be nearly triple digits, again, and I can't drink water fast enough. To make things trickier, the shoulder narrows to a sliver and the white line separating me from passing cars disappears altogether. Sharp turns are overgrown, which makes it impossible for motorists to see me until the last possible second. I hobble along the roadside and doubt my last-minute choice to take this shortcut. Turns out it's not a shortcut after all. I kick myself. Should have listened to my gut. My belly brain always knows more than my head. But I rarely listen to it.

*

I didn't realize this route is the only way to get to Claytor Lake, a popular boating and recreational area. Thundering pickups with oversized boat trailers hog the narrow path. Unfriendly horns, grimacing faces, and lots of discarded beer cans on the roadside. Dehydration begins to take hold and I start nodding off, per usual. Halfway through the 24-mile stretch, I decide to throw in the towel. It's simply too dangerous and my physical condition is deteriorating rapidly. I'll hitch a ride to the highway and figure things out from there. But I never actually put my thumb out. I just figure I'll say yes if anyone offers safe passage. Nobody does.

I bob and weave from one side of the road to the other, choosing the avenue that affords the longest line of sight. In the throes of it all, a young woman, Cynthia, pulls into a driveway ahead. She wants a photo with me and her three sons. She gives me a big hug and her boys all shake my hand. My spirits lift. I'm suddenly awake. Shortly thereafter, an EMT stops to give me more waters and my energy perks up more. She looks closely at my face and tells me to be careful. I wonder what she sees.

*

I drink and I drink and I drink. Down nearly four gallons total before calling it a day at 38 miles. But four gallons wasn't enough. I know because at dinner I can't use my fork. The tiny muscles in my fingers keep cramping up. My hands shake and crabclaw inwards toward my body. I ask my server to box up what's left of my burrito and brace myself in the booth to keep my eyes from tunneling closed. I stumble back to the hotel then sit on the bed and watch as the muscles in my calves ripple as if trying to escape through the skin. It's like there's a baby in there. An alien baby. I drink water until my stomach is uncomfortably full. Absentmindedly finish what's left of my burrito and disregard the shreds of cheese and lettuce that fell onto the bedsheets. I write a quick post on social media. "Tonight I feel how I usually feel after running a 50-miler. Eyes sunken in. Muscles firing like they're on electric stim. All in all, I'm a woozy hot mess."

Comments start dinging in. The one from Hoboallie catches me off guard. "Tom. It seems the ending of a journey always is the most difficult part. You have done an amazing job so far. We've been reading about you since we met at the Valentine, TX Prada Shop. If you ever come to upstate NY please text us. We have travel tales to share. Stay safe and always in motion." I remember meeting Hoboallie and her husband while they were on a cross-country road trip. But I'd never have guessed they were following along. She's right, the end of this trek is proving to be the hardest. But it's made even more difficult by this searing heatwave currently blistering the southeast.

*

I lie prone, all the sheets pulled back. I'm hot and shivering. I have clammy hands and an irregular heartbeat. My eyes burn. I breathe with my mouth open. I can't think straight. It's after 1:00 a.m. by the time I'm able to fully lie down. It's even later before I finally fall asleep. But then I'm up a thousand times to stretch out a cramp or pee out the water my body has been desperately hoarding. A woozy hot mess is right.

Day 182

I can't stop yawning. And no amount of electrolyte intake seems to make the water quit sloshing in my belly. Still, I set out on Lee Highway and figure I'll just take it easy. Straight away, a man stops to give me an egg and cheese biscuit he just bought at Hardee's. Soon after, Jennifer, an Asian woman whose husband is currently bicycling the Pan American highway from Argentina to Alaska, dishes off some homemade banana bread, salty potato chips, a massive orange, bottles of water, and a bag of ice. But neither salty snacks nor the extra water help to equalize my body. After seven miles I've sunken in. I'm dizzy and more exhausted than ever. And worst of all, I'm not peeing. Not one drop all day. Which is evidence of a bigger problem.

Chuck, an old ultrarunning friend, posts a comment on my social media. "Please tell me you're taking today off to recover from that dehydration," he writes. Moments later, Marti, a woman from my MFA program, wires money to cover tonight's hotel stay. Without another thought, I do a 180° turnaround and head straight to a hotel I passed a couple miles back. Soon as I check in, Bobcat, a buddy from back home, texts me asking for my exact location. His daughter Allie, a student at nearby Virginia Tech, is on her way over with a stash of coconut water and other goodies to aid my recovery. Today others did all my thinking for me. And, evidently, it's exactly what I needed.

Day 183

I've been drinking so much electrolyte liquid that now I can't walk 15 minutes without having to urinate. Normally I'd try to be discreet. Hide behind a tree and wait for traffic to clear. But today my only rule is, don't face the road.

I get a message on social media from a woman named Steph. "Heard you are headed to Christiansburg!! If you know where you might be I'd love to bring you water and snacks." We exchange a flurry of texts consisting mostly of her asking what I'd like on my sandwich. Ham or PBJ? Cheese or no cheese? Mayo or mustard? Dijon or yellow? Steph confirms my route and asks if I need any additional supplies. "Maybe a spray bottle? Or a bandanna?" Then she and her son, Gabriel, track me down at a solitary turnout about 10 miles out of Christiansburg. She gets out of the vehicle with Gabriel in one arm and a grocery bag in the other. "I'm that hippie girl who always brings more than I need in case others need it," she says. She hands over the abundance. Included with the snacks is a blue bar of homemade soap branded with a sticker that says "Body Treats By Steph."

Gabriel peers at Little Buddy and asks how my water bottle stays hanging from the handlebar. I demonstrate how the fixed carabiner works. He's unimpressed. "Hey! Maybe next time we'll come to your house so I can meet your kids, OK?" he says, looking at his mom. She nods and tells him that would be a nice idea. "Look," Gabriel then says, pointing at the ground. "Did you know we all have shadows?" I adjust my position so our shadows can do a high-five. Gabriel laughs. "Our shadows are us —but down there!" he says, pointing at the ground.

*

For the rest of the day I charge along, staying barely a step ahead of another bout of severe dehydration. In a coherent daze I think of Steph and Gabriel and of the children I always thought I'd have but never did. My unwillingness or inability to fully say yes to any one place or person or job has made it easy to become a middle-aged, single, childless man without a certain career path. I'd love to have some kids to introduce to the likes of Gabriel. And though it's still a possibility, I feel like that ship has sailed.

Roadside ponderings of parenthood make me think of my own father. I imagine him sitting at his desk back home, making lists or organizing things into neatly labeled bins like he does. I imagine him painting a still life in his studio. Maybe flowers in an empty Coke bottle. I wonder what he thinks about as he passes the time. Then I wonder what I'd do if I had a son who was hoofing it across the United States.

I imagine I'd have a paper map tacked to the wall. Every day I'd read his posts and track his route. I'd mark his progress with a highlighter. I'd do a little Wikipedia research on the random places he passes through and learn each town's claim to fame. When I meet up with my buddies, for a beer or whatever, I'd brag about my kid who's out there doing this cool thing. And though I'd want to hear his voice, I'd at least make sure he hears mine. Leave him voicemails saying he's on my mind and that I love him dearly. I'd tell him to make it home safely so he can tell me all about his trip. Because my child's journey would be mine, too.

Day 184

It's the 4th of July. I'm hoping to get in a bunch of miles before it gets too late. I don't want to be on the road as people drive home from festive holiday barbecues.

The 4th of July is the day I headed off to basic training in 1990, and when I honorably discharged in 1994. On this day in 1991, I was based in Darmstadt, Germany, worried that my unit would deploy to the desert. But for this one day, no soldiers were concerned with war. We all had the day off, and every unit organized various feasts that made our post resemble a giant hometown neighborhood. Men went shirtless, women wore bikini tops, and everyone temporarily disregarded rank and status. Captain Jolly, normally straightlaced and heavy-handed, didn't look quite as tough in his Cape Cod tank top.

On the parade field in the center of Kelly Barracks, my buddies and I passed around someone's half bottle of Wild Turkey until it was empty. I smoked my first joint, hash actually, while sitting beneath the flagpole. Then we drank warm racks of Darmstadter Pils as midday came and went.

At some point someone changed out Metallica's *Master of Puppets* CD for Wilson Phillips' self-titled debut. The opening song, "Hold On," shifted the mood, and within minutes we all were lying on our sunbathing towels, leaning up occasionally for a sip from our tall bottles. For hours we played the album on loop. By the third time through we all were drunk, dancing badly and singing along to the lyrics: "I know this pain. Why do you lock yourself up in these chains? No one can change your life except for you. Don't ever let anyone step all over you."

I walk in a fog of nostalgia and sing this song at full blast. Then I pay 10 bucks to download the record on iTunes and sing along with it all the way into Buchanan, Virginia, where a sign outside a bank says it's 98°F. Purgatory Mountain hazily looms in the distance. I blame the heat for my fit of tears. But I let the feelings flow freely as I accompany Carnie, Wendy, Chynna, and all my skinny Army buddies from those days in the early '90s. Even after nearly 30 years, I still remember all the words to the song.

*

A note on my social media from Aurora, a new Facebook connection, says, "I read an article last night through my local news channel that said in places where there is a lot of corn, the humidity can feel worse because the corn sweats into the air and makes it more sticky. Not sure if this applies to where you are right now, but it sure does here in Illinois."

*

Something in my heart has settled. Katie and I are regularly talking and texting again. But unlike before, I'm not wondering what's going to happen between us. I'm not concerned at all with my speed or distance, either. Or even with finishing, even though I've got a day locked in for when it's likely to happen.

My new perspective has added a freshness to the times we do connect. I'm aware that I'm not trying to prove anything. Or demand any attention. Or wishing she'd do something that isn't in her nature. I reach out now because I want to hear the calm of her voice and chit chat about the little things I'm not making public. Like, how I've been picking up business cards I randomly find on the road, then emailing the person to let them know our paths have virtually crossed. Or the the time I walked down a raised median in the middle of a busy highway because it was the safest place to avoid traffic. I tell Katie about the couple I met who wore matching blue outfits fully branded with the Chicago Cubs logo, the woman telling me she "married into the faith" as her man proudly nodded his head. And the two old ladies, one Black and one white, who checked me into the Wattstull Inn tonight from the comfort of their cigarette-burned recliners beneath a wall of mounted deer heads.

Who knows, maybe Katie and I will stick it out after all. Or maybe my reentry to real life will muddle the clarity I suddenly have.

Day 185

Heavy traffic creeps near Natural Bridge. More people sneak photos of me from the passenger seat and I wave to prove I caught them. I imagine bad photos of me and Little Buddy are popping up on strangers' newsfeeds. I make a mental note to wear a QR code next time around.

A man ahead waits for a break in the traffic parade so he can cross the highway to get his mail. As I near he calls me over. "Must be an accident on the interstate," he says. "It's never this bad." We chat in the shade outside his property gate. "When I was in my twenties," he says, "I wanted to float down the Mississippi on a raft like Huck Finn. But I met a lady who said it was a bad idea, so instead I did the Missouri from Sioux City to Omaha. I had no money, but I never went hungry." He says that just like the Credence Clearwater song, "people on the river are happy to give."

"I'm Mark," he says. "I'm actually kinda famous. Not the sort of guy who waits for life to happen." I apologize for not recognizing him. "It's fine," he says. "I'm obscure. But go look me up. Was on HBO last month. Been on the Travel Channel and done lots of news spots. I'm good filler material." He hands me his card. It says he's a Fiberglass Sculptor for the Amusement Industry. "I ship my stuff all over the US," he says. "If you've been coming up the Eleven, you may have seen the headless Indian in Kingsport. That's mine too. It's damaged. I've been down there all this week fixing it. They wanted it done by Independence Day which to me seems a little ironic."

Mark invites me into his lot and offers a quick tour of the various buildings. There are massive fiberglass sculptures everywhere. Ghosts and cowboys and snowmen and mythical creatures and clowns and camels and hippos. "I can do cartoony stuff, or I can do Remington," he says. "Just depends what the client wants." Mark says he was working on a Robert E. Lee bust, but then he learned one of Lee's dying wishes was to not have any honors done in his name. "What about Lee Highway?" I ask. Mark shrugs. "Yeah, apparently he wouldn't have wanted that," he says. "When the Civil War ended, Lee hoped everyone would put away their Confederate flags and begin healing the broken country together. And make no mistake, I come from the south. But this whole 'south will rise again' mentality is based on nothing but ignorance. If folks knew their history, they might change their ways." I ask Mark if he thinks disseminating this information would actually influence change. He scratches his head. "Well, maybe not," he says. "Lots of folks aren't really interested in changing."

*

Not far ahead at the Pink Cadillac diner, a white guy in an orange polo waves me down from across the street. "What?" he shouts. "You walking across the country or something?" He motions for me to wait, then runs across when the coast is clear. "I was kidding!" he says. "I didn't even see your sign!"

Steve's from Long Island and on his way to Chattanooga for his son's wedding. "Man, I've always wanted to ride a horse across America," he says. "Or do a Gobi desert adventure. But I'm just too busy." Steve asks where I'm finishing. "Probably Brighton Beach in Brooklyn," I say. "Dive in the ocean and call it a day." It's his neck of the woods and he rattles off the names of a handful of Uzbek restaurants. I try to take note, but immediately forget his recommendations. "But let me tell you this," he says. "I wouldn't go in that water. Last time I went swimming in the ocean I got some sort of infection that ate away the flesh on my leg." He pulls up his pant leg to show me the scar. It looks like a smooth continent. "I want to give you a bottle of champagne for the finish," Steve says. "But don't tell my wife. It's supposed to be for the reception." I stash the bottle in LB's trunk. Steve gives me a hug and asks me to call him when I reach New York.

*

Back in West Texas, transcon cyclist Bill insisted I give him a shout if I ended up anywhere near Harrisonburg. I do, and he and his wife Lucy offer to put me up and keep me fed while I'm within range.

On our first night together, Bill brings me as his guest to a long-standing weekly gathering of his best friends. "We call ourselves the 'philosophical militia.' We rarely talk politics, but when we do, I just listen," he says. Bill tells me he's the group's token liberal. "Though I think they all lean left in their own way," he says.

Tonight they're meeting in one of the member's massive garage. Tall roof with boats in the rafters. Power tools and beautifully crafted workbenches. The men scoot chairs to make room for me in their circle. Someone pours me a whiskey. "Sometimes when we come together we build boats," one of the guys says. "But sometimes we just sit around talking about life and drink bourbon." I raise my dram. "Or, if we don't want to do that, we shoot guns," another guy says, which makes everyone laugh before taking another sip from their highball.

When they first started coming together, their goal was to build a wooden canoe from scratch. Nobody had ever done it, and they figured it would be a purposeful and fun reason to gather. They've since built a handmade canoe for every man in the group. Each one turning out better than the last. A few of the gorgeous boats are stored in an adjacent barn. A couple guys give me a quick tour and point out which one was made first and how they worked this detail and that. The meticulous and artful craftsmanship of each canoe is stunning. Even the guys who made it seem impressed by what they've done. "Wow. It's been a while since I've looked at these older boats," one fellow says. "We've gotten pretty damn good at 'em through the years."

The men catch up on life's happenings. Someone tells a story, one that's been told many times before, apparently. Then they pepper me with questions about my walk. I tell them the story of Lion. "Damn," one guy says. "That's a good one." A couple wipe their eyes. One guy thanks me for the reminder to say yes to kindness. "It's a reminder I need, too," I say. "I feel so fortunate to have crossed paths with these folks and so many others who will forever influence how I move through life." Someone raises their glass again. We cheers, sip, and refill.

Day 186

The next morning Bill drives me to where he picked me up in Lexington. En route we talk about spirituality, yoga, God. I share the story of my grandfather's near-death experience. Gramps cried as he told me that after his second heart attack he saw a light. The light told him it wasn't his time yet. That he needed to go back and do what's right. "Did he?" Bill asks. I'm not sure, and I say as much.

Bill turns up the stereo volume and asks if I know much about bluegrass. I don't. All I know is an album I've been listening to since Texas. Becca had bought me a ticket to join her and Jeff at an Old Crow Medicine Show concert but I didn't make it to town in time. "Oh bummer," Bill says. "They put on a good one. Maybe one of these nights Lucy and I will play a little on the back porch. I'm still learning the guitar, but Lucy has the voice of an angel."

*

Jeff, a white man about my age, stops me as I enter Staunton. I recognize him from a mile or so back when I passed him in the parking lot of a dry cleaners. He welcomes me to town. Jeff's an entrepreneur. Years ago he lived in his pickup as he adventured through South America. He's also done a lot of boating on Chesapeake Bay. "Someday I'd like to do an extended boat trip on the open ocean," he says. "But I don't want to wait until I'm old to get it done."

Jeff gives me money for lunch. Tells me to go to the farmers market. "Find the yellow food truck that sells papusas," he says. "Then check out the coffee shop adjacent to the booths. You won't be sorry." The market is only two blocks off my route, so I take his advice. The vibrant scene reminds me of my farmers market back home. Vendors sling local produce and artwork while shoppers peruse the shady rows with armfuls of reusable bags. I do as Jeff recommends, then park Little Buddy in a cool spot under a tree and take a seat on the grass. The band's on break, so I close my eyes and absorb the white noise of conversation. The papusas are an explosion of flavor. I eat slowly and savor each nuance.

*

As I'm packing up to go, a woman approaches, looking back and forth between LB and me. Conversation with her draws in more folks, and before long I'm standing in the center of a group as locals ask curious questions. A few hold their phones up, taking video. Someone asks how I prepared. "Well, I'm not much of a planner," I say. "I like to just let things shake out how they want to shake out." Once the standard questions are out of the way, the conversation turns more thoughtful. I'm surprised by my own honesty and candor as responses to heavy questions roll naturally off my tongue: Do you think your skin tone makes it easier to do this walk? What have you learned about yourself along the way? How has your walk explored the current political state of the country? What are you excited about and afraid of? What will you do on your first day home? Each question becomes less about my answer and more of a conversation with the engaged circle of marketgoers. "This walk is a metaphor for so much more," someone says, and I agree.

Then, channeling Art again, I tell the group I may be the one walking, but the most important part of the journey is what's happening right now among us. All of us strangers coming together to commune like this. Heads shift to make eye contact with others in the circle, and a few people start to cry. Then someone opens their arms to hug an adjacent stranger, which inspires all of us to do the same. We embrace, and not in a one-armed sorta half hug, but in a way that feels genuine. I wipe away tears as folks exchange further niceties and contact information. "Minutes ago we were strangers," a woman with a stroller says. "And now, look at us! This is what a community looks like."

*

After the exchanges in Staunton, I call Katie. "This is what I am meant to do!" I say. "I should be out here walking for a living! Never stopping!" I know this sounds over the top, but there's something mutually beneficial going on the longer I'm out here. "It's a win-win!" I say. "I think this walking thing is why I am here. I think it's why I'm alive! I mean, if that's the case, how the hell could I ever stop. Like, for real?"

I hastily ramble on as I process the magical experience at the market. Katie just listens. When I finally pause for a breath, she proclaims how happy she is for me. And I can tell from the uplift in her voice that she really is, which is cool, but her response is also nowhere near the level of intensity I'm feeling, so I take it as a miss. I suddenly question why I'm calling. And not just her, but why am I calling *anyone* right now? I'm in the clouds, and Katie's words kill my buzz a little bit. So I clam up and tell her I'd better get going. I hang up and start walking again, unable to define how I'm truly feeling. I am elated, energized, angry, resentful, alone, confused. I am all of these at once.

But there's one thing I know for sure. In the wake of that powerful circle of people at the Staunton farmers market, I wish I'd been better able to validate my own happiness and sudden feeling of purpose. My buzzkill has got nothing to do with Katie at all. Nothing.

I make another promise to myself. That I'll work on being my own biggest fan. I stop and make write this quick note in my journal, adding the caveat, "...and not just on this walk." Then I return to the road.

Day 187

When buckets of water start falling from the sky, I take shelter under a tarpaulin roof at a motorcycle repair shop. I text Bill to let him know I'm done for the day. Fight off falling asleep as we drive back to his place.

After another one of Lucy's homemade dinners, I relax on the screened-in back porch and sip homemade gin as I listen to her and Bill sing and play bluegrass. Jampa, their goldendoodle, whose name is the Tibetan word for unconditional love, sits at their feet. Lucy jumps from the fiddle to the guitar with mastered ease, while Bill holds his own on a guitar he made by hand. When they play "Wagon Wheel," I sink into my chair and reflect on all the miles I've walked with that song as my soundtrack.

Later, we share the same space reading quietly. Bill's got a novel and Lucy's on her Kindle. I'm nosed into a local newspaper article about Bill's bike trip with Tim. Had they not done that adventure, none of us would have met. I am grateful for our time, fellowship, music, and meals together. I am grateful for Lucy's clafoutis dessert and the leftovers I'm finishing off tonight. Everything is more fun when we do it with others. And as much as I enjoy being alone on the road—briefly interacting with strangers I'll likely never see again—I prefer togetherness.

11

One's destination is never a place
but rather a new way of looking at things.

- Henry Miller
Big Sur and the Oranges of Hieronymus Bosch

Day 190

WHEN I ENTER WEST VIRGINIA, tall corn stalks sway in the gentle breeze. Tin-roofed houses sag and send end-of-day shadows across the highway. I take an off day in Martinsburg and restock my food and water. I scrutinize my map to strategize a route into New York City. I figured I'd approach via Washington DC, Baltimore, Philadelphia, and Trenton. Four giant cities in a row with challenging byways and expensive hotels. But today I stumble upon a ferry system that, weather permitting, shuttles tourists between Manhattan and the Gateway National Recreation Area at Sandy Hook, New Jersey. It gets people out of the city and onto the beaches. I'm relieved to scrap my big city plans and head for the northeast coast of Jersey. I'll still have to navigate through Philly, but one city crossing is a million times better than four.

*

My hands shake as I plan my trajectory to Sandy Hook. My path looks to be about 250 miles long and passes through historic towns like Gettysburg, Lancaster, West Chester, and Freehold. If I average a relaxed pace of 23 miles per day, it should take me 11 days to get there. I'll score a campsite and take a couple days off to ensure my arrival in New York coincides with Katie's. We'll walk the final day together just like we did the first.

To lock things down, I jump on Gateway's online reservation portal. It's a good thing I do because it's high season and there aren't many spots left. With 3,000 miles behind me, I finally know exactly when I'll reach the opposite side of America.

July 22. It's crazy to think everything is about to wrap up, but I know better than to celebrate. Because nothing is certain. Lots can and will happen between now and then. I rub my thigh, still smarting, and commit to the plan. "Process over product," I repeat like a mantra. "Process over product."

Day 191

As I sit on the curb of a gas station and down my espresso and honey bun, a man exits the quick mart and stops directly in front of me, blocking the morning sun. He points to a grove of trees near the railroad tracks across the parking lot to show me where he's been camping the past few weeks. "Man, you remind me of Steinbeck's *Travels With Charley*," he says. I perk up. "Yeah, except for maybe the Charley part," I say, referring to Steinbeck's travel companion—a tall, blue, gentleman poodle, as Steinbeck called his dog. "Although maybe my cart, Little Buddy here, counts as mine."

I first read this novel in high school, but recently it popped up again while I was stranded at a train station in Erfoud, Morocco. A local man noticed my predicament and invited me to wait out my six-hour bus layover with him at his trinket shop. We did our best to communicate using hand signals and journal drawings. At some point I traded him my banged up iPod shuffle for a trilobite fossil and a tattered copy of the Steinbeck classic.

Reading about Steinbeck and his dog traveling across the US while I explored Morocco proved unexpectedly relevant. Human interactions are pretty much the same worldwide. Good connections begin with openness.

*

I talk with no less than a dozen people before lunch. Most folks hand off a snack or a few bucks, while others want to hear or share a little bit more. I'm game for all of it. Cars stop, neighbors holler, fellow pedestrians ask for a minute. Store clerks hold up the line, cyclists double back, and people living on the street want to commiserate.

I've stopped noticing the changing landscape or bleak road conditions and recall only an endless line of friendly faces. A true mixing pot of color, age, gender, sexual orientation, and economic status, all united by curiosity and a willingness to slow down in order to have a random interaction with another human.

Day 192

My rationed miles quickly become a joke. Seems the closer I get to the coast, the faster I gobble up the miles. I cross the Potomac River and enter Maryland at Williamsport. By the time I reach Hagerstown, I'm already halfway across the narrow section of the state and still cruising along.

The city architecture reflects early America. Narrow streets, tall skinny houses built up against each other. I use the generous bike lane and breeze through the midday rush. I'm overjoyed to walk in a town with bike friendly infrastructure. A rarity on this trip.

*

On Charles Street, I near a group of shirtless Black men hanging out on the corner. "Man, what the hell you doing out here in this heat?" someone asks. It's pushing mid-90s and feels hotter on the pavement. Plus, it's superhumid. *Must be all the corn*, I've lately been thinking to myself.

The men stop what they are doing and form a circle around me. "You're doing *what* now?" a guy asks. "I know you must have hitchhiked somewhere along the way!" another man says. "Come on!" yet another adds. "Really now, how long you been out here?" I tell them today is day 192. The crowd swirls, howling in disbelief like I just did some kind of David Blaine magic trick.

They settle, and all eyes focus again on me. "Damn, man! I know this guy ain't lying! Take a look at his calves!" Men cover their mouths as they stare at my lower legs. "It looks like there's something wrong with them!" a woman jokes. "Yeah, I know," I say. "They're like Popeye. It's genetics. I have my mom to thank."

One at a time, folks on the street corner shake my hand or pat me on the back. The loudest voice in the group offers a blessing. "We're all going to pray for you," he says. "And hey, congratulations." I choke up as he shakes my hand and gives me a hug, then I continue rolling up the street. "Yo!" someone shouts from the group. "Don't forget about us!" I raise my fist. Then I make sure I flex my calves a little bit extra as I walk away.

*

At mile 30, well past my daily mileage ration, I unexpectedly cross into Pennsylvania at Washington Township. I knew I was close to the state line, but I didn't expect to enter a third state today. But once I do, I'm inspired to knock out another few miles before finding a stealth camping spot behind an old cemetery.

As the sun sets, I relax, thrilled to be camping again. I lay outside my tent and watch the quiet, blanketing sky, the winking stars. I imagine I'm back in the desert and there's nobody for miles. Headlights occasionally slice across the field as folks turn from Ringgold Pike onto Harbaugh Church Road. But I don't worry about anyone stopping. Not here. Because at night, most folks leave graveyards alone.

The air turns cool and I adjourn to my tent and tune into the sounds outside, now louder. Bugs chirp in unison, the breezy friction of cornstalks growing heavy with dew, small creatures inspect Little Buddy. I hear a faint breathing. Then something chewing. Though I know it's some sort of critter, I close my eyes and pray to the cemetery ghosts. "Keep me safe," I say. "Just for a few more days."

Day 193

I break camp extra early, and it's not long before I'm climbing again. Ascents rise from the flats and shoot straight into the sun. These are by far the steepest grades of the entire trip. On Old Route 16 I cross the Appalachian Trail and wonder if someday I'll bisect this highway with a pack on, halfway into my thru-hike from Georgia to Maine. But I shelve the fantasy and stay focused on the gnarly gradient.

The soles of my feet burn as I white-knuckle the downhills. These roads are paved mountains. Replete with umpteen hairpins and squiggly ups and downs that resemble an EKG reading. I'm amused by the ancient Speed Limit 10 signs. These days cars idle faster than that.

The acclivity is so great I have to careen into LB's bars. I'm as much holding him steady as I am pushing his weight upward. My standing angle is so sharp that my forehead is level with my wrists. The barbed highway makes preposterous demands on my Achilles tendons. What if today is the day one pops? I'm the perfect age for it. If it does, I'll probably hear the thick tendon snap like a stressed branch. I'll fall to the ground and grab my heel. Wince and curse and squirm. I'll release my hold on LB and he'll be off like a downhill drag race while I helplessly watch him get smaller and smaller, coursing down, down, down. His tires will heat up as he trips over pebbles, catching them like ramps. Maybe he'll launch over the unrailed cliff like Evel Knievel. He'll go out with a bang.

This imagined catastrophe fills in my head as I wrench upward, one grueling step at a time, feeling my heartbeat on my tongue. I lick salt as it drips from my mustache. My mouth and teeth are dry, my palms soaking wet, and each step inches me closer to the crest. I'm motivated simply by the prospect of catching my breath before having to endure it all over again.

At some point I mutter notes of encouragement to LB. "Come on! We got this!" If he could, he'd side-eye me and shake his head. "Dude, why you sweating us?" he'd say. "Of course we got this. Just do your part and I'll do mine. Quit fucking worrying."

*

Finally the road levels out and I'm on a flat and fast straightaway into the next big town, Gettysburg. I break at a corner store where the Middle Eastern man ringing me up says business is going to be good because it's bike week. "Oh cool," I say. "I love bikes!" Back outside, I keep an eye out for people in colorful kits zipping by on their carbon fiber customs. But the abundance of roaring Harleys sharing the road into town confirms my mistake. Bike Week in Gettysburg is like a mini-Sturgis. I'll arrive in the thick of it, sans leather or any degree of coolness.

*

All day they pass me, one thunderous engine after another. Riders acknowledge me with extended arms flashing low peace signs, which makes me feel included in their rebellious roar. I reply with quick waves as I try to keep LB true on the slanted and partial shoulder.

Silence slices the air between rumbles of riding groups. The rolling hills turn fragile. I assume every open field is a Civil War battle site. Tall grasses sway like weary soldiers in the intermittent breeze. Chaos ahead and chaos behind. But for a brief moment, peace.

*

In Gettysburg, I need refuge from the noise and bustle and stop in an empty shop where a sign above the door says Palm Reader. I browse the meager retail options, crystals and magic wands and books about past lives and meditation, and consider the possibility of having been drawn in here for other reasons.

I linger, expecting someone to join me in the waiting area, and pass time looking at a menu of offerings: Tarot readings, palm readings, crystal balls, past life analysis, magical remedies. I have so many looming questions. Like, what will come of Katie and me? Will I stay in Carrboro? How should I reinvent my business? Should I about-face and do this walk all over again? Or hop on a plane to Ushuaia and start a double continent crossing? I'd love for someone, or something, to help me find clarity. But I'm alone. Just here with myself and fretting about my future. Which is nothing new, really, except I'm doing it in this tourist trap.

The room suddenly feels hollow and contrived. Poorly lit and cold. I head for the door. Soon as I turn the knob, I hear footsteps and a woman's raspy voice. "Hello?" she says as she appears from behind a beaded doorway, rubbing her eyes. I stop and return her greeting. Her brown hair is disheveled, her shirt wrinkled. "Is there anything I can help you with today?" she says. Her tone is bothered. Like maybe I've interrupted something. A nap, most likely. "Um...no thanks," I say. "I think I got what I needed." I open the door and reenter the turbulence.

Day 194

The morning is quiet and hung over. I take foggy back roads out of Gettysburg, past placarded battlefields and memorial statues. I imagine the opposite of serenity, sprays of bullets and rivers of blood. Actual soldiers, not brass ones, waving victorious colors skyward. Eyes closing for a final time.

I step over a small American flag laying crumpled and stained in the street gutter. I stop to gather it, inspect its stem, then stab it into an adjacent lawn.

Up the road in Thomasville, I pass a couple sitting on the porch with their black lab. The man is shirtless. His white chest isn't used to the sun. "Hey!" he shouts, getting up from his chair. "Hold up a sec!" His name his Mike. He, his wife Pat, and their dog Samson come down to the sidewalk to say hello. They offer me water and Pat runs inside to grab it.

Mike's from Long Island, but he doesn't think of New York as home anymore. He's happy to be out of the rat race. "Everybody there does drugs," he says. "We just wanted to get away from all that." I ask if they've seen the motorcycles heading toward Gettysburg. "How could we miss 'em?" he says. "They just keep on coming!" Mike and Pat went to Gettysburg Bike Week once, and once, he says, was enough.

Mike asks about my route into the city as Pat hands me a glass of ice water. I empty it in one slug then answer. "York, Lancaster, Philly," I say. "Then a straight shot east to the coast. I'll take a quick ferry into Manhattan from Sandy Hook for my last day of walking from Manhattan to Brooklyn." Mike rubs his chest with both hands. "So, then what?" he asks. "Then it's over?" I nod. "Yeah I suppose it is," I say. He pauses and Samson pokes my leg with his snout. "It must feel weird," he says. "Yeah, it does," I say. "But I think it's about time for me to take all I've learned out here and get back to real life." Mike wishes me good luck as Pat reaches for a hug. "Hey, before you go," Mike says. "Let me give you some advice—be careful in York and Lancaster. But especially in York. People get killed over there every day. That place is trouble." Pat crosses her arms, nodding.

Outside a beauty shop in York stands a sandwich board that says Just Breathe. I stop walking and follow its direction. Deep inhale. Deep exhale. The first mindful breath I've taken all day. Shoot, the first one I've taken in a while.

Farther up, I approach a group of Black people sitting on the wide steps of a brick house stoop. Everyone's eyes are locked on Little Buddy. I stop and interrupt their staring. "You folks look like you're curious what's going on here," I say. They laugh. I introduce myself. "Well, I'm Adelia," says the eldest woman. A swatch of grey hair perfectly set atop her head and a red towel draped over one shoulder. "This is Buster, Nicole, and Kevin, my children." They all give me a wave. "You really walking?" Buster asks as he adjusts a velcro strap on his sandal. "No rides at all?" He shakes his head at my answer. "And now that I'm this close," I say, "a ride doesn't sound tempting at all. Not that it ever did."

Adelia looks toward Kevin. Ankle weights hang loose above his laceless Nike sneakers. "Hear that, Kev?" she says. "Might be the only man alive who could keep up with all the walking you do." Kevin slaps his hands on his muscular thighs. "Well, godspeed, my friend," he says. "You basically made it."

Day 195

Ahead, a rickety white truck tucks in alongside the walk ahead. As I approach, a white guy leans out the open passenger side window. Uses his hand to get my attention. "Man, we saw you a couple hours ago on the bridge," he says. "Wanted to stop and give you this twenty bucks. You can get you some lunch or something. I'm Ray and this is Harry." Our conversation gets them riled up and has a similar effect on me. "What are you going to do when you're done?" Harry asks, and I assume he wants to know about my work. It's been so long since I've thought about my business that I have a hard time describing exactly what I do for a living. So I simplify and tell him I'm a consultant, which has the effect it always does—it halts the conversation. When I don't elaborate, he leaves it alone. But his face tells me his question had nothing to do with my job.

"I know a guy who goes to Drexel who's about to do a wild adventure," Harry says, raising his tattooed hands. "Starting in

Philly, he's driving across the US, then up to Alaska, then hopping a freighter across the Bering Strait, going into Siberia, and somehow making his way from there to Bhutan on foot." They tell me I ought to link up with him. "Shit, forget that consulting thing!" Ray says. "This is your exit plan! You can't stop now! You've come this far already. Keep going!"

"Hey man, let me ask you this," Ray says. "What kind of cool stuff have you learned along the way? You must have had some pretty epic moments in your head. Shit, I know I would have." My mind races as I pause. I want to say something profound, but it's a hard question to answer in a roadside exchange. I tell Ray I'm still trying to process my experiences. "But you know," I say, "I'm pretty sure the overall lesson, if there is one, has something to do with kindness. The kindness of strangers—like you guys. There's a whole lot of goodness out there if we're open to it. But I don't know—so much has happened and I'm still trying to sort it all out." Ray shades his eyes from the sun. He reaches out the truck window and pats my chest with his heavy palm. "You got this, brother," he says. "You got this. Now go finish it and figure it all out." My eyes fill with water.

*

Once again, I surpass the mileage plan and creep closer to another 40-mile day. Coming this close to my longest day of the trip—41 miles—makes me want to push just a little farther for a new record. But such thoughts dissipate as I turn weary from the heat. No amount of honey buns and espresso is enough. No amount of water or medical-grade electrolyte replacement keeps me steady. But unlike the countless other times I've dealt with a similar predicament, today it's accompanied by something new. Emotional outbursts.

When I think about finishing, I lose my shit. My face explodes like a popped water balloon and I bellyache uncontrollably. When I picture Katie's face, or imagine her voice saying, "Hi Sugarpie," I repeat the outburst. When someone stops to say something nice, I crumble. Each wave of grief is followed by an instant of pure elation, but it only lasts a second before it quickly returns to more sorrow, more heartbreak. I sink into a despair saddled by that same nightmarish feeling I felt back on day one. I'm as afraid of returning to my so-called real life as I was to begin this walk across America.

My consciousness floats above my body as I walk along a tired backroad. Past windmills. Past "The Place That Made Shoo Fly Pie Famous." Past souvenir shops advertising Amish furniture and pretzels. Past a man in a black hat driving a horse-drawn buggy. I watch from above as he "woahs" his horses and offers me a safer, quieter alternate route toward the coast. I take it.

I step over another broken handgun. Past scatterings of construction workers who look right through me. Past the an empty gas station with an attendant who stands like a hood ornament. A young man stops me and asks if I'm a vegetarian. Then he hands me a bag of beef jerky. "You need this more than me," he says.

*

I see everything, every little detail, but it's all some kind of wonky surrealist painting. I'm the felled tree in the shape of an axe. The stomping clothesline with a porpoise head being pursued by a pterodactyl. I'm the clock melting across the back of the stilt-legged elephant. I'm a hamburger.

I know I need shade and rest and water and food, but such practical matters are unreachable behind the symphony of voices filling my head. It's Art and Lion and Leann and Jennifer and Q and so many others I never want to forget. I'm trying to hold them all in. I picture their faces and wish they could all be with me when I reach the water.

297

Day 196

As soon as I get on Strasburg Road in Gap, I wave at an old white woman who's walking gingerly on the opposite shoulder. She waves back, looks both ways, and quicksteps to my side. She steadies herself on LB's handlebar. "Oh boy. It's sure is hot," she says. She extends a fragile hand. Says her name is Billie. "Come with me inside real quick, won't ya." she says. "There's someone I'd like you to meet." We cross the highway together, and as she leads me up her driveway she twice asks where I started. "Los Angeles! Oh, that's just wonderful!" she replies both times.

She opens the screen door and I follow her inside. It slams behind us. "John!" she says in two syllables to a shirtless old man sitting in a recliner watching TV. "Guess who I found? The man from the newspaper who's walking across America!" John cuts off the television and slowly stands up. Dark brown splotches dot his loose, beige skin. He's 93 years old. Served in the South Pacific during World War II. He scoots toward me and I meet him halfway. Shakes my hand with a crushing grip and asks if he can make me a ham sandwich. "Go on! Sit down," Billie says. "Oh dear! You must be so tired."

Billie tells me she and John are friends. After their spouses passed away, they moved in together to keep each other company. "I worked at Pillsbury for 40 years," Billie says. "You know, the Jolly Green Giant. Only missed one day in all that time. I loved to work. Drove a forklift most of the time." She said one day a bigwig watched her working and told the supervisor to hire more women. "They said I did a better job than the men did," she says as she folds her hands in her lap. "Now, where did you say you started again?" she says.

John returns with my sandwich on a plate and says he wants to see my cart. We all go outside. John rubs his chin as he gives Little Buddy a once over. "How's she holding up?" he asks. "A little rickety," I say. "But I think it'll make to the end." He squeezes LB's handlebar. "Boy do I know that feeling," he says.

John's attention shifts to the highway. "I've lived here my whole life, you see," he says. "My wife is passed. Got no kids. I'm just waiting here with Billie as we both near the end."

Billie goes inside and returns with another sandwich. She hands me a ziplock filled with dark purple cherries, stems attached. "There you go,"she says. "Now you can spit the cherry pits at bad drivers," John says. The way he says cherries sounds like *churries*. "Tell me again where you started?" Billie asks. "Los Angeles," I say again. "Oh wow. I've never been to Los Angeles!" she says. "You hear that, John? He started from Los Angeles!" I drink another cup of water, eat the second sandwich, and it's time to go.

"Give me a kiss before you leave," Billie says. "And please write me a letter. I promise I'll write you back." I tell her I'll send a postcard from New York. "Oh, I would like that very much!" she says. "Please do that!" Billie and John stand in the driveway as I turn out of sight. I open the baggie and run my fingers over the fat cherries. They're big as plums. I bite into one and its juice stains my fingers. One leads to more and I stash the pits in the corner of my mouth until there's too many to hold. Then I aim and spit them out like a machine gun. The stones hit the ground with a soft tap. "Churries," I say. I repeat the new word over and over until it sounds like gibberish.

*

I'm sunken-eyed and road-weary, itchy under my arms and between my legs from prickly heat. Sweat drips in a steady stream down my sleeve and my shirt smells like ammonia. I've considered trashing it, but I'm too sentimental. I catch my reflection in a West Chester storefront window and worry my tomato face is a bad sign. I tune into my heartbeat, it seems normal, but everything can change in a second.

Finally on a sidewalk, with the sun low and the humidity losing its bite, I'm within range of my hotel. Two young people— a white woman in a long orange dress and an Asian woman with two-tone braids—call at me from a parking lot. I perk up. "Hi! You want a beer?" one asks. "It's not very cold but—" I interrupt. "Absolutely!" I say. Erin and Liz, students at West Chester University, are returning from the grocery store. Liz has big plans to travel, too. She understands the allure of following her dreams, even though she says it's hard to make things happen. She offers me a cigarette. I tell her I don't smoke. "Yeah, I guess I should have figured that," she says, tucking the pack back into her pocket.

They congratulate me for coming this far. "All the way from California to West Chester, Pennsylvania. Damn, dude!" They ask for a hug and I warn them about my soaking wet and disgusting shirt. But they don't care and they squeeze me like a sponge. For a moment I am weightless.

Day 197

Last night, any time I'd start to fade, I'd wake to stabbing charley horses in my legs. But then my body finally let go, and I crashed hard. So hard that I woke this morning in the same position I flopped. Now, I look at myself in the mirror and see someone an unfamiliar face. I run my fingers over my cheeks and eyelids. I'm an extra in an western film. The suncooked guy who comes crawling out of the desert begging for water.

I take the elevator to the free breakfast and fill my belly with three packs of maple oatmeals and a dozen shriveled sausages. I go back for seconds. And thirds. I fill my cargo pocket with prepacked mini bear claws and a stale raisin bagel wrapped in paper towels. The clerk asks how I enjoyed my stay in West Chester, which suddenly reminds me I am in West Chester. Time and place has grown increasingly difficult to differentiate. Seems just yesterday I was in Harrisonburg, Huntsville, Little Rock, Silver City, Phoenix, Palm Springs. Seems like just yesterday I was home.

*

Soon as I'm on West Chester Pike, a big yellow sign warns "Beware of Aggressive Drivers." Defensive walking has been my rule, but the alert amplifies my regular traffic anxiety.

After a long stretch of aging strip malls and industrial centers, I enter West Philly along Market Street. Old, decrepit houses sit so close together they hold each other up. The train crackles past on the elevated rail. People of color congregate on street corners and stop what they're doing to say hello.

Handshake after handshake, hug after hug, I feel more like a politician than a wanderer. I gradually make my way downtown where tall, white buildings and congested traffic dominate the landscape. Well-dressed people, mostly white, rush past wearing earbuds and sunglasses. People give way to LB but nobody stops us, nobody except one man, Willem, a tourist from LA on a road trip across the US. He stops me on Independence Mall near the National Constitution Center. "Our auras brought us together!" he says. Willem tells me he believes that what we put off is precisely that which we attract.

*

The Benjamin Franklin Bridge is pedestrian friendly. It spans nearly two miles over the Delaware River into New Jersey. I cross into another state and take selfies with the City of Brotherly Love's skyline behind me.

I enter a desolate corner of Camden. No pedestrians or commuters. No bikes. Just empty shells of buildings, broken windows, and abandoned cars. The landscape is pocked with overflowing trash cans and unkempt swatches of grassy weeds. There's obvious fire damage in a lot left to rot. Tree roots push up through sidewalk cracks and I think of resilience. Here, the quiet openness seems like something's been forgotten. Especially in contrast to the other side of the bridge.

I chug along Federal Street and stop for a break in a shady park. An older man wearing a bright yellow shirt and matching hat stands with a rake in one hand, and a wheeled garbage can in the other. He introduces himself as Juni. He works for the city. "See all these planter boxes," he says. "I keep them looking nice. Add mulch, plant flowers. Throw away trash. I also sweep the walks. Sometimes I paint over graffiti, but not often."

Juni is from Puerto Rico. He's in the Latin gospel choir at his church. "When I was a kid I wanted to be a singer," he says. "God told me if I visited five churches I'd learn all I need to know. So I set out alone to do just that. At each church, I identified the lead vocalist and listened to what they did. Watched how they moved. And now I'm a combination of all of them." He places his rake into his cart and puts his hands over his heart. "Tom—do you mind if I sing you a song?" He softly clears his throat. Then his voice breezes into a melody. with pitch-perfect vibrato. He accentuates Spanish words with his hands, his body. I can't translate fast enough to know exactly what he's singing about, but it doesn't matter because I don't need to know the words. I can feel them. My shoulders relax. My teeth stop clenching. Juni finishes the song with his hand on my shoulder. His eyes peer deeply into mine. "You see, Tom. That's the sound of God working through me. It's my honor to offer kindness in this way."

I ask Juni what he's doing today. "Oh, a little of this and a little of that, like always," he says. "But maybe a little extra, too. We'll see."

*

A couple blocks later as I near a barber shop, a Black man with a long goatee beard sits on the concrete steps and messes with his phone. He looks up as I pass, then hollers for me to stop. We introduce ourselves. He's Jerry. "I want to be a part of this," he says.

Our conversation turns immediately deep. We share thoughts on personal energy. About setting intentions and choosing happiness. "The world could be falling down around us but ultimately we choose how to respond to it," he says. "I haven't always seen things this way, but I'm starting to believe it's possible."

"So there must be a reason why you're doing all this?" Jerry says. I tell him I've struggled with answering that particular question since day one. "Yeah, there is," I say. "But my response is never the same. What started as a personal goal has evolved into something I didn't expect." I tell Jerry the reason has evolved to be less about me, and more about meeting a bunch of random strangers. "But still, there's even more to it," I say. "Even though I'm about to be done, I don't quite have the exact words for it yet." Jerry's brows raise. "I get it," he says. "Lately I've been learning a lot about myself, too. It's not always easy to explain the shifts as they happen. Time will likely shine a light on it all."

Jerry's brown irises turn iridescent as the midday sun illuminates his face. I'm struck by his kind eyes and tell him so. "You can tell a lot about someone by their eyes, you know," I say. He thanks me. Looks down at his feet for a second, then back up at me. His hand shades the sun glare. "It really matters to me that you noticed that," he says. "Because I'm trying. Really trying. And I'm finally starting to believe these things about myself, too."

I tell Jerry that maybe we just need to trust our gut and not try to understand things so much. That maybe *just being* is what it's all about. We exchange contact information and hope we'll cross paths again. "And hey, I'd like to hug you if that's OK," I say. "Yeah man, come on," Jerry says as he opens his arms like wings.

12

I knew long ago
and rediscovered
that the best way to attract
attention, help, and conversation
is to be lost.

- John Steinbeck
Travels With Charley

Day 198

AFTER NEARLY 200 DAYS OF WALKING

I still don't have my *why* locked down. Flashes of certainty happen on occasion when, for a brief moment, everything about this walk makes perfect sense. But just like with a dream, the lucidity often vanishes as soon as I try to put things into words. I find myself grasping at a certainty that was so clear only seconds ago.

But I've stopped beating myself up for not having an eloquent or certain why to share with others. I've come to accept the fact that today's answer is the correct one. Sometimes I'm walking because it's been the plan for nearly a quarter century. Sometimes I'm walking to better tune in with myself, or live life at a slower pace, or make unexpected connections with others. Sometimes I'm walking because being out here makes me feel most alive. But sometimes it's to escape and to be alone. And sometimes the likely prospect of a random hug makes it all worthwhile. Yet sometimes I don't have a reason at all—I'm just walking.

I've stopped believing my life needs a mission statement. I'm the best version of myself when I honor what's truly happening inside of me—when I stop trying to formulate a contrived version of reality. For far too long I sought profundity in an attempt to make myself more interesting, and frankly, I'm over it. My goal now is to seek out the delight of each day. To celebrate the glorious minutiae. And when I look for it, I find it. Without fail. I believe this is enough.

I also recognize that my perspective of this walk will likely change with time. I may uncover a deeper driving reason for this walkabout. My memories will likely change as I change, too. But right now all I know is I don't want to make the walk any more than it is. I want to stay open to the myriad possibilities that come along with it. Right now I want to tune into the beating of my own heart so I might be better able to tune into others. Today, this is my why. And I'm fine with it.

Day 199

As I funnel toward the ocean, I meet more people than ever. And even though I can taste the salt in the air, I am grateful these conversations delay my final stretch to the beach.

I remind myself to savor these last few days. I make sure I'm taking time to breathe, to be present, to see. I know full well my privilege and good fortune are to thank for my near arrival. Sure, I want to be done. To end my journey of six million steps. But at this moment, I am here. In rural Jersey. Nothing else is but now.

*

With four days left to knock out the remaining 60 miles to the coast, I take my time. I sleep in a bit and enjoy an actual cup of coffee before setting out. I normally walk at a clip just faster than four miles per hour, but today I halve it. I slow my pace to a *saunter* and recall the possible origins of that word as described in Henry David Thoreau's essay, *Walking*. It may come from "a la Sainte-Terre," which means "to the Holy Land" and describes people who roved about accepting charity on their pilgrimages to Jerusalem. But it also may derive from "sans terre," meaning "without land or home." A person who is equally comfortable anywhere. I think both etymologies apply to some degree. But the second one especially resonates and I daydream of a future sans terre. Forever roaming about at a snail's pace, calling anywhere I happen to lay my head down, home.

*

Midmorning near Hainesport, a man walks toward me on the wide shoulder. I can read his body language—he's coming to meet me. We near and he introduces himself. Mike. Clean-shaven white guy, Adidas ball cap on his head, and strong hands that give themselves away when we shake. His are the hands of someone who uses them for a living. Construction, maybe. His accent rings with sounds I've often tried to imitate when doing my impression of an east coast mafioso. He wants to help. "Food, money, place to stay, whatever you need," he says. I'm craving a sandwich, like a big-ass east coast hoagie, and I tell him so. A half hour later, he returns with a couple bags of food. We grab a picnic table at a nearby park and eat lunch together.

Mike is retired. He used to build bridges until one day he fell multiple stories onto a concrete slab. Landed flat on his back. "I was in a medical coma for a couple weeks," he says. "I pretty much forgot everything in the days leading up to the accident. I'm a big Phillies fan—and I don't even remember watching the no-hitter the week before. That should tell you something!"

Day 200

The blacktop shoulder narrows, forcing me to keep Little Buddy's left wheels on the unpaved surface. Normally this is fine since it's grass or packed dirt. But I've reached the end of the hardpack and now it's sand. When the loose grains take hold of LB's wheels, all his forward momentum comes to an abrupt stop and I nearly go over his handlebars. Traffic thickens.

The same Mike from yesterday stops again and suggests we take lunch at a coming pizzeria. We talk sports and Mike explains the difference between North Jersey and South Jersey loyalties. "Here we're all about the Eagles and the Phillies," he says. "But if you go to North Jersey, everybody likes New York's teams."

Mike asks me what's next. "You mean next like *today*, next?" I ask. "Or like after the walk, next?" Mike says today. I tell him I'm hoping to get to Freehold. Mike finishes chewing the last of his crust and takes a swig of Coke. He sets down the styrofoam cup. "Don't be surprised if you see Bruce," he says and I stop chewing. "That's right. That Bruce."

For the rest of the day the sun rages down. The approaching ocean hasn't really cooled things off yet. I walk singing Bruce's "I'm On Fire," as its tempo sets the perfect pace for my afternoon into his hometown. Step—step—step—step. "Hey little girl is your daddy home? Did he go and leave you all alone? I got a bad desire." I'm amazed that I still know all these words to the song even though the last time I listened to it was probably the same year the album came out—1984. But it's carved into my brain, a permanent part of me. "Sometimes it's like someone took a knife, baby edgy and dull, and dug a six-inch valley through the middle of my soul." I think of Katie. In four days I'll see her again. *Four days.* "Woah-oh-oh, I'm on fire."

*

I make it to Freehold and keep an eye out for the Boss. I get the last room at an overpriced mall hotel where the front desk clerk asks me if I'm here for the wedding. "Nope," I say. "I'm walking across America. And tomorrow, if all goes well, I'll see the ocean after two hundred and one days on the road." He sticks to the script. Hands me my room key and rattles off details about the exercise room, the pool, and the free morning breakfast.

In the hallway, housekeeping staff have to move their cleaning carts to make way for Little Buddy. I have a minor anxiety attack thinking about whether or not I'll have to disassemble him to get him in the room. It's always such a crap shoot, but expensive hotels are usually the least accommodating. I let out a whoop when the doorway is just wide enough to fit his girth. "Glory days!" I sing out loud. Then give the housekeeping crew a thumbs up.

Day 201

Butterflies flicker and whiz around me and Little Buddy. They land on his bars and lid, on my hands and hat brim. What was it Amena said back in Alabama? That the abundance of butterflies means something? I think right now it simply means I'm paying attention.

*

In West Park off of Rumson Road, I take a break on a bench overlooking the Shrewsbury River Bridge. The Atlantic Ocean teases me from periodic vantage points. A horn blows and the bridge draws to allow passage of a sailboat. Two blonde women approach with a yellow poodle. They are mother and daughter, Carol and Bridget, and their dog Tucker. They saw me earlier in the day. "We read the sign on your back," Carol says. "And for the rest of the morning we've been talking about you. We were even inspired to go for a walk. We're three miles in." They ask how far I'm going today. "I'm figuring I'll total about twenty-seven," I say. "But maybe a little less. However long it takes me to get to Sandy Hook." They look at each other and laugh. "And we thought three was a lot," they say. I tell them I'm procrastinating a bit right now. That I'm not sure if I'm ready to see the ocean yet.

Bridget looks at my feet. "How many pairs of shoes have you gone through?" She guesses seven and she's spot on. "So, what kind of food do you eat?" asks Bridget. "Like, granola and stuff?" I crack up. Make some kind of joke like, of course I only eat granola. Then I lift LB's flap to show them my food stash. There's not much left. Just a couple cans of refried beans, a half pack of tortillas, some instant oats, peanut butter, and a few apples. "I'm not eating five star," I say. "But I'm definitely not going hungry."

Before leaving, they both give me hugs. "Thank you so much, I really needed this," I say. "This morning's been a bit of a mental rollercoaster." Carol nods knowingly. "Probably because you are about to be done," she says. Her words are just what I need to get going. I load up LB and head to the bridge as it lowers. When I'm finally across the Shrewsbury River, the Atlantic Ocean comes into full view. "I made it," I say. I enter the town of Sea Bright and take a sharp left, heading north on Ocean Avenue.

*

The heaving wind warns of weather to come and I hope to make it to Sandy Hook before it arrives. Whitecaps crest on waves. The sound of seagulls and vacationers fills the space between gusts.

I could park LB and run out on the beach right now. Dive in the ocean and call this walk a wrap. But I don't, and I won't. I refuse to touch the ocean until four days from now.

*

I'm a solid day ahead of schedule, and my camping reservation at Gateway National Recreation Area is for tomorrow. Earlier today, their online portal showed some available sites, but now there are none. I've still got about five miles before I make it to the ranger station, and odds are I'll arrive after hours. If I do catch a ranger, I'm sure they'll help me figure something out. Worst case I'll just find a stealth spot to crash. But right now, my biggest concern is the coming weather. A fine storm is brewing and I'm going to need cover soon.

*

I move along at my normal clip, wave at a parade of out-of-state cars, and field an occasional question or drive-by photo. A pair of scooters pull up. The two riders hit their brakes and flip their helmet masks. "Hi! I'm Candance," one says. "Spelled like 'can-dance.' And this is Jojo." Jojo says hi and promptly asks if I need any food. I tell her I'm good to go—and I am—I've managed to whittle down my stash to precisely all I need before boarding the ferry to Manhattan in a couple days. "Well, I'm going to get you some food, anyhow," she says. "My husband runs that restaurant over there." She points to a massive resort on the ocean side. "I'm going to have them make you up something." Jojo asks what sorts of food I like and if I have any dietary restrictions. Then she flips her visor back down and scoots into traffic.

Candance and I chat about my trip. "And what about the people?" she says. "How have they been?" She's surprised when I tell her that every day strangers sought me out to do nice things. "Just like you and Jojo are doing right now," I say. "Kindness is everywhere in America. And it'll find you if you're open to it. It found me, that's for sure." Candance takes off her sunglasses and wipes her eyes. "It's such a relief to hear that," she says. "We are all so inundated with the opposite. It's exhausting, I swear."

Jojo returns with four young people, staffers from the restaurant. One's lugging a big bag of food and hands it over. She describes its contents: "Chicken fingers and dipping sauces, a salad, a cheeseburger, some chips, and some other things we tossed in." Jojo asks if I have a reservation at the Hook. "I do, but not until tomorrow," I say. "I made it here a day too soon. No matter how hard I tried, I couldn't slow down." Candance and Jojo offer to ride ahead and tell the rangers I'm en route. We exchange phone numbers, I give everyone giant hugs, and I continue plodding north. Soon I get a text from Candance confirming the rangers have gone home for the night. Says to call her if I get in a pinch.

*

As I'm peeking in the high window of the ranger's empty registration trailer, a woman exits an adjacent restroom. Her name is Miel. "The campsite is completely full," she says. "But hey, my group has two sites booked and we're only using one. How about you just take the other? It's D-16, right over there.

And when you have a chance, stop on over to our site. We're a fun bunch and we'd love to have you."

I set up my tent and get situated for the night. I take a quick sink shower in the bathroom and feel a thousand times better. I dig through my food stash to collect a couple packs of peanuts and some individually wrapped Twizzlers. Then I enter Miel's camp with candy in hand. "Knock knock!" I announce. "I come bearing gifts." Miel introduces me to everyone—Scotty and Thui, Tasha and Ted, and Miel's partner, Goose. "Your timing is perfect," Miel says. "We're just about ready for dinner."

Someone puts a beer in my hand while others make room on an inflatable couch under a makeshift awning. "We're hoping this is enough cover," Ted says. "It's supposed to really come down tonight." Miel insists I grab a plate and help myself. I pile it high with wings and ribs, barbecued veggies, cole slaw, and potato salad.

When I return to my spot on the couch, it starts to rain. The temperature drops as we eat, and soon we're all packed-in on the slippery seat. Someone's playlist thumps softly to trance beats.

During a break in the downpour, everyone scatters for more food except Scotty and Miel. Scotty enters an adjacent tent and Miel messes with a strap on her sundress. She stops me as I head to the food table for seconds. Asks me if her shoulders are sunburnt. I squint to see better in the dim lantern light. "Ooof. Looks painful," I say. Miel shrugs, then tugs at the ties and her dress drops off. She quick catches it and covers up again. "Whoops," she says with a smile. "How rude of me not to ask— you aren't offended by nudity, are you Tom?" I stammerlaugh and she rephrases her question. "I mean, you wouldn't mind if I took my clothes off, would you?" I stand immobile, my plate catching droplets of rain that fall between us. I glance down at remnants of my potato salad, spicy barbecue sauce, and crumbs of Cool Ranch Doritos as it all mixes with splashing water. I reluctantly look back up at Miel. I haven't seen a naked body in more than six months and am flash frozen by her question. I collect myself and clear my throat. "Well. It's your party," I say.

"I'm totally fine with whatever." Miel smiles. Then, slowly this time, she lets her dress fall completely to the ground and kicks it away. "Oh my God!" she exclaims. "This is *so* much better!" Her body literally glows—everything that was covered by her dress is adorned with swirls of neon pink and green paint.

"So, mister Tom, let me fill you in," Miel says playfully with her hands on her hips. "All of us here are nudists and swingers. And we really, really, *really* like to do drugs." Someone shouts a "cheers" and the group clinks beer bottles. "But don't misunderstand," Tasha interrupts. "We're also just regular, normal people. I'm a CPA, she's a lawyer, he's a schoolteacher. We just like to party in—how should I say it—a *particular* kind of way." I look back and forth at the group, expecting someone to reveal the practical joke. "Believe it, my man!" Scotty shouts from inside his tent. "And in a bit we'll show you what we've got cooking up in here."

*

The rain starts again and we form a tight huddle on the couch under the sagging tarp. Goose pushes the heavy water from where it puddles and Miel positions herself underneath the showering cascade. "It's so warm!" she says, as she dances in the waterfall.

Eventually, the group decides it's time to upgrade the booze to something stronger. One at a time, folks go into Scotty's tent as he dispenses a dose of ecstasy. "Go in and visit Molly!" folks say when it's the next person's turn. Each comes out encouraging me to go next, but I'm still on the fence.

Besides the time in the early '90s when I snorted a line of coke in a bar bathroom, my experimentation with drugs has been limited to marijuana. And even that's old news. Middle age has altered my metabolism to such a degree that a third beer now puts me over the edge and takes multiple days to fully leave my system. I have no context for ingesting a psychoactive drug and

I'm afraid what might happen if I partake. But I'm also intrigued, so I'm staying open to whatever ends up happening.

I watch others intently as the drug takes effect. Their auras seem to peacefully glow as they settle into a relaxed buzz. "I'm pretty sure you'll like it," Miel says. "And Scotty will make sure you don't take too much." I tell her I'm apprehensive, and she validates my concern. But she also assures me it's not that big of a deal. "Plus, we're all looking after each other," she says. I remember one of my mantras for this walk—*Say yes as often as possible*—and decide what the hell. "Fuck it," I say. "Let's do it." The group applauds when I start moving toward Scotty's glowing tent. "Come in and visit Molly!" he beckons.

Inside, Scotty asks my weight and tells me he'll cut me a quarter hit so we can see how my body responds. I watch as he scoots powder onto a scale like one from my high school biology class. Adds a little, subtracts a little. Then he expertly taps the powder onto a small piece of thin paper and folds it up just-so. He hands it over like it's fragile. "This is a partial dose for someone your size," he says. "Just swallow it with some water. It'll take about twenty minutes to kick in. You may need more to truly feel it. And there's plenty more where that came from." I down it with a sip of beer. "There ya go!" he says proudly. "But hey, don't drink any more of that beer. It'll ruin it." Scotty pats me on the back and I exit the tent to a standing ovation. I give the group a thumbs up. Tasha, now also completely naked and cuddled against Ted on the couch, pats the empty space beside her. The tapping sounds like a beach ball. "Get back over here, new guy," she says, "I need someone else to keep me warm."

My dose was minuscule compared to everyone else's, but within minutes I feel it starting to take hold. My skin is warm and prickly and my mind fully at ease. I feel the heat from where my legs press against the plastic chair, and the piercing coolness of each occasional raindrop. In group gatherings I usually have to manage some sort of social anxiety, but right now I'm completely at home amongst these strangers. "You feeling it yet?" Scotty says as he exits the tent. "I am," I say, as I slouch back on the plastic couch. He laughs as he motions for Thui to join him and they excuse themselves to another tent. Thui exchanges looks with us like, *see you later on.*

Ted gets up to go to the bathroom, and without his balancing weight on the inflated couch, Tasha and I suddenly press tightly together. Her hand falls onto my knee and she leaves it there. She looks up at me and bites her bottom lip. "Hey everyone," she announces without breaking eye contact, "I don't think anybody's kissed the new guy yet." Her hand touches my cheek and Miel throws her head back, laughing. "Nope," she says. "I don't believe they have!"

Day 202

My body regularly awakens at the exact same time, 5:13 a.m., and today is no exception. But this morning I'm up with a throbbing headache from last night's shenanigans. It won't get any better lying in a tent already thick with the day's humidity, so I fumble to get dressed and stumble to the bayside of Sandy Hook. It's a good thing I'm not walking today. I'm a wreck from my MDMA quarter hit.

The rain has stopped but a steady wind remains. Waves of water bounce off the land and crash into themselves in a confusion of foamy ripples and cresting whitecaps. A high-pitched screech directs my attention upward where an osprey kites, scoping out its breakfast prey. Alongside the gliding bird are three others doing the same thing. They chatter, one at a time, long and short calls. I've watched osprey hunt before, but never have I seen them do so in a group like this. Cool gusts shove them into each others' space. Unphased, they adjust position and reset their formation. Occasionally one dives like a rocket toward the bay, hits the surface with a tiny splash, and talonhooks a fish, then disappears down the coastline. But even when one flies off, there are always four birds hovering in wait, patiently engaged in the hunt.

A fisherman casts his rod off the muddy beach. Pulls it up empty. He greets me as I near him. I wonder if he's catching anything. "Nah," he says. "I'm the only guy stupid enough to be out here fishing today. Everything's churned and messy. All I'm catching is lettuce." He reels in the line and pulls up a clump of slimy seaweed. "Maybe it's more about being out here than it is catching the damn fish?" I say. He unhooks the green clump and hurls it into the ocean. "All I know for sure is I'm the only guy dumb enough to be out here," he says. I give him a look. "Well, maybe not the only one," he says.

*

Jojo sends a text offering to bring me coffee and breakfast. "I'll have to drop and dash," she writes. "I'm off to cater a movie set in Brooklyn." Just as I get back to my site, she shows up with a feast: a ham and cheese omelette, a pile of home fries, a biscuit with strawberry cream butter, two perfect bananas, a granola bar, two cups of piping hot coffee, and a tall cup of fresh squeezed OJ. "You're an angel," I say. "I bet you met many angels along the way," she replies. "Yeah, I definitely did, but you're today's angel." She gives me a big hug and rushes off, hoping to beat traffic.

I hear Miel's voice. "Morning!" she says as she enters my campsite. "That was fun last night, wasn't it?" She looks cozy with her hands tucked into her hoodie's pockets. "Totally," I say. "But I'm paying for it today. My body's not used to pretty much anything we did." She laughs. "Hey—we want to invite you over for breakfast," she says. Her timing is perfect, because the pile of food from Jojo is way too much for just one person.

At Miel's camp, I sit on the reinflated couch and fill my belly with food again. Tasha puts her head on my shoulder and closes her eyes. "Was nice to meet you, new guy," she says. I wrap my arm around her. Pretty sure I'll never see any of these people again.

The wind picks up and offers breaks of sunlight and blue sky. "Finally!" someone exclaims. Though conversation revolves around the naps to come, they've got to get home first. I help them break camp, and follow their lead as they haphazardly pile soaked gear into three vehicles. I thank them for taking me in and making a seventh wheel feel so welcome. "It's what we do," Miel says. "And what we all should be doing, all the time."

Day 203

I spend the next two days on the Hook. Get to know rangers Gage and Bear, and offer counsel to TJ, a young guy beat down by a week long music festival and issues with his girlfriend. "We're here to rest at the nude beach. And to hopefully reconcile. We both made some really bad decisions at last week's event. We said and did mean things to each other. But I blame it on the drugs." I suggest he gets some rest, then talk to her about it when they are both in a better state of mind. As I walk back to my site, I laugh at the irony of me giving any sort of relationship advice.

*

I walk to Fort Hancock at the end of the peninsula. Take a guided tour of the Sandy Hook Light, the oldest working lighthouse in the US. The fort's old barracks and parade grounds remind me of my time at basic training at Fort Jackson, South Carolina. White, colonial-style buildings remark on a time long past. They make me nostalgic, and I spend time walking in circles, unwilling to leave the pull of memories. The past is often reshaped as something attractive, even if in reality it was a version of hell.

*

At the opposite end of Sandy Hook I find a food truck that sells empanadas. I sit in a shady spot and write postcards. Later, back at camp, I notice a man who keeps walking back and forth from his truck to his site with a loaded dolly. Turns out he's an independent construction foreman who travels around doing various jobs. To save on hotel expenses, he always stays in campsites. "I'm a full time glamper," he says. "You're welcome to come on over anytime to check out my setup. Feel free to use my solar shower even if I'm not here.

When the sun gets low, I sit at my picnic table and watch my neighbor like a voyeur. He lounges on a blow-up easy chair inside a large, screened-in tent. The tall lamp above him sends a dim glow over his digs. It's a proper living room. On my final night, the aroma of mesquite from his mini-barbecue tempts me to join him. As does his classic rock playlist that's spun no less than three big-hair metal songs in the past hour. Poison, Great White, and Ratt. But when Emil, a touring cyclist, parks his rig in the site shared with mine, we get to talking and my neighbor's dinnertime comes and goes. Emil is from Germany. He's finishing his transcon in New York City the day after tomorrow, just like me.

Emil and I share a large roofed pavilion that will offer cover from the rain in tonight's forecast. It's going to pour, so we scoot the heavy tables out of the way and set up our tents on a concrete floor under the permanent shelter. I assume we'll eat our evening meal together, so I hold off cracking open one of the two cans of Bud Light I've been lugging for more than 500 miles. I'm just about to offer him one when he says goodnight, crawls into his tent, and zips a wall between us. Within minutes he's snoring.

I eat my final New Jersey dinner alone. The last can of chili, my final apple, bruised and damaged, the remaining spoonfuls of my chunky peanut butter, and a large Snickers I grabbed a few days back for this very night. I crack open one of the cans of warm beer. Try to picture the face of the man who gave it to me. I look toward Emil's tent and silently raise my can toward him. I finish it as the rain starts, then drink the other, too, so it doesn't go to waste.

All night the rain thunders on the shelter's tin roof. Water drips and drains into a perimeter of puddles around the foundation. By morning, the storm is gone. And so is Emil. Just a perfectly straight tread mark through damp sand leading toward the NYC finish line.

Day 204

I tear down camp for the last time of this trip and load up Little Buddy. He feels weightless and extra-nimble. The five-gallon jug of water that usually anchors him down is empty. My food stash is gone. And the extra water bottles I've been reusing since Arkansas now lie in the bottom of the camp dumpster. I get emotional as I dispose of the Albertsons grocery bag that's served as my daily trash receptacle since day two. As it leaves my hands and settles atop a mound of others' rubbish, I pridefully revel in having reused it so many times. And since it's still got some life left in it, I also feel sort of guilty for chucking it. Part of me wants to save it as a momento to show my nonexistent grandkids. *And this here is the trash bag I used for my entire walk across America. Ain't it something!* I think of all the waste I generate in my life and make a mental note to be more mindful. Because if a disposable garbage sack can last more than six months, what else in my life am I throwing away too soon? Probably a lot.

*

Back on the footpath toward the ferry stop, I'm shocked by how wide Little Buddy seems. How did I ever manage him on narrow roads with speeding cars? Or worse, on roads without a shoulder? How the hell did we navigate without incident? The journey seems like someone else's miracle as I steer him to the side to make way for a young couple on a pair of yellow beach cruisers. It's amazing how we adapt to things, and equally curious how quickly these adaptations are forgotten.

A lifetime of travel has taught me the importance of being time-cautious with public transport, so I arrive at the dock more than an hour early. Yesterday they cancelled this seasonal stop due to inclement weather. Today's blue skies find me optimistic. But you never know.

A woman rides up on her bike. The panniers are a dead giveaway and I ask how far she's come. Marie is cycling from Orlando to Montreal. We commiserate about how we'll get our rigs on board and where we'll stash them thereafter. Fifteen minutes before launch, buses of day-use beachgoers arrive and folks line up behind us in a queue. Ranger Kathleen preps the gates for passenger entry. Greets us both with a wide smile. "You folks traveling together?" she asks. "No," I say. "But Marie here has ridden her bike all the way from doggone Florida!" Ranger Kathleen throws her arms in the air. "I've been working this route for years and have never met anyone doing that sort of thing." Kathleen asks about my baby jogger. "Well then! Who'd have figured?" she says. "Today I meet two people doing unthinkable things! Must be my lucky day!"

*

Little Buddy fits just fine on the ramp leading to the ferry but once on board I'll need to stash him in a cordoned section for safety's sake. "The best view is from the roof," a deckhand says, then walks me to the closest stairway. Up top the seating is empty, and only a few folks are standing along the rail, peering at the distant view of Staten Island beyond Lower New York Bay. The ferry sounds its horn, and soon Manhattan's skyline towers in the distance like unexpected mountains. I'm overcome by the shock of suddenly being in the presence of something massive. I think of what a man in Texas told me as he kicked a rock with his worn alligator boot. "There are no destinations, just a string of temporary stops," he said. "And though we try to touch the horizon, we know in our heart it's futile."

Today, New York is my horizon. My temporary stop. I work to catch my breath as the ferry rises and falls over the ripples of the bay. I catch the eye of an older woman leaning on the rail. Her hair blows wildly as she motions her head toward the coming skyline and nods at me. I return the gesture, and that is enough.

*

When we dock in New York, my gurgling stomach calms. I disembark on East 35th Street where Katie's brother, Andrew, meets me. He guides us six miles back to his place in Harlem via a handful of inconvenient photo op detours to 42nd Street, Times Square, and the Apollo Theater.

At Andrew's apartment I disassemble Little Buddy for the last time and stash him in the stairwell. Tomorrow, on my final day of walking, I'll leave him behind. I definitely don't need to carry anything substantial to Coney Island. Plus, he'll only further hog the already congested New York City sidewalks. And though the decision to leave him behind makes perfect sense, it also makes me sad that he won't be with me at the end.

*

While Andrew and I chat in his kitchen, I get a text from Katie. Her flight landed on time at La Guardia and she's a few blocks away. Our reunion is muted by the presence of her brother, but for the evening's duration we stay close at each other's side. The three of us hit a Sengalese place for dinner and catch up. Just like at the cafe on day one with Joel and Brittany, I'm present but not fully here. My mind carries me above our table to spectate these final moments before it's all over. But unlike that day more than six months ago, I am not afraid. I am ready.

I make the excuse that I ought to get a good night's rest for tomorrow's walk into Brooklyn. But really, tomorrow's mileage is no big deal. Seems forever ago that a 20-mile day was substantial. Now it's what I do every morning before lunch.

Back in the apartment, Katie and I scoot living room furniture out of the way to make room for our nest of blankets. We spoon on the floor. "This time tomorrow I'll be done," I say. Katie waits for me to say more, but I don't. "How do you think you'll feel?" she asks. I take a deep breath and try to imagine myself in this same place 24 hours from now. "I don't know," I say. "Same as I do now, I suppose." Katie challenges my answer. "Well then, how do you feel *now*?" she says. I wiggle my body to get closer to her. My bruised hips appreciate the thick layer of comforters we've made on the hardwood. My pause lengthens until I assume she's no longer awaiting my response. "It's going to be cool be able to say that I walked across America," I say. "But really, I think I'm ready to do it all over. Not necessarily another walk, but something that brings out what this walk did. Because I really like who I became out here."

Day 205

We're in no rush. We get up when we wake up, eat a little breakfast, and put a few snacks in a day pack. After the sun's been up for a couple hours, Katie, Andrew, and I head out. Outside the apartment I snap a selfie of the three of us and post it on social media. "Final Day: And we are off!" I write.

We stop at Lenox Coffee, my favorite neighborhood spot for espresso. I order an americano and cinnamon roll then we sit and watch people file in. I take another photo and post a note on social media. "Lenox Coffee, Harlem! Hell yeah!"

*

It's weird walking without Little Buddy. Without bars to push on, I'm not sure what to do with my hands. Every now and then I catch my reflection in a window. I'm super lean. My neon construction vest is now a dull yellow. The Walking Across America sign is fraying at its edges, attached with rusty safety pins. My floppy hat, version two, has holes worn through the top. My rank and threadbare shoes probably should have been replaced 100 miles ago. I'm wearing the less stinky of my two snap-up long sleeves. I stand tall. My strides are long and confident. My sidewalk clip is brisk. I am careful to monitor the speed of my pace to avoid a gap between us three. But still a divide grows. I keep having to stop so Katie and Andrew can catch up.

*

In the early weeks of this journey, I was laser focused on achieving daily mileage goals. When I interacted with folks, I'd secretly hope we'd wrap things up quickly so I could get back on the road. I raced toward the Atlantic like it was my job. Like I had something to prove. Spent each day obsessing over time, progress, and what folks would think about me after all was said and done. Back then, this journey was all about me.

The early injury that sidelined me for a month challenged me to reframe my reasons for doing this walk in the first place. I *thought* I was walking to finally check a long-term goal off my list, and I sort of was. But I was also unconsciously digging into my deepest self in an attempt to find the truest version of me.

After a month of rehab I restarted the walk with a new intention. To let go. I gave myself permission to release control of the outcome. Every day I asked myself to be vulnerable. I allowed myself to stay open to others and to opportunity. My new perspective changed everything. Without this reset, I would have completely missed the abundance of love and goodness awaiting me on the roadside. I would have missed out on the journey itself.

Post-injury, I did my best to embody Art's words about this walk not being about me. I regularly channeled Lion and said yes to kindness whenever it showed up, even if it derailed my plans. And though Art's and Lion's transformative voices were the loudest, every person I met as I walked across America added something important. Something that collectively nudged me along. Each person offered breadcrumbs that I followed to fuel my forward movement. I learned something from each of these thousand teachers that brought me in better touch with myself. Remove them from this experience and the transcontinental journey doesn't really matter.

*

If it's true that we attract the sorts of people who energetically resemble us, it's obvious I have not been giving myself enough credit. For the majority of my life, I've believed myself to be inadequate. But the wealth of kindness I attracted on this walk suggests I'm not such a bad person after all. In fact, I'm pretty amazing. Pretty badass, actually.

*

I write another post. "5th Ave. toward Brooklyn Bridge!" Andrew guides us out of Harlem and along the east side of Central Park. We turn when he says turn and stop when he says stop. It's a luxury to not be in charge of the day's route and I give myself over to it. I just walk while looking closely at one of my favorite cities.

On 5th Avenue I peel away from Katie and Andrew to say hello to a man who's drawing in a notebook. His name is Eddie. "I figured you must have a cool story," I say as I sit on the bench next to him. "Ha! That's why you stopped? For real?" he asks. Eddie flips through his sketchbook, shows me cityscapes of buildings and trees. Detailed pencilwork and shading. He's darn good at what he does. I ask if he makes art for a living. "No. Just for fun," he says. "I don't want my hobby to become a chore and stop bringing me joy, you know?"

*

"Washington Square Park!" I write in another post, marking our path for anyone who might be interested in tagging along. Last time I was here, a man was playing classical piano in the middle of the park. This is as far as Andrew can go with us this morning. He'll meet up with us later before I take the plunge at Coney Island.

*

"Brooklyn Bridge!" I write as Katie and I join the mass of tourists heading across the iconic landmark. I think of my friend Big John who used to work on the fishing boats below. I lean over the rail and watch the bustle of workers doing whatever they do on the docks. I tell Katie a story about when I unloaded fishing boats in Alaska. The one about a guy who put a 300-pound halibut's eye in his mouth and called himself a triclops. Nearly swallowed the golf ball-sized orb in a fit of laughter. She's heard it before. She's heard all my stories before.

We march across the bridge and drop into Brooklyn.

*

"Trying to find us?" I write. "Here's where we are at 1:30—Going left on Atlantic and right on Flatbush, into Prospect Park and along Ocean Ave. More updates to come!"

We pass the Barclays Center then take a pedestrian path into Prospect Park. Signs are everywhere for the Celebrate Brooklyn Festival starting today, and temporary fencing surrounds the Bandshell. We stop to listen as someone does a sound check. We assume it's the headliner for tomorrow's show, Brandi Carlile, who Katie and I both confuse with Belinda Carlisle. We burst into bad renditions of songs by the Go-Go's. "Vacation, all I ever wanted!" I sing. "Vacation, had to get away!" Katie responds. "Vacation, meant to be spent alone!"

*

"Almost there!" I post. But this time with a video update of where we are and where we plan to be. "It's about 2:45 and we still have about eight miles to go which, at the pace we're going, is like three hours. But it's come down to this and I'm still trying to figure out how I feel. Which, I guess, will all sorta come to pass before too long." My phone constantly vibrates. I stop to read the likes and comments but there's too much to sift through.

*

Tremaine, a UPS driver, stops to ask what we're doing. I tell her it's the last day of a long-ass walk. "I'm a marathoner," she says. "I can appreciate that." She asks for some data points. "When I finish, it'll be more than three thousand two hundred fifty miles over two hundred five days," I day. "Fourteen states, seven pairs of shoes, and countless generous strangers." She nods like it all makes sense. "So what's next?" she asks. My mind races, and in a flash I think about a million things. But I keep my answer simple. "A dip in the ocean, a giant dinner, and some beers," I say. She hugs me, then hits the horn as she shoves into traffic.

*

I get messages from two people who plan to meet Katie and I before we reach the beach. Marti is a friend from my MFA program and Holly was a second grader in the first PE class I ever taught back in 1994, the same year I was inspired to do this walk.

Marti and her husband Tom have been following my social media updates and will catch up before too long. Holly's text says she'll meet us at the beach. The thought of having a posse at the end chokes me up. I don't even bother trying to hold back. Katie rubs my back with her hand as I cry openly. "You got this, baby," she says, which makes me cry even harder.

*

"In case you are following or planning to meet up," I write, "we are on Ocean Ave, turning right on Neptune, then left on Coney Island Ave, ending on Brighton Beach! Boom!"

Southbound along Ocean Avenue, the beach isn't far ahead. Marti and Tom chase us down, sweat dripping off their foreheads, and join us as the pace quickens. I don't really know Marti all that well, and it's the first time I'm meeting Tom. So we walk in a two-by-two formation, occasionally switching partners so we all can get acquainted. My camaraderie with Marti can be traced back to a buzzed bus ride from Oak Knoll winery to the Pacific University campus during one of our writing residencies in Forest Grove, Oregon. I remember noticing the summer scarf she wore. Its color and wisp accentuated her generous smile. I remember her telling me about a book she wrote titled *Conversations With George Bush*. An odyssey of interviews with regular Americans who shared the name with the then-leader of the free world. "In some cases, people with that name couldn't even get a pizza delivered," she says. "God help any of our current president's namesakes," I say.

*

An hour later the ocean comes into view. We four make the final right turn onto Neptune Avenue and link up with Holly, then the final left onto Coney Island Avenue where Andrew, his wife Carrie, their kids Egypt and Aariana, and Aariana's brand new baby, Adelina, join the group. We are 10 strong, the same number of folks who were with me when I started in Santa Monica. Everything's coming full circle.

*

We stand in a warm clump, shielded from the driving wind. The crashing surf is only a couple hundred meters away. I'm fidgety and restless, eager and mesmerized. My heart pounds. The ocean is a magnet. I'm ready but I'm not. I need something. I excuse myself from the group and run toward a public restroom. "Hey! Where ya going?" someone hollers. "Just a sec!" I shout without looking back.

Inside, I stand at the urinal, unable to pee. I throw my head back and laugh hysterically, filling the dim space with a burst of noise. I take a giant inhale, then scream until my throat cracks. My voice echoes on the hard tile like a Tibetan singing bowl. The resonance dies, and is chased by silence.

Under the florescent lights, my skin is extra-tan and the hairs on my arms are translucent blonde. I run my fingers over my tattoo of the hobo sign on my right wrist. I trace the arrow zigzagging through the circle. *Keep on. You're going the right way.* It was right. It *is* right.

I flush nothing down the drain, then walk to the sink mirror. It's scratched up so bad I can barely make out my face. I bob and weave for a recognizable glimpse. Then, knees bent, I hold steady in a tiny, unblemished nook and examine myself. I am old. Slight. My skin is flushed and ruddy. I have more wrinkles than I remember. Crow's feet and laugh lines course across the tattered map of my face. My beard is full and unkempt and my teeth look yellow. My tongue is fat and chalky. I am a version of what I've always known.

I flap my hands and shake my head, kick my feet one at a time. "Well, Griffen. This is is it!" I say aloud. Then I spin around and open the door with a forearm shiver as I bound out of it. I glide down the steps, then jog along the boardwalk to rejoin my people. I am ready.

*

I want to hurry up and get to the water, but I also want to make sure we do this right. Lots of people have been following my adventure from afar and I want them to be able to watch as I reach the water. Holly volunteers to do the camerawork for a Facebook live video, and Katie removes from the daypack the warm bottle of champagne I've been hauling since Virginia. I look at everyone's faces, thank them all profusely, then thank them a hundred more times.

*

Though it's mid-July, a prime time for beachgoers, Brighton Beach is empty. Not a soul besides us down the length of the blustery beach. Even the shops look closed. There's a minor sprinkling here and there, but no real threat of rain. Storms are coming, that's for sure, but all day they've been getting pushed back to later and later. As dark clouds thicken overhead and reflect the churning ocean, I joke that the sky is waiting for me to be done before unleashing. "Quit stalling!" someone says, which inspires similar chides to ripple throughout the group. "OK, OK. I hear ya," I say. "Let's do this."

*

I grab Katie's hand and we lead the group down the temporary pathway over the sand. Though the group is on our heels, it feels like it's just her and me. We exchange a quick look and I pick up the pace, my long strides reaching long down this final bit. Once again, my steps are faster and wider than hers, and before long I let go of her hand and burst ahead. When I reach the end of the walkway, I wait for her to catch up. I empty my pockets and hand the contents over to her. My wallet, my Burt's Bees, a handkerchief, and the dice-sized wooden house she gave me in Santa Monica the night before I started. "To remind you that no matter where you are, you are at home," she said. It's been in my pocket for more than 3,000 miles.

I thank Katie for everything. Then I give her another hug, turn around and walk to the water's edge. I hesitate. Then I turn and look back at my group. I faintly hear them cheering over the slush of waves. They motion for me to *go, go*. I turn to face the ocean again and it yanks me in.

*

My legs sprint to the surf line and my body dives into a curl of mushy beach break. All sounds disappear as my head submerges, floppy hat and all. I keep my eyes closed. When I surface, I aim my face to the sky, outstretch my arms like wings, and howl until I'm light-headed and all turns silent. The faint cry of another person hooting and hollering gets my attention. It's another man, maybe 50 feet away, further out in waist-deep surf. When our eyes meet he mirrors my ecstatic celebration. He jumps up and down, pumping his fist. Together and separate we celebrate from a distance. I dive under again and let my body go limp. The waves press against me as I twist and roll beneath them. I hold my breath for as long as I can before breeching. And when I come up, I am heavier than ever and want to sleep.

*

Waterlogged, I slog back to the beach and embrace Katie, slow and long this time. She holds my face in her hands. "You did it, baby! I knew you would." The she squeezes me. Runs her hands up and down my shoulders and arms. "I'm so proud of you," she says. Which makes my eyes burst and I let it all out as I tuck my face into the warm crook of her neck.

When we let go I give everyone else a salty hug, too. Katie picks up the bottle of champagne and reaches it toward me. "Well?" she says. "Hell yeah!" I say as I take it from her. I step back and ceremoniously tear the foil and untwist the wire. I edge the cork side to side until the carbonation shoots it into the sky. The contents cascade up and out until the bottle is nearly empty. I woot and raise the bottle for a slug. "It's gone!" I shout, then laugh like it's the most hilarious thing I've ever experienced. Everyone else does, too.

Holly videos my sign-off. I thank everyone for following along. I tell them I'm lost for words and right now I'm looking forward to a celebration with friends. When she cuts the feed, we all fill the moment with more hugs and expressions of disbelief, mostly by me. "This is unreal," I say. "I can't believe I did it. I can't believe it's all over." I rub my face and scratch my head, befuddled. "No—this isn't the end," someone says. "It's just the beginning."

13

Having arrived, when I was finally allowed to stop,
drink some tea, and look out across the Himalayas,
I felt moved and could feel a growing lump in my throat.
I stood up tall and reached my arms into the sky.
But my joy dissipated quickly when,
after only a few minutes, I asked myself:
"How the hell am I going to get down?"

- Erling Kagge
Walking: One Step at a Time, regarding the author's Everest ascent

July 2018

I SLEEPWALK IN MY OWN HOUSE. Hobble amongst furniture and bump into walls. I look for my tent and worry I might trip on Little Buddy. My dream shifts, and suddenly I'm standing on a rooftop, watching the first flickers of sunrise. I know I'm asleep, but I can't wake up. I struggle, half-confused, half-desperately hoping my blind hand will happen upon a light switch. "You OK in there?" Katie says from the bedroom. Her sleepy voice is just enough to rouse me and I'm suddenly aware I'm standing in the bathroom. *My* bathroom. Not a hotel. Not a campground. Not in a desert or forest or RV park. I know this place, but still I am lost in it.

Less than a month ago, every day had a distinct purpose—I'd wake up, walk, eat, and sleep. Then I'd do the same thing the next day. Now I have no routine to guide me and I wander, purposeless, from kitchen to living room to porch fiddling with things, then end up on the couch where I watch birds take turns at the feeder. A pair of cardinals is most frequent—the graceful female who eases onto the ledge, finding her balance before pecking at seeds, and her bumbling male counterpart who mounts the seedcake haphazardly, often losing his grasp and causing the feeder to dangerously swing like a wrecking ball. I grow bored of that and turn on music, then turn it off. The playlist I obsessively listened to during the walk has grown tired and unappealing.

I sort through the assortment of boxes I mailed home from small towns along my route. Each parcel contains artifacts I collected that added unnecessary weight to Little Buddy's rear compartment. Interesting rocks, tattered license plates, poker chips, plastic army men, coins, arrowheads, pocketknives, business cards, motorcycle club patches, and more than 100 steel spoons. I don't remember why I picked up that first spoon back in California. But once I did, they never stopped appearing on the roadside. They are broken and bent, scraped and burnt, crusted with a layer of muck, or gleaming like a new mirror. They represent nourishment in all its forms. I lay them out on my dining room table, bowls up, and they form a perfect square. I lean over them and my face reflects in convex. Then I put them all in the dishwasher and stand at the sink listening to the hum of the hottest cycle. It reminds me of traffic. The neighbor's dog sees me through an adjacent window and barks. She wants me to come outside and throw a few sticks.

I rummage through my closets and drawers and consider how much stuff I have. I am disgusted by my excess. Most everything I needed for the last six months fits in a two-gallon dunk bag. So why do I own four winter jackets? Do I really need so many just-in-case items? What am I doing with this 20-pound chunk of brown onyx from Baja? And why am I hanging onto this wooden trunk filled with old things I never look at: baseball cards, school yearbooks, Cub Scout patches, my childhood teddy bear. I fixate on my abundance, then obsessively make two piles —one for a future yard sale, one for the trash can. Clearing clutter provides an afternoon of activity. But once it's done, I'm back to staring at birds.

The mail comes. Mostly junk and nothing for me. I write a New York City postcard to Billie and John in Gap, Pennsylvania, the folks who made me sandwiches before sending me off with a fresh bag of cherries. I text Little Paul in New Mexico to thank him for the great conversation at Denny's in Silver City, New Mexico. I call Ray and Bart from the used tire shop in Texarkana to tell them I made it. "Yep, yep, yep," Ray says. "Good for you." I text Becca to tell her I miss her family. I reach out to all my brothers and sisters. "Just checking in," I write. I scroll through my phone contacts and look at all the new names from the walk. Then I send a text to Singing Juni, Champagne Steve,

Whataburger Jason, New Jersey Mike, Mustache Pat, Barber Jerry, Texas Michelle, AT Steve, and Floppy Hat Eric. I picture their surprised faces as they open my message.

I quietly visit Midway Barbershop where Step, the owner, edges my receding hairline. He shares his theory of humankind. "Nine out of ten people are good," he says as he shuts off the electronic clippers and stands directly in front of me. "But it only takes one person, one goddamn person out of ten, to make us question this truth." I suggest that maybe we should go ahead and assume all 10 are good. Step shrugs, flips the clippers back on, and resumes my haircut. When he spins me around and hands me a mirror, I give a thumbs-up. Then I take the long way home, occasionally stopping to brush the itchy clippings from my ears. From afar I see familiar faces and detour to avoid contact. I'm not ready to socialize with people who actually know me.

Back home, I make a list of action items that will get my consulting business back up and running: fresh marketing ideas, new workshop content, innovative blog post topics, clients and leads I should reach out to. After I fill the page, I crumple it up and toss it across the room. Then I spend time wondering why my work even matters.

I eat a bowl of tasteless cereal and start reading a poetry book I agreed to review. After a few pages I lose interest. I take ibuprofen for a headache I could have avoided by stopping for an espresso while I was out for the haircut. I stand in the middle of the living room and peer out my bay window. An occasional car drives past. Neighbors walks by with their dogs on a leash. One dog shits in my yard and its person looks around then covers the pile with a handful of yanked grass. Normally this would piss me off, but right now I couldn't care less.

I log onto Netflix, browse a bit, then log out. I crack open the front window and listen to cicadas. I close my eyes and imagine the swarm of green dragonflies at my stealth campsite in an Arkansas farmfield. Nostalgia traps me in misery and I'm overwhelmed by how much I miss the roadside. I walked across

America and now I am home. But the whole of me is scattered across 14 states.

When I finally muster the courage to purposely interact with people, I feel uneasy. "How was it?" many ask with enthusiasm. Others bypass the question and want to know what I learned. I don't know how to respond to these inquiries so I say, "It was amazing—but I'm still trying to figure it all out." And though this is true, it's also a conversation squasher. I wish the truth went something like, *The walk gave me what I needed to get my life back on track*! Or, *Because of the walk, everything is finally clear as day*! But no such revelations occurred. So the reunion turns awkward and I feel like I let the person down.

Soon I'm back in the flow of life—work, relationships, chores, and exercise. As my schedule returns to normal, questions about the walk grow less frequent. Soon it's as if nothing happened. Like I blinked and seven months passed. The walk is like a book I read. Or a movie I saw. It's someone else's story.

Fall 2020

It's now the second half of 2020. More than two years have passed since I completed my walk across America and I've moved on in so many ways. Shortly after I returned, Katie and I agreed to finally split up. Then, in late 2019, I shut down my business and accepted a job that heaved me across the country. If it's true that growth comes from change, and change comes from loss, well, then I am growing *a lot*.

My lessons from the walk deepen with the passage of time. Things become clearer as I distance myself from them. In writing and rewriting this book a half dozen times, I've relived the journey as a bystander, and in doing so I've realized the profundity of many roadside exchanges that, in the moment they occurred, seemed benign. The more obviously pivotal interactions have taken on even greater meaning.

When I met Art at that Pomona stoplight, I couldn't have guessed that his words about the walk not being about me would become a daily mantra. These days I find myself meditating on this simple truth whenever I'm unhappy or inconvenienced. I paraphrase Art's words aloud—*It's not about you, Tom*—and immediately check myself. I may be the one moving through this life, but how I respond to everything affects others. If I ignore or forget this truth, I spread my funk around. I don't want to do that, and Art's words keep me from giving into my selfish tendencies.

I repeated Art's words like a prayer during last spring's coronavirus quarantine—*It's not about me, it's not about me*—and simply speaking them kept me from feeling sorry for myself. I had just moved to the Pacific Northwest and barely had my bags unpacked when everyone got locked down. In the most difficult times, Art's words extracted me from the fearful sludge of the unknown. Chanting *it's not about me* helped me stay grounded in the collective mess we all found ourselves in. It was a reminder to reach out. To virtually give others the sort of hug I so desperately needed.

I've also often channeled Lion's insistence to always say yes to kindness. Having spent most of my life trying to be self-sufficient and hyper capable, accepting help of any kind has rarely felt like anything but weakness. But Lion taught me otherwise. When I tell the story of our coming together, I always say that had I stopped walking on the day he and I met, the trajectory of my life would still have been forever changed. His words, "Don't say no to kindness," were precisely what I needed to hear. And though his words shifted my perspective for the remainder of the walk, they too grow more meaningful with time. Never before had I been encouraged to willingly let my guard down. But once I did, I never wanted to put it up again.

I set out to walk across America, and I did it. I accomplished a long-term goal, met an abundance of wonderfully kind and interesting people, and spent a lot of time thinking deeply about what I want the second half of my life to look like. But really, so what? Because if I am not careful, my walk will take on the qualities of the art hanging in my living room—at one point the pieces moved me to tears, but now I take them for granted. I see them without truly seeing them. If I stop listening to the resonating wisdom of Art and Lion and so many others, my walk will become a useless, dusty trophy and the 3,000 miles will have been done in vain.

In my real life—which is to say, my life *not* on the roadside —nobody ever asks me *why*. I never have to bumble through a question about my reasons for living my life as I do. The responsibility is now mine. It's up to me to regularly challenge myself with such an inquiry. It's up to me to make sure I have a purposeful direction. And just like during the walk itself, my answer is always evolving. And I believe if I'm doing it right, it always will be.

*

Back on day five in California, I altered my route to include San Timoteo Canyon Road, an 18-mile serviceless highway stretch alongside a railroad into Beaumont. It would be my lengthiest stretch without services up to that point. I started the day quietly. I was afraid, yet laser-focused on getting it done.

Halfway through the canyon, I encountered Sergio and Griselda as they operated a fruit stand in a dirt turnout. They offered me the sort of generosity I more commonly questioned than accepted. The day was unseasonably hot and I was suffering from exertion. Sergio noticed this and insisted I rest in their shade. Situation forced me to open myself to their grace. He handed me a plate of fresh fruit and told me to fill my belly.

Sergio kept thanking me for walking. "What you are doing is a hard thing," he said. "And that makes it important." I couldn't comprehend why he was thanking me. After all, he and Griselda were the ones helping me out—shouldn't I be thanking them?

After spending time looking at family photos on Griselda's phone, it was time to go. Sergio handed me a couple oranges and wished me safe travels. "Vaya con dios," he said. Then he told me he had one more thing to say before I left, and it was important. For a moment all was silent—no traffic, no wheels in the dirt, no squeaky brakes. Sergio positioned himself directly in front of me and placed his hand on my shoulder. He took a breath then held his other hand up, tapping his index finger gently toward my chest. "You started this walk with a good heart," he said, each word slow and deliberate. "Make sure you finish with one, too." I nodded and promised him I would.

As I walked away, the next customer rolled in, kicking up a cloud of dust. I covered my face and waved at Sergio and Griselda, who waved back. Then I found my pace on the narrow roadside and set out to follow the distant blast of train's thunderous horn.

AUTHOR'S NOTE

At the outset of this adventure, I had no plans to write a book. I shared my journey by writing a daily Instagram post detailing something that impacted me on that particular day. My posts were raw. Fresh memories loaded with typos.

I did, however, keep a detailed record of each day on the road. Some notes I wrote in an old school journal, some I typed on my phone's Notes app, but the majority were verbally dictated. Recording audio quickly became a boredom-fighting strategy. I passed a lot of time detailing elements of the mundane.

Upon my return home, I boarded an Amtrak and rode the perimeter of America. I thought a seated view of the nation's landscape would help me reassimilate into normalcy. As I watched the scenery race by, I compiled my myriad notes into a massive log of thoughts and experiences. This document became the primary source material used to reconstruct the particulars of in this book. Without it, the majority of my random interactions and sporadic memories would be lost.

In the retelling of my journey, I've recreated countless conversations. I've taken great care to maintain the integrity of each exchange without including any embellishment. I've also tried my best to stay true to the themes of what people said, while also paying homage to specifically *how* they said it. I've put people's words in quotations to aid in the written aesthetic, but in every case I am paraphrasing. In a few instances I've changed names to ensure privacy.

This is my story. And I am humbled for this chance to share it.

Tom Griffen
Spokane, WA
November 2020

MILEAGE & ACCOMMODATIONS

CALIFORNIA
Day 1: Santa Monica pier to Glendale (homestay / 20 miles)
Day 2: Glendale to Azusa (homestay / 20 miles)
Day 3: Azusa to Rancho Cucamonga (hotel / 20 miles)
Day 4: Rancho Cucamonga to Redlands (hotel / 20 miles)
Day 5: Redlands to Beaumont (hotel / 21 miles)
Day 6: Beaumont to PCT section south of I-10 (camp / 22 miles)
Day 7: PCT to Palm Springs (hotel / 16 miles)
Day 8: Injured (hotel / 0 miles)
Day 9: Palm Springs to Coachella (hotel / 28 miles)
Day 10: Coachella to Salton Sea (camp / 22 miles)
Day 11: Salton Sea to Bradshaw Trail (camp / 22 miles)
Day 12: Bradshaw Trail backtrack to Gasline Rd (camp / 20 miles)
Day 13: Gasline Rd. to I-10 electrical line road (camp / 15 miles)
Day 14: Electrical line road to Blythe (hotel / 15 miles)
Day 15: Off day (hotel / 0 miles)
Days 16-21: Injured, recovery in Phoenix (homestay / 0 miles)
Days 22-24: Injured, recovery in Blythe (hotel / 0 miles)
Day 25: Blythe to Ehrenberg, AZ (homestay / 15 miles)
276 miles in California

ARIZONA
Day 26: Injured (homestay / 0 miles)
Days 27-41: Injured, recovery in North Carolina (home / 0 miles)
Day 42: Return to Phoenix (homestay / 0 miles)
Day 43: Drive to Brenda, AZ (camp / 0 miles)
Day 44: Brenda to Vicksburg (camp / 15 miles)
Day 45: Vicksburg to Wenden (camp / 16 miles)
Day 46: Wenden to Aguila (camp / 20 miles)
Day 47: Aguila to Forepaugh (camp / 15 miles)
Day 48: Forepaugh to Morristown (camp / 25 miles)
Day 49: Morristown to Surprise (homestay / 22 miles)

Day 50: Surprise to Arizona Canal Trail (homestay / 13 miles)
Day 51: Arizona Canal Trail to homestay (homestay / 20 miles)
Day 52: Off day (homestay / 0 miles)
Day 53: Homestay to Arizona Canal Trail to Mesa (homestay / 22 miles)
Day 54: Mesa to Apache Junction (camp / 20 miles)
Day 55: Off day (homestay / 0 miles)
Day 56: Apache Junction to Florence Junction (homestay / 24 miles)
Day 57: Florence Junction to Superior (camp / 20 miles)
Day 58: Superior to Globe (hotel / 16 miles)
Day 59: Globe to Peridot, San Carlos Apache Reservation (camp / 23 miles)
Day 60: Peridot, San Carlos Apache Reservation to Bylas (camp / 24 miles)
Day 61: Bylas to Safford (hotel / 31 miles)
Day 62: Off day (hotel / 0 miles)
Day 63: Safford to BLM land (camp / 23 miles)
Day 64: BLM land to Duncan (homestay / 18 miles)
368 miles in Arizona

NEW MEXICO
Day 65: Duncan to BLM land (camp / 25 miles)
Day 66: BLM land to Lordsburg (hotel / 10 miles)
Day 67: Off day (hotel / 0 miles)
Day 68: Lordsburg to Continental Divide (camp / 23 miles)
Day 69: Continental Divide to Silver City (hotel / 23 miles)
Days 70-72: Injured (hotel / 0 miles)
Day 73: Silver City to BLM land (camp / 20 miles)
Day 74: BLM land to BLM land (camp / 20 miles)
Day 75: BLM land to Deming (hotel / 13 miles)
Day 76-77: Off day (hotel / 0 miles)
Day 78: Deming to BLM land (camp / 16 miles)
Day 79: BLM land to Hatch (camp / 25 miles)
Day 80: Hatch to Radium Springs (camp / 26 miles)
Day 81: Radium Springs to Las Cruces (hotel / 20 miles)

Day 82: Las Cruces to Anthony (hotel / 26 miles)
106 miles in New Mexico

TEXAS
Day 83: Anthony to El Paso (hotel / 22 miles)
Day 84-85: Off day (hotel / 0 miles)
Day 86: El Paso to Clint (hotel / 25 miles)
Day 87: Clint to Plainview Lake (camp / 18 miles)
Day 88: Plainview Lake to Esperanza (camp / 27 miles)
Day 89: Esperanza to Sierra Blanca (hotel / 27 miles)
Day 90: Sierra Blanca to Allamore (camp / 24 miles)
Day 91: Allamore to Van Horn (hotel / 10 miles)
Day 92: Van Horn to BLM land (camp / 29 miles)
Day 93: BLM Land to railroad tracks (camp / 25 miles)
Day 94: Railroad tracks to Marfa (camp / 21 miles)
Day 95: Off day (camp / 0 miles)
Day 96: Marfa to Alpine (hotel / 27 miles)
Day 97: Alpine to Marathon (RV Park / 31 miles)
Day 98: Marathon to Dry Creek culvert (camp / 30 miles)
Day 99: Dry Creek culvert to Sanderson (hotel / 30 miles)
Day 100: Off day (RV Park / 0 miles)
Day 101: Sanderson to roadside generator (camp / 31 miles)
Day 102: Roadside generator to Langtry (camp / 31 miles)
Day 103: Langtry to Comstock (hotel / 30 miles)
Day 104: Comstock to Del Rio (hotel / 30 miles)
Days 105-106: Off day (hotel / 0 miles)
Day 107: Del Rio to Brackettville (hotel / 33 miles)
Day 108: Brackettville to Cline (camp / 18 miles)
Day 109: Cline to Uvalde (hotel / 22 miles)
Day 110: Uvalde to Sabinal (camp / 24 miles)
Day 111: Sabinal to Castroville (camp / 34 miles)
Day 112: Castroville to N. San Antonio (hotel / 35 miles)
Day 113-114: Off day (hotel / 0 miles)
Day 115: N. San Antonio to Spring Branch (camp / 31 miles)
Day 116: Spring Branch to Austin (homestay / 26 miles)
Day 117-119: Off day (homestay / 0 miles)

Day 120: Austin to Hutto (homestay / 26 miles)
Day 121: Hutto to Thorndale (homestay / 25 miles)
Day 122: Off day (homestay / 0)
Day 123: Thorndale to Rockdale (hotel / 15 miles)
Day 124: Rockdale to Hearne (hotel / 28 miles)
Day 125: Hearne to Marquez (hotel / 35 miles)
Day 126: Marquez to Buffalo (camp / 17 miles)
Day 127: Buffalo to Palestine (hotel / 34 miles)
Day 128: Off day (hotel / 0 miles)
Day 129: Palestine to Flint (camp / 30 miles)
Day 130: Flint to Owentown (camp / 26 miles)
Day 131: Owentown to Gilmer (camp / 29 miles)
Day 132: Gilmer to Avinger (camp / 28 miles)
Day 133: Avinger to Atlanta (hotel / 29 miles)
Day 134: Atlanta to Texarkana (hotel / 29 miles)
1042 miles in Texas

ARKANSAS
Day 135-136: Off day (hotel / 0 miles)
Day 137: Texarkana to Hope (hotel / 32 miles)
Day 138: Hope to Gurdon (camp / 28 miles)
Day 139: Gurdon to Caddo Valley (hotel / 25 miles)
Day 140: Caddo Valley to Perla (homestay / 23 miles)
Day 141: Perla to Little Rock (homestay / 25 miles)
Days 142-146: Off day (homestay / 0 miles)
Day 147: Little Rock to England (homestay / 31 miles)
Day 148: England to Stuttgart (homestay / 25 miles)
Day 149: Stuttgart to Clarendon (camp / 27 miles)
Day 150: Clarendon to West Helena (hotel / 40 miles)
Day 151: West Helena to Lula, MS (camp / 15 miles)
271 miles in Arkansas

MISSISSIPPI
Day 152: Lula to Sardis (hotel / 36 miles)
Day 153: Sardis to Oxford (hotel / 25 miles)
Day 154-155: Off day (hotel / 0 miles)

Day 156: Oxford to New Albany (hotel / 38 miles)
Day 157: New Albany to Booneville (homestay / 27 miles)
Day 158: Booneville to Cherokee, Alabama (camp / 25 miles)
151 miles in Mississippi

ALABAMA
Day 159: Cherokee to Florence (hotel / 30 miles)
Day 160: Florence to Rogersville (hotel / 24 miles)
Day 161: Rogersville to Madison (camp / 29 miles)
Day 162: Madison to Huntsville (hotel / 9 miles)
Day 163: Off day (hotel / 0 miles)
Day 164: Huntsville to Hollywood/Scottsboro (camp / 28 miles)
Day 165: Hollywood/Scottsboro to Kimball, TN (hotel / 32 miles)
152 miles in Alabama

TENNESSEE
Day 166: Kimball to Chattanooga (hotel / 33 miles)
Day 167: Chattanooga to Cleveland (hotel / 22 miles)
Day 168: Off day (hotel / 0 miles)
Day 169: Cleveland to Niota (camp / 33 miles)
Day 170: Niota to Lenoir City (hotel / 30 miles)
Day 171: Lenoir City to Knoxville (hotel / 18 miles)
Day 172: Knoxville to Blaine (camp / 25 miles)
Day 173: Blaine to Mooresburg (camp / 34 miles)
Day 174: Mooresburg to Kingsport (hotel / 38 miles)
Day 175: Off day (hotel / 0 miles)
Day 176: Kingsport to Bristol (hotel / 28 miles)
261 miles in Tennessee

VIRGINIA
Day 177: Bristol to Marion (hotel / 41 miles)
Day 178: Marion to Max Meadows, hurt quad (hotel / 33 miles)
Day 179: Off day (homestay / 0 miles)
Day 180: Off day (hotel / 0 miles)
Day 18: Max Meadows to Christiansburg (hotel / 38 miles)
Day 182: Christiansburg to Christiansburg (hotel / 7 miles)

Day 183: Christiansburg to North Roanoke (hotel / 27 miles)
Day 184: North Roanoke to Buchanan (hotel / 26 miles)
Day 185: Buchanan to Lexington (homestay / 23 miles)
Day 186: Lexington to Staunton (homestay / 27 miles)
Day 187: Staunton to Harrisonburg (homestay / 32 miles)
Day 188: Harrisonburg to Mt. Jackson (homestay / 25 miles)
Day 189: Mt. Jackson to Strasburg (hotel / 25 miles)
Day 190: Strasburg to Martinsburg (hotel / 40 miles)
344 miles in Virginia

WEST VIRGINIA / MARYLAND / PENNSYLVANIA
Day 191: Off day (hotel / 0 miles)
Day 192: Martinsburg, WV (through MD) to Waynesboro, PA (camp / 34 miles)
Day 193: Waynesboro to Gettysburg (hotel / 23 miles)
Day 194: Gettysburg to York (hotel / 34 miles)
Day 195: York to Lancaster (hotel / 24 miles)
Day 196: Lancaster to West Chester (hotel / 37 miles)
Day 197: West Chester to Broomall (hotel / 16 miles)
Day 198: Broomall to Mount Laurel, NJ (hotel / 25 miles)
193 miles in West Virginia, Maryland, and Pennsylvania

NEW JERSEY
Day 199: Mount Laurel to Wrightstown (hotel / 18 miles)
Day 200: Wrightstown to Freehold (hotel / 24 miles)
Day 201: Freehold via to Sandy Hook (camp / 27 miles)
Days 202-203: Off day (camp / 0 miles)
69 miles in New Jersey

NEW YORK
Day 204: Sandy Hook (ferry) to Harlem, NY (homestay / 6 miles)
Day 205: Harlem to Coney Island (homestay / 20 miles)
26 miles in New York

ACKNOWLEDGEMENTS

Special thanks to all the roadside saints—Art, Lion, Sergio & Griselda, and everyone else I connected with whose impact continues to shape me. Your guidance, wisdom, fellowship, and generosity is what made my walk across America worthwhile. I am forever humbled and grateful for the crossing of our paths. This walk is meaningless without you.

Huge thanks to all of the people en route who gave me water, food, groceries, money, supplies, stories, songs, hugs, love, information, advice, opinions, or a place to safely sleep. You, quite literally, kept me going.

Huge appreciation to my old and good friend, Tom Raynor. You made it possible for me to shelve everything except the writing of this book. I appreciate our lasting friendship and your undying support of artists and the creative process.

To my big sis, Lisa Murphy. I celebrate your generosity and forever support.

Thank you to the following people who, via my GoFundMe campaign or otherwise, made my walk financially possible: Jennifer Murvin, Andrew Hume and Carrie Walker, Joel and Brittany Griffen, Jo Haraf, Jennifer Perena, Bryan Bresnan, Gram Dorothy Whitworth, Dustin Shinholser, Betsey Elbogen, Katherine Jane Desrochers, Adrian Bischoff, Jennifer Ellis, Katy Puckett, Dave Bardin, David Smith, Scotty Larson, Frank Pitts and Marsha Hamilton, Margaret Sonnefeld, Kathleen Coe, Erin Jobe, James Lalonde, Audrey Layden, Medina Korda Poole, Michelle Johnson, Eduardo Corral, Michelle Wells, Vievee Francis, Chandra Farnham, Stephen Brandt, Jason Jabaut, Krystle Gray Larrabee, Leah Shlachter, Mort Nace, Kyle A. Rosko, Matthew Willey, Liz and Andrew Love, Allison De Marco, Kurt

Rosenkrantz, El Guapo, Nana Morelli, Ed Malley, Maria Kelly, Kim and Chris Hornberg, Bridget Laye, Shelby Bishop, Carly Erickson, Justin Lau, Derek Powers, Ann Thompson, Kitty Lowry (RIP), Bob and Kathy Benwell, Tom Raynor, Sandy Campbell, Viktor Fursov, Mark Johnson, Bethany Chaney, Rod Foley, Becca and Jeff Sandoval, Craig Samuels, Jenny Bilmes, Andrea Bishop, Nat Clubb, Leslie Carboni, Emma Powers, Kelly Goode, Johan Borutzki, Kurt Periolat, Jim Kruse, Darren Fields, Tom Talbot, Pamela Challender, Scott Campbell, Molly De Marco, Martha Hoelzer, Steve Cohn, Rita Martinez, Jon Parker, Maggie Martinez, Harold and Jenny Hill, Julia Le-Thi, Chris Farley, Susan Donovan, Austen Musso, Nick Hernandez, Ernie Hernandez, Jimbo Gothers, Vincent Mourou, David Schultz, Luke Kramer, Catherine Dekanic, Rose McCool, Lewis Webb, Cynthia Burkins, Kimberly Hupp Van Norden, Mary Woo, Tess Kramer, Ann Donaldson, Teresa Finch, Joseph Millar, Leslie Kelen, Emily Mah-Nakanishi, Eric London, Al Valenti, Marc de Mahy, Peter Boisvert, Jeff Phillips, Nancy Severance, Kathy and Dan Talbot, Wendy and Jason Benwell, Frank DiPane, AL Nesbitt, Daniel Yant, Michelle Fritz, Zayas Jose, Kevin and Raquel Garofalo, Jennifer Check, Shawnda Rogers, Sara Earle, Nova Trailhead, Alexandra DeSiato, Claudio Arweiler, Adeline Kline, Kelly Bodie, Rumi Muraoka, Chris Cook, Lisa Morgan (RIP), Sandra Polizzi, Bill O'Luanaigh, Meredith and Paul Terranova, Adam Greene, Amy Owens, Pete Vaughn, Marti Mattia, Rremida Shkoza, Kara Hume and Family, Lisa Murphy, Mickey Duval, Denise Corey, Ryan Wetter, Kevin Goldenbogen, Duncan and Meg Morgan, David Hume, Lucy Bauman (RIP), Wade and Julie Pannell, Lorraine Johnson, Richard Oosterhof, Anissa Gainey, Colin Sheffield and Amanda Corbett, Patty Hume, Huru Price, Farmer John Soehner and Nichole Soehner, Victor Jimenez, and also to all the random folks who passed me their hard earned money while I walked through their neck of the woods.

Giant gratitude to everyone who generously donated to this book's crowd-funding campaign: Andrew Wolfsfont, Terri

Schneider, Bart Surminski, Katy Pucket, Jo Haraf, Roisin Kilcoyne, Eric Marshall, Andi Rathbone, Andrew Hume and Carrie Walker, Ruth Horn, Dan Robinson, Nancy Severance, Doug Thurston, Lorraine Johnson, Ernie Hernandez, Andrew Wood, Pete Vaughn, Leslie Kelen, Joseph Millar, Craig Samuels, Joel and Brittany Griffen, Charlie Morris, and Richard Oosterhof.

Love to Zayas Jose (RIP), Darrin Caldwell (RIP), Kitty Lowrey (RIP), and Lisa Morgan (RIP).

To the folks along the way who offered up their contact information and told me to reach out if I had any problems: Sadiqa (Q) and Amena in Alabama, Jason in Texas, Brendan in Texas, John in Mississippi, Carolyn in Tennessee, Juni in New Jersey, Steph in Virginia, Mike in New Jersey, Travis in Tennessee, Deborah in Arizona, Christine in New Mexico, Champagne Steve in New York, Michelle in Texas, Huey in Texas, Brandi and Vicki in Texas, AT Steve in Tennessee, John in Texas, Pat in Texas, Nathan in Alabama, Tammy in Texas, Jojo and Candance in New Jersey, Angelica in Texas, John in Texas, Ray and Bart in Texas, Little Paul in New Mexico.

Special thanks and love to Transcon cyclists Tim McDonald and Bill Gardner. So happy to now call you my dear friends.

Big appreciation to the international cyclist extraordinaire with the awesome orange bike—Richard Oosterhof. You are a true *badass*.

Major gratitude for the warm beds and home-cooked meals during my homestays: Joel and Brittany Griffen (pre-Oliver) in California, David Hume in Arizona, Kim and Chris Hornberg and Family in Arizona, Mike and Amy Griffen and Family in Texas, Becca, Jeff, Enzo, and Ociee Sandoval in Arkansas, Scott and Ann Robinson in Mississippi, Bill and Lucy Gardner in

Virginia, and Andrew Hume and Carrie Walker and Family in New York.

Big appreciation to Mark Sullivan and *Running Insight Magazine* for accepting my risky idea to write about the running shops I visited along the way. It was a lot of fun to type 1000-word articles on my iPhone, and even more exciting to see them publish while I was on the road.

Thanks to the running stores I stopped in who let me take up their time and space: Nathan and Rebecca at Tortoise and Hare, Chris at Up and Running, Garrett at Fleet Feet San Antonio, Jen at Ready to Run, Gary at Go! Running, Noelle and Sean at Fleet Feet Little Rock, David and Brittany at Terra Running, Dink and Suzanne at Fleet Feet Huntsville, Carter at Fleet Feet Chattanooga, and Steve at Brooklyn Running Company.

Major love to the following folks for their medical guidance and healing: Dr. Justin Lau at Elite Spinal & Sports Care (Sacramento, CA), Lino Cedros at Kinections (Sacramento, CA), and Brian Beatty PT at Balanced Movement Studio (Carrboro, NC).

To my professional friends who kept me shod, socked, nutritioned, CBD'd, and magically herbed: Jody Herzog and team at Fleet Feet Cleveland, Wade Pannell and team at Fleet Feet PNW, Dusty and Staci Robinson and their team at Fleet Feet Sacramento, Luke Rowe at CEP, Thom Abrams at Superfeet, Jon Parker at GU, Luke Childers at Generation UCAN, Casey McCombs at Oofos, Steve Carter at Fleet Feet Chattanooga, Noelle and Sean Coughlan and team at Fleet Feet Little Rock, Chris Pluchos at Asics, Chris Landry at Medi-Dyne, Joel and Sheryl at Theramu, Dom Godfrey at Steigen, Jeff Oberlatz at Fleet Feet Sacramento, and Stephanie Cimmarusti at Mystic Moon Tree.

Thanks to fellow crossers who provided inspiration, intel, or support before/during/after: Peter Jenkins, Andrew Forsthoefel, El Guapo, Lindsay Monroe, Erin Parete, Brett Bramble, Don Muchow, John Price, and everyone on the USA Crossers Facebook page.

Thanks also to the guiding spirits of Helga and Clara Estby.

Ongoing peace and love to my dear friends who never stop with their moral support and general wonderfulness: Scotty Larson, Kent Treptow, Dusty Robinson, Becca Sandoval, Derek Pye, Big John, TR, JP, and Ginger Dust.

Giant gratitude to my first readers (and fellow Pacific MFA Program peeps) who offered invaluable insights and revision suggestions on a way-too-beefy initial manuscript: James Lalonde, Sam Chamberlain, Dan Tremaglio, and Ronit Plank. Your comments made me a better writer.

Thanks to KH for the close edits and brilliant feedback.

And to my family—we are complicated, we are wonderful. I love you with every ounce of my heart.

Finally, to Katie Hume. Through it all you have been my guiding light. My foundation. Though I long for what we could have been, I am delighted by all we are and all we're sure to become.

And to anyone else I forgot to include here: this walk was about *all of us*, and my oversights, I assure, are unintentional.

TOM GRIFFEN was born in a California cowtown but spent his formative years along the Erie Canal in upstate New York. Tom is a freelance writer, visual artist, and a leadership trainer. He resides in Spokane, WA on the third floor of an old printshop. In his spare time he carves wooden spoons and enjoys a well-crafted 6 oz. americano or hazy IPA.

Find Tom on Instagram @tomgriffen. For more info on his long walk, to book him for speaking engagements, and for links to his accompanying poetry collection, *Imagine the Sea*, please visit tomgriffen.com.

Photo © Tom Womack 2018
Staunton, Virginia